Literature and Language Teaching

Literature and Language Teaching

edited by
Christopher Brumfit
and
Ronald Carter

Oxford University Press

Oxford University Press
Walton Street, Oxford OX2 6DP

Oxford   New York
Athens   Auckland   Bangkok   Bombay
Calcutta   Cape Town   Dar es Salaam   Delhi
Florence   Hong Kong   Istanbul   Karachi
Kuala Lumpur   Madras   Madrid   Melbourne
Mexico City   Nairobi   Paris   Singapore
Taipei   Tokyo   Toronto

and associated companies in
Berlin   Ibadan

Oxford and Oxford English are
trade marks of Oxford University Press

ISBN 0 19 437082 8

First published 1986
Fourth impression 1996

No unauthorized photocopying

Typeset in Sabon by
Hope Services, Abingdon

Printed in Hong Kong

For Arnold Kettle

Contents

Preface

Although this book is called *Literature and Language Teaching*, it does not pretend to offer a comprehensive or synoptic account of the relationship between the two elements, literature and language teaching. We have selected contributors who provide reasonable and well-argued cases which, though they represent different viewpoints, are united by a recognition of the varied ways in which language and literature study are related and can be integrated. Literature is not regularly discussed as a coherent branch of the curriculum in relation to language development in either mother-tongue or foreign-language teaching. However, classroom development cannot proceed before key theoretical and practical issues are identified and debated. We hope that this collection, though not exhaustive, may lay a basis for this further exploration and debate.

C. J. Brumfit
R. A. Carter

December 1984

Acknowledgements

The ideas in this book have been developed in reaction to (and sometimes in opposition to) those of many people who have been generous in time, argument, and suggestion. Particularly, we would like to thank participants in seminars supported by the British Council in London in April 1982, and in Naples in December 1983. Late in the preparation of the book we both discovered independent early debts in our thinking to Arnold Kettle. Others who have been particularly generous with help have included Roy Boardman, John McRae, Liz Moloney, Simon Murison-Bowie, Walter Nash, Doug Pickett, Cristina Whitecross, and Henry Widdowson. In spite of the fact that we know that none of these will be entirely satisfied with the final product, we are most grateful to all of them for their varied, substantial, and indirect contributions.

Acknowledgements are made to the following from whose texts the papers and extracts below have been taken.

British Telecom for *Dialling Instructions and Call Charges* (1970).

Leonard Cohen and Jonathan Cape for 'All There Is to Know About Adolph Eichmann' (from *Selected Poems 1956–68* by Leonard Cohen).

Margaret Drabble and Weidenfeld and Nicolson for an extract from *Jerusalem the Golden*.

East African Publishing House for 'Literature Teaching in Tanzania' by C. J. Brumfit (from the *Journal of the Language Association of Eastern Africa*, Vol. 1 No. 2, 1970); and for 'Literature in East Africa' by R. D. Pettit (Vol. 2 No. 1, 1971).

Faber and Faber Ltd. for an extract from 'Mundus et Infans' by W. H. Auden; and for an extract from 'The Love Song of J. Alfred Prufrock' (from *Collected Poems 1909–1962* by T. S. Eliot).

The Executors of the Estate of Robert Frost and Jonathan Cape for 'Dust of Snow' (from *The Poetry of Robert Frost*, ed. by Edward Connery Latham).

Robert Graves for 'The Persian Version' (from *Collected Poems, 1975*).

Heinemann Educational Books for 'Literature in Schools' (from *Writers in Politics* by Ngugi wa Thiong'o).

The Controller of Her Majesty's Stationery Office for permission to reproduce part of a British passport.

The Executors of the James Joyce Estate and Jonathan Cape for an extract from *Dubliners*.

Bernard Malamud and Chatto and Windus for an extract from *The Natural*.

The Executors of the Estate of W. Somerset Maugham and William Heinemann for 'The Man With the Scar'.

Methuen Children's Books for extracts from *The House at Pooh Corner* by A. A. Milne.

Modern English Publications for 'Testing Language with Students of Literature in ESL Situations' by J. P. Boyle (from *Language Testing*, ed. by J. B. Heaton, 1982).

The Modern Languages Association for 'Literature in the School Foreign Language Course' by William Littlewood (from *Modern Languages* Vol. 56, pp. 127–131, 1975).

The National Association for the Teaching of English for 'Is Literature Language?' by S. J. Burke and C. J. Brumfit (from *English in Education*, Vol. 8 No. 2, 1974).

Penguin Books for an extract from *Return to My Native Land* by Aimé Césaire (1969).

Pergamon Press Ltd. for 'Reading Skills and the Study of Literature in a Foreign Language' by C. J. Brumfit (from *System* Vol. 9 No. 1, 1981).

A. D. Peters and Company for an extract from *Decline and Fall* by Evelyn Waugh.

Craig Raine and Oxford University Press for an extract from *A Martian Sends a Postcard Home* (1979).

The Editor of *RELC Journal* for 'The Non-native Literatures as a Resource for Language Teaching' by Braj Kachru (*RELC Journal* Vol. 11 No. 2, 1980).

The School Library Association for 'Wider Reading for Better Reading' by C. J. Brumfit (from *The School Librarian* Vol. 27 No. 1, 1979).

Charles Scribner's Sons for 'Richard Cory' by Edward Arlington Robinson.

Teachers of English to Speakers of Other Languages for 'Literature in the ESL Classroom' by Sandra McKay (from *TESOL Quarterly* Vol. 16 No. 4, 1982).

The University of London Institute of Education (Department of English for Speakers of Other Languages) for 'Texts, Extracts, and Stylistic Texture' by Guy Cook, taken (re-titled) from *Working Documents 2: English Literature for EFL* (1980).

The University of Pennsylvania Press for Figure 5.1, taken from *Language in the Inner City* by William Labov (1972).

Denis Warner and *The Daily Telegraph* for 'Dingo Appeal Rejected'.

Introduction

This is a book about the interaction between language, literature, and education. It consists of four parts: this Introduction, in which a number of fundamental issues are discussed in some detail; a section of papers on linguistics, literature, and the implications of the interaction between linguistics and literature for education; a section of papers on general educational issues raised by wanting to include literature in the curriculum; and a final section which looks at one very important issue with specific reference to one overseas setting and to British education.

The book includes papers of varied levels of abstraction, in order to explore both general principles and specific problems of implementation. Similarly, the papers in Part Two may be more immediately accessible to the general reader than some of those in Part One. None the less, we feel that the book can be read as a consecutive set of papers, for there is a progression in the argument from general principles, to consideration of the role of language in literature, to implications of that for educational and curricular discussion. At the same time, we would be unwilling to make excessive claims for the discussion here. Literature teaching is by no means secure in many educational systems, and its role as an ally of language is not infrequently disputed. This collection can only open up further discussion in an area which is increasingly important.

English Literature and English Language

This part of the Introduction consists of four sections in which some seminal issues in the study of literature and language are addressed. These issues are: the relations between *stylistics* and literature study (Section 1), questions of what is understood by *literary language* and literature as a particular type of *discourse* (Sections 2 and 3), and the issue of the kinds of *literary competence* involved in reading texts (Section 4). The book as a whole is intended to offer a selective introduction to issues which will require careful thought to enable further progress in this important area to be made. The issue of 'literature and language teaching' is generating a great deal of interest at present, but we wish to avoid being either programmatic or synoptic—although we do hope to argue clear cases for particular emphases and directions. Our examination in this introduction to the book will be largely theoretical and necessarily selective but, wherever possible, we will focus on issues which we and our contributors judge to be relevant for methodology and pedagogy in the domains of language and literature teaching. In both its parts, this Introduction should provide a framework within which the papers that comprise the volume can be understood, interrelated, and evaluated.

1 Literary stylistics and the study of literature

The main starting point in this section is the relationship between *practical criticism* and *stylistic analysis* of literary text. It is assumed here that most teachers of English will be acquainted with or will have had direct experience of practical criticism in relation to the interpretation of literary works. (For a clear introduction to the aims of practical criticism, its development, and a number of examples in practice on modern English poems, see Cox and Dyson 1963.) Practical criticism shares two main presuppositions with the discipline of stylistics: first, that literary text is made from language and its primary focus for analysis will be the patterns made by language. In a basic sense, this is the only 'material' the analyst has to go on. The literary text is seen as self-sufficient as a language artefact, and, as it were, as an object in itself. The second presupposition is that practical criticism, or 'close reading', is opposed to belletristic or aestheticist waffle about literary texts, and attempts to locate intuitive responses to the meanings and effects released by the text in the structure of the language used. In this respect, the critic will attempt to show *how* what is said is said and *how* meanings are made. Any interpretation which does not give due attentiveness to the base of language organization is not, it is claimed, worth very much, though a main difference between stylistics and practical criticism is in the *degree* of detailed systematic attention given to the analysis of language.

Intuitive responses to a text are central to the process of reading and re-reading literature. They are a necessary starting point for fuller investigation of what a text means to us. However, it is not altogether clear what exactly is primary in our response to a text. Is it an experience evoked in us exclusively by what is referred to in the text? Does it result from a relationship between a particular text and material we have read previously on related themes or in a special 'cultural' tradition? Or is the initial response a linguistic matter of reactions to striking phrases or to an unusually evocative stretch of language? Or is it some combination of these separate reactions? Crucially for non-native speakers, how much of the text do we have to understand linguistically before reading gives rise to productive responses and intuitions? It is important to keep an open mind about these under-investigated issues.

Not uncommonly, constant exposure and re-reading is felt to deliver to students the necessary intuitive awareness. A problem here, and one often noted by stylisticians, is that exposure may serve only the most able and linguistically proficient students. Advocates of stylistics (including most of the contributors to Part One of this book) consider that stylistic–analytical procedures provide a principled method by which reading and interpretative skills can be developed, and recognize that some students have to learn how to analyse language before they can respond subjectively to a text. In any case, it is argued, the continuing processes of systematically formalizing intuitions can lead to ever-increasing appreciation of a writer's artistry in and through language. It is not clear, however, what precise form language analysis should take, and much depends on the aims of the course, the level of language competence, whether the literary text is studied in a language class or a literature class, and so on. For this reason, some papers in Part One of the book advocate *language-based approaches* prior to linguistic–stylistic analysis. These can involve the application of tried and tested language teaching techniques (e.g. types of questioning strategy, small group and pair activities, paraphrase, cloze work, etc.) to literary text study. Papers by Long, Carter, and Nash illustrate such procedures and discuss some of the problems involved. In fact the *familiarity* of such procedures to students of English as a foreign language is not normally a difficulty. The second part of our Introduction, 'Literature and Education', discusses further questions of primacy, interdependence of language and response, and the issue of whether competence can be 'caught' or 'taught' in literature teaching.

There is insufficient space in this introduction for detailed illustration of stylistic analysis, but readers will find examples in Part One of the book which draw on systematic linguistic analysis of syntax, lexis, discourse, phonology, etc., to support interpretations or discussions of a literary text. (For further examples with a pedagogic orientation see papers in Carter 1982a and Brumfit 1983 and a review by Carter, 1985.) We support the view that a sensitive stylistic analysis of a text can produce facts about its linguistic organization which cannot be ignored. More importantly for the student a firm basis in language analysis is given from which he or she can proceed to say with some precision what it means to them, how it means what it means, and why the text is liked or disliked by them as a piece of literature. Analytical tools are supplied, or, as is often the case with foreign students, where explicit discussion of language is already a familiar feature of the classroom, existing analytical tools can be used to extend individual interpretative skills. The case for linguistic–stylistic analysis has been well put by Roger Pearce (1977):

> Linguistic analysis becomes an integral aspect of the process of understanding literature, a means of formulating intuition, a means of objectifying it and rendering it susceptible to investigation and, in so doing, a means of feeling out and revising our initial interpretation.

Such study is clearly not a case of remembering what the teacher said about a poem, or what interpretation was given in the books of criticism in the library.

We believe that students and teachers of literature should engage in stylistic analysis when studying literature, and that this can ensue with varying degrees of systematicity at different levels of literary study. But we also acknowledge that there are limitations to this procedure. Sometimes these result directly from teachers' attitudes to stylistics. For example, some teachers consider it to be mechanical and destructive both of responsive enjoyment and imaginative participation in literature, and they complain that too exaggerated a claim has been made on behalf of stylistics. (For a representative and provocative argument, see Roger Gower's review of *Poetry and the System* by Brian Lee, in *ELT Journal* Volume 38 No. 1, 1984.) We agree that stylistic analysis cannot be the only approach to literature study, and that there are dangers in analysis which is independent of responses to a text or for which, where appropriate, students have not been prepared by selected preliminary or 'pre-literary' language-based activities (see especially the paper in this volume by Carter). In the second part of this Introduction, readers are referred to material in this book and elsewhere in which arguments are provided for studying literature as translinguistic discourse—that is, as a discourse involving more than mere systems of language (see especially the paper by Burke and Brumfit)—and where the admission of a wider social, historical, and political 'context' is seen as essential to the teaching of literature. To this extent the question of depth v. breadth raised by Pickett and others in this volume is engaged. Thus, we acknowledge that there are potential limitations in focusing analytically on language, but we believe that the following statement, made by Roman Jakobson in 1960, is just as relevant today to literature and language teaching debates:

> A linguist deaf to the poetic function of language and a literary scholar indifferent to linguistic problems and unconversant with linguistic methods are equally flagrant anachronisms. (Jakobson 1960: 377)

2 What is literary language?

Increasingly, linguists and linguistic critics are addressing themselves to questions such as: is there a language of literature? And what *is* literary language? Anyone interested in the study of literature would have to admit that these are important and fundamental questions. Indeed, some may argue that investigating such aspects of literature is more important and fundamental than writing yet another interpretation of Keats's 'Ode to a Nightingale' or a Shakespeare sonnet. It is the kind of investigation which often serves to generate further questions, but one which many teachers believe can help students to explore in an open-minded way the *nature* of literary text. (For fuller argument see Widdowson 1975: Chapter 6, as well as section 4 of this Introduction.)

Our focus in this section is on questions which are specifically concerned with language. We begin, however, with an assertion. *We believe that there is no such thing as literary language.* When we say this, we mean that we find it impossible to isolate any single or special property of language which is exclusive to a literary work. It does not mean we deny that language is *used* in ways which can be distinguished as literary.

For example, it has been conventionally thought, from Romantic critics such as Coleridge onwards, that metaphor is the distinguishing mark of literature. In fact, it requires only a little linguistic introspection to see that metaphor is pervasive in our daily discourse and, as a property of language, is not in any way unique. Metaphors are not found only in Shakespeare or Donne.

The world of discussion and debate, parliamentary, journalistic, academic or otherwise, is impregnated with metaphors which regularly compare argument to the conduct of a battle. The following are just a few instances of an abundance of military metaphors: *marshal an argument*; *have* or *defend a position*; *buttress an argument/position*; *concede a point*; *conflict of opinion*; *his strategy in the debate was to . . .* ; *she manoeuvred her points skilfully*; *to be entrenched*, etc. One parliamentary reporter wrote recently that 'the argument of the leader of the opposition was quickly so badly wounded by the prime minister that for the rest of the debate crutches were needed and he ended up looking a very old soldier'. (A fuller argument and range of examples can be found in Lakoff and Johnson 1980.)

It is also regularly noted, particularly in respect of poetry, that a striking phonological pattern is a distinguishing mark of poetic language. Yet there are several instances in 'ordinary language' where patterns of contrast, similarity, or parallelism are to be found. Proverbs, for example: 'a stitch in time saves nine'; 'where there's a will there's a way'. Or children's songs and games: 'London Bridge is *falling down, falling down, falling down*'; 'Incy-win*c*y spider . . . '. Or in advertisements: 'Drin*k*a pin*t*a mil*k*a day'; 'You'll never *b*ite a *b*etter *b*it of *b*utter in your life'. (See also the essay by Nash in this volume for further discussion and examples.) It is also worth noting here that advertising copy can also play with density of social–cultural allusion in ways which, it is often claimed, can only be the province of poetry. The subtlety of this reference to a Great Train Robber and the pun on 'nips in and out' (Biggs regularly escaped from British prisons) makes for a striking and memorable advertisement for a British Leyland Mini car:

Nips in and out like Ronald Biggs.

However, this last example points to a possibly more substantial claim that semantic density of language is more properly associated with literature. We would not necessarily disagree with such a claim, but would point out that playing with the double-sidedness or even multiple valency of certain word combinations is regularly to be found in jokes, for example:

Q. How do you make a Swiss roll?
A. Push him down a mountain.

or

Q. What's black and white and red all over?
A. A newspaper.

(where the structural ambiguity i.e. *roll* [verb and noun] and *red* [adjective and verb (read)] is exploited). Or in advertisements such as:

You can't beat the experience (of PAN AM flights)

(where the lexical value of 'experience' as something which you have and something which you can undergo is utilized). And:

You can't see through a Guinness

(where the ambiguity of 'see through' because it is not transparent—Guinness is a dark, opaque beer—and because it is a good honest beer—you 'see through' things which are deceptive—is very subtly played upon).

In case it is thought that we are saying that all language is literary and that all language users are as creative and imaginative as each other, we are *not*. Clearly when Ted Hughes in his poem 'Wind' describes the wind blowing across hills in the following metaphorical terms:

The tent of the hills drummed and strained its guyrope

or Auden—describing a train's progress—deploys phonological

pattern in his poem 'Night Mail':

> Written on paper of every hue
> The pink, the violet, the white and the blue
> The chatty, the catty, the boring, adoring,
> The cold and official and the heart outpouring.
> Clever, stupid, short and long
> The typed and the printed and the spelt all wrong

there are a number of linguistic features which can be isolated (rhythm, rhyme, alliteration, assonance, metaphor, etc.) and which are combined in such a way as to reinforce the message conveyed and to link with other linguistic devices *across the whole text* so that a unity and consistency of effect is produced. Such 'layering' of linguistic features is not so pervasive in the so-called 'non-literary' examples we have examined.

Above all, however, it is important to recognize that questions of value, judgements of relative merit, effectiveness or classic status do not fall directly within the remit of linguistics. Linguists may, indeed should, face such questions, but they must take off some linguistic hats if they want to provide an answer.

In other words it is stressed again that there is no such thing as literary language which can be recognized and isolated in the same way as, for example, the language of newspaper headlines, or legal language, or the language variety of weather forecasting. That is, with the exception of what are loosely identified as poeticisms (e.g. 'eftsoons', 'steed', 'verdure', 'azure') there is no specialist lexis to the extent that 'trough', 'anti-cyclone', 'low pressure', 'isobars' belong unmistakably to the register or language variety of weather forecasting. Neither are there unique syntactic patterns such as:

> Lord's son weds kitchen maid
> Polls freeze out frosty Foot

(articleless substantives, simple present tense) common to newspaper headlines, or:

> The vendor undertakes to exercise no further claim on the aforementioned property

which is restricted to the context of legal contracts and the like.

Literature is not a language variety. This can be demonstrated by pointing out that literary text is almost the only 'context' where different varieties of language can be mixed and still admitted. Any deviation from norms of lexis and syntax in legal documents would be inadmissible, but in these lines from a poem by W. H. Auden different levels of formality, mutually exclusive lexis, and variable syntax (varieties of journalism, military discourse, slang, archaism, etc.) co-exist because Auden judges such heterogeneity as appropriate to his purpose:

> Kicking his mother until she let go of his soul
> Has given him a healthy appetite; clearly, her role
>   In the New Order must be
> To supply and deliver his raw materials free;
>   Should there be any shortage,
> She will be held responsible; she also promises
> To show him all such attentions as befit his age.
>
>   Having dictated peace,
> With one fist clenched behind his head, heel drawn up to thigh
> The cocky little ogre dozes off, ready,
>   Though, to take on the rest
> Of the world at the drop of a hat or the mildest
>   Nudge of the impossible,
> Resolved, cost what it may, to seize supreme power and
> Sworn to resist tyranny to the death with all
>   Forces at his command.

> (W. H. Auden, 'Mundus et Infans')

Similar features are to be observed in the poem by Robert Graves, 'The Persian Version', discussed in the chapter by Graham Trengove in this volume. Another notable example is the 'Nausicaa' section of James Joyce's *Ulysses*, in which the language commonly associated with sentimental pulp fiction is employed, or the 'Proteus' section in which, sometimes within the same clause, different historical varieties co-exist in order to embody, it might be said, the gradual gestation of an embryo—simultaneously of a child and the modern English language—and in order to serve to remind us that any non-literary linguistic form can be pressed into literary service. Writers will exclude no language from a literary function.

To conclude this section, it is necessary to establish two central points.

1 Linguistics *as a descriptive science* can reveal some interesting aspects of language use in what are 'conventionally' literary or non-literary contexts. Such linguistic analysis should assist students of literature to consider in a rational way some of the questions raised, and to re-examine their own presuppositions about literary

language and the nature of literature itself. It does mean that proverbs, jokes, ambiguities, metaphors, etc. can be exploited in the 'literature' class. In fact, we have come to believe that it may be more productive for us to talk about language and *literariness* rather than 'literary language'. (See Werth 1976 and Carter and Nash 1983.) This points to the fact that what is literary is a matter of relative degree, with some textual features of language signalling a greater literariness than others. The category is one best identified along a gradient or cline, rather than seen as a yes/no distinction. This whole area of language and literariness is examined further in the following section, and pursued with reference to classroom teaching strategy in a number of articles in this book, most notably by Nash and by Short and Candlin, who offer a slightly different emphasis for this point by stressing the reading procedures and strategies used for processing texts, and advocate comparison of different discourses in order to explore these 'readings' rather than to illuminate the nature of 'literary' discourse itself. (See also Haynes 1976.)

2 Linguistics as a *descriptive science* is not able to comment on, evaluate, or otherwise account for the *significance* of the instances of language examined here. Linguistic analysis might be able to reveal *how* Ted Hughes constructs a line of poetry or a journalist a newspaper headline, but other non-linguistic criteria are much more important for its 'appreciation'—that is, for our recognition of it as a text worth our consideration. Criteria for this decision will be based on the arguments (which might be political, moral, or any other) which the formal analysis is intended to illustrate.

3 Literature, language, and discourse

In the previous section we explored the operation of language in a range of contexts, including a literary context. We attempted to demonstrate that features of language, conventionally assumed to be literary, occur in contexts not normally considered to be literature. We concluded that it is productive to talk about *literariness* in language where some uses of language are more or less 'literary' than others. A natural concomitant of this would be an approach to the teaching of literature in which language study and literary study are more closely integrated and harmonized than is commonly the case at the present time.

It must be recognized that such proposals generate some important questions as well as some knotty problems. One is that we concentrate conveniently on short texts, single lines of poetry, and on literary extracts. Reasons of space do not permit otherwise, but we openly acknowledge the dangers inherent in this and advocate that, where practicable, opportunities should be found in the classroom for students to try to explore some of the questions and test out the limits of the problems by using complete, self-contained texts. We share the reservations expressed by Guy Cook in his chapter on this topic in this volume.

Another 'problem' is that examination of literariness in language leads inevitably to the question: what is literary discourse? That is, given these conclusions or discoveries about the nature of literariness in language, how is it that some texts are read as literary and others are not? It is a question which in a number of important respects goes beyond formal linguistic analysis, though its implications for the use of literature in language teaching may be significant. This section will be devoted to the question, although it will be possible to do no more than indicate some of the parameters necessary to an answer. This is partly because the issues are complex, but also because our constant pedagogic aim is to suggest areas for investigation and interpretation that the learner might find interesting, rewarding, and useful to pursue.

A framework for a working definition of the nature of literary discourse can be supplied by examining the texts on page 12. Both 'texts' are about telephones and how they are used. In a basic sense, Text A is expected. We expect there to be imperatives in an instructional text; we expect variations in paragraphing and print size for purposes of clarity. The context for Text A is that we would read it with a telephone in front of us; in other words, it is dependent for its meaning on a medium outside the text itself. After reading Text A we might expect to be able to perform an action in the world (making a phone call) in a more accomplished manner. The language used is, as we would hope, unambiguous in its reference to the specific features of the depicted object. We make sense of what is communicated without paying attention to it as a communicative act. We would only notice it as a text in language if expected frames of references were broken (e.g. if interrogatives were used instead of imperatives, or if words became ambiguous or began to rhyme). By contrast, Text B does not even mention the word telephone. We work out the referent for ourselves and are given no unambiguous guidance by the text. It is not a prerequisite

Text A

When You Make a Call

First check the code (if any) and number.

Lift the receiver and *listen for dialling tone* (a continuous purring).

Dial carefully and allow the dial to return freely.

Then wait for another tone:

Ringing tone (burr-burr) the number is being called.

Engaged tone (a repeated single note) try again a few minutes later.

Number unobtainable tone (steady note) replace receiver, re-check the code and number, and then re-dial.

After dialling a trunk call there will be a pause before you hear a tone; during this time the trunk equipment will be connecting your call.

At the end of the call, replace the receiver securely because timing of calls stops when the caller hangs up.

When You Answer the Telephone

Always give your name or telephone number.

If you hear a series of rapid pips, the call is coming from a coinbox telephone. Wait until the pips stop and then give your name or telephone number.

General Post Office: *Dialling Instructions and Call Charges* (GPO, 1970)

Text B

......

In homes, a haunted apparatus sleeps
that snores when you pick it up.

If the ghost cries, they carry it
to their lips and soothe it to sleep

with sounds. And yet, they wake it up,
deliberately, by tickling with a finger.

(From Craig Raine: 'A Martian Sends a Postcard Home')

for our reading it that we have a telephone or any other object in front of us. Having read it, we will not expect to be able to use the telephone better. We have not been 'instructed' in anything. The poem does not conform to our expected frames of reference; rather, such frames are dislocated. With the Martian we come to see the telephone in a different or new way; it is *represented* from a fresh angle as it were, and we negotiate the extent to which an alternative world is represented. We might enjoy reading it, be amused by it, want to read it again because it is worth reading for itself. Such claims could not normally be made in respect of Text A.

Further exploration of such questions from a pedagogic perspective can be found in contributions by Short and Candlin, Carter, and Nash.

There are, however, a number of relevant 'teaching' points to be made here. The main one is to reinforce the importance of studying literature in regular conjunction with other discourse types. In the first place, this can serve to assist students in identifying and understanding the operation of language for different communicative functions and sensitizing them to what Widdowson terms the 'conventional schemata' of 'ordinary discourses'—in itself an important feature of language development in foreign-language learning. As far as 'literary' studies are concerned, students also acquaint themselves with the nature of literary discourses and therefore are studying literature in a very primary and essential sense. But there is a more subtle and ultimately more substantial purpose in a teacher of a foreign literature using literary text in this way. It has been framed very clearly by H. G. Widdowson in a recent interview (*ELT Journal*, 37/1, 1983):

. . . If you're a sensible teacher you use every resource that comes to hand. But the difference between conventional discourse and literature is that in conventional discourse you can anticipate, you can take short cuts; when reading a passage, let's say, you often know something about the topic the passage deals with, and you can use that knowledge while reading naturally in order to find out what's going on in the passage. This is a natural reading procedure: we all do it. The amount of information we normally take out of something we read is minimal, actually, because we simply take from the passage what fits the frame of reference we have already established before reading. Now you can't do that with literature . . . because you've got to find the evidence, as it were, which is representative of some new reality.

So with literary discourse the actual *procedures for making sense* are much more in evidence. You've got to employ interpretative procedures in a way which isn't required of you in the normal reading process. If you want to develop these procedural abilities to make sense of discourse, then literature has a place . . .

We would agree with Widdowson here in claiming that literature can encourage in students an ability to infer meanings by *interacting* with the text. That is, things are often deliberately left unclear in literary text. The nature of the communication can be problematic, and the student has to search both backwards and forwards, in and across and outside the text for clues which might help to make sense of it. The meaning is self-contained in the language but it is not to be discovered by appeal to neat, simple, conventional formulas. It has, as Widdowson puts it, to be *inferred by procedural activity* (our italics). Such training in deciphering the communication, in working out its *status* as a communication, is a crucial factor in the development of language learning abilities. It is also, we want to stress, the case that when literature is used (though never exclusively), it can be much more enjoyable and stimulating for the learner. In Craig Raine's poem, the world of the Martian, for example, is not real in an absolute sense, but it stands in a relation to the real world and offers us a perspective on it which, for us at least, is original and exciting and thought-provoking. In a number of respects, therefore, we would want to claim that a focus on literature as discourse can have an important contribution to make to language study and learning and can help students to appreciate more fully the nature of literature as literature.

The whole question of literary versus 'informational' text in the language classroom has been framed very clearly by Littlewood (1976) and this paragraph serves as an effective summary of this part of our Introduction:

Literary texts have a different relationship to external reality. They, too, depend upon it for their raw material and for their interpretability, but after selecting elements from it, aim to combine these elements into a new portion of reality which exists only within the text. The reader is asked to recreate this reality in his mind, using evidence from the language of the text and from his own knowledge of the world. His relationship to a literary text thus differs in important respects from that of a reader of an informational text. The reader's creative (or rather, 'co-creative') role, and the imaginative involvement engendered by this role, encourage a dynamic interaction between reader, text and external world, in the course of which the reader is constantly seeking to form and retain a coherent picture of the world of the text. The possibly static and unquestionable reality of the informational text is replaced by a fluid, dynamic reality, in which there is no final arbiter between truth and falsehood. The possibility exists for a meaningful dialogue with the text or, at group level, about the text.

In conclusion, then, we would want to argue for a re-definition or re-orientation in the use of literature in both the foreign-language and mother-tongue classroom. First, a literary text is authentic text, real language in context, to which we can respond directly. It offers a context in which exploration and discussion of *content* (which if appropriately selected can be an important motivation for study) leads on naturally to examination of language. What is said is bound up very closely with how it is said, and students come to understand and appreciate this. Literary texts provide examples of language resources being used to the full, and the reader is placed in an *active* interactional role in working with and making sense of this language. Thus, literature lessons make for genuine opportunities in group work and/or open-ended exploration by the individual student. Not all works of literature are fiction, but the reader does not read literature for factual truth or information, and this fluidity of representation prohibits restriction to formulaic language practice. (See the contribution by Michael Long in this volume for a more extended discussion.) It is this open, questioning spirit with which we would hope students might face a literary text. It also helps them to explore the nature of the object itself and learn about it as a communication. It is a basis for students to work out why they like reading what they read, and for extending their language into the more abstract domains associated with increasingly advanced language competence.

4 Literary competence and reading literature

Although our focus in the previous three sections has been on language and on the contributions of linguistics to literature study and teaching, we have also pointed out areas of literary studies to which linguistics cannot be easily applied. Our examination in this section of some parameters for a definition of literary competence shows that, while integrated language and literary study should form an important section of any proposed literature teaching syllabus, it is not and cannot be the whole story.

As we have stressed above, what makes us read a work of literature is a highly complex matter. It is in part to do with language and style, in part to do with authorial intention (a writer can call his or her work 'a novel' or 'a drama'), in part to do with certain readers and critics in certain influential journals and educational institutions assigning the work to such a category. Primarily, however, it is to do with how readers decide to read it. In this respect, what the work is called is not important. Indeed, there are many works which are read or studied as literature which do not fit the standard categories of novel, poem, or play—for example, Edward Gibbon's *The Rise and Fall of the Roman Empire*, Sir Winston Churchill's *The Gathering Storm*, both of which are history books, or William Cobbett's *Rural Rides* or Darwin's *The Voyage of the Beagle*, which are factual travelogues. In fact, one working definition of literature is that we read something as literature when we forego the need to assign it a function. The above books are certainly still read today, but no longer for the function for which they were originally intended. We do not read Gibbon primarily for information. We read it as literature, not as history. Conversely, if we read Blake's 'Tyger' for the information it gives us about a particular species of animal, we would not be reading it as literature. In other words, we are interested in the general state of affairs to which literature refers, rather than in any particular pragmatic message.

However, in reading Gibbon or Darwin as literature and, by implication, reading Adam Smith's *Wealth of Nations* as non-literature, the reader is involved in choices and preferences. We are, in effect, saying that one writer is better than another and are involved thereby in the kind of value judgements to which we were and are probably exposed in educational institutions when teachers suggested that we ought to be reading Hardy rather than Mickey Spillane or Ian Fleming or, across media, to receive greater edification from *Daniel Deronda* than from *Dallas*. To decide in favour of one writer or one work rather than another is generally assumed to involve the exercise of 'taste'. Literary education is seen by many as the inculcation in students of the kind of sensitivity to literature which allows discrimination of the 'good' from the 'bad'. When we have achieved defined capacities of judgement, then we have acquired a literary competence and can be awarded appropriate 'qualifications'.

We are not for the moment challenging this view of literary education as the development of taste. Attention should be drawn, however, to the obvious fact that value judgements are not immutable and that values are as subject to change (from one period of history to the next or from one culture to another) as any other human capacities. In the allocation of the label 'great literature' to a literary work we cannot be making a judgement which is objective or factual, however much we might like to think we are. A value judgement is constituted by the social and historical conditions which determine our particular ideology. The teachers and professors who have the power to decide which books make up an English Literature syllabus reflect in their choices, and in the knowledge of the literature which they purvey, a fundamental structure of beliefs and interests which reflect the particular culture or section of society into which they were born and in which they grew up. There is nothing, in principle, wrong with this or with the fact that they have an ideology; but it is wrong to be so naïve as to proclaim that such choices of texts are value-free or free from a theory of what literature is, and not impregnated with their own ideology or the ideology of their social or national group. As Terry Eagleton puts it in a perceptive opening chapter to his book *Literary Theory* (1983: 14):

> The claim that knowledge should be value free is itself a value judgement.

There can in turn be no discussion or definition of literature which can be objective or value-free, and that includes the analyses which we have offered in this book so far.

Two main pedagogical issues emerge from the above discussion, and they will be briefly discussed here with an eye on some possible practical implications for the classroom teacher. These are difficult issues for all teachers of language and literature, and especially for the teacher working in a context of English as a Foreign Language and Literature.

The first is that different cultures will value different things and that for students from other cultures, attention needs to be given to the selection of material which on the one hand is representative of different traditions, discourse-types, writers, etc. in English literature but which on the other is also 'valued' appropriately by the readers to whom it is taught. As we recognize in the second part of our Introduction, this is an immensely complex issue and it is taken up on several occasions throughout the book.

The second point is no less crucial to classroom teaching. This is that teachers need to make provision for sensitizing students or, to put it another way, developing in them the necessary literary competence to be sensitive to the kinds of styles, forms, conventions, symbolization etc. which a writer communicating in the Western European English-medium literary tradition would assume his or her readers were acquainted with and to which they might be expected to respond accordingly. These are effectively strategies of reading, but they form a component of a culture-specific set of norms and expectations which often need to be explicitly taught in the development of literary competence. Certainly for students of a foreign literature, but for native-speaking students, too, any higher-order pedagogic aims are founded on the fostering of reading skills of this kind. We draw particular attention to them in this section of the Introduction because the 'competence' is an interesting combination of linguistic, socio-cultural, historical, and semiotic awareness.

For example, it cannot be taken for granted that all students of English literature appreciate references to the seasons. Consider this stanza from Wilfred Owen's poem 'Futility':

Move him into the sun;
Gently its touch awoke him once
At home, whispering of fields unsown.
Always it woke him, even in France,
Until this morning and this snow.
If anything might rouse him now
The kind old sun will know.

One important feature is the association of the cold weak sun with winter and death. In many parts of the world a cold sun is unimaginable, and hence such symbolic equations may not be possible. Not all cultures may share the view of the sun as an animate, life-giving entity. Similarly, the equation of autumn and falling leaves with the process of dying is not necessarily easily transferable. By the same token, do all cultures associate yew-trees with death, or death with the colour black, or see it as final in the way that a writer such as Owen sees it? Do all students share the symbolic associations generated for competent readers of English literature by water, or towers, or the apocalyptic resonances of horses, or even the colour red? If not, then major classics of twentieth-century literature such as T. S. Eliot's *The Waste Land*, D. H. Lawrence's *The Rainbow*, or W. B. Yeats's *The Tower* and *The Winding Stair* remain not simply 'difficult' in a linguistic sense. Are students familiar with the notion of a special poetic diction in eighteenth-century English literature or with the semiotic and formalist properties of a sonnet (notably the fact that the form is appropriate to relatively elevated treatments of love and death)? If not, then the sonnets of the American poet e. e. cummings, which deviate from standard expectations in both form and content, will prove difficult for some students to understand and appreciate. Just as there are rules and expectancies in spoken discourse exchanges, so literature, as a communicative act, relies on expectations and norms forming an important element in the channel of communication between writer and reader, and the teacher of literature needs to help students to acquire the requisite literary competence.

Finally, to conclude this section on 'reading' literature, a further dimension must be acknowledged. This is an under-researched area which exposes to some extent the necessarily ethnocentric focus of our concerns so far and reflects also on the use of the terms 'literature' and 'English literature'. It does not require us to point out that there is a vast and growing body of literatures in English in different parts of the world and that, thus far, stylistic analysis has only in very rare cases addressed itself to the kinds of language issues brought about by the existence and increasing study of these literatures in conjunction with, in opposition to, or in exclusion from the canons of English literature. Mention of writers such as Chinua Achebe, Amos Tutuola, Raja Rao, and Salman Rushdie (to name writers from only two countries—Nigeria and India) raises the issue of 'creative writing by non-western bilingual users of English in typical non-western settings where English is primarily used as an institutionalized second language' (Kachru 1983a). Such 'contact literatures' exhibit stylistic and discoursal characteristics which differ markedly from the traditional canons of English literature and bring with them related culture-specific problems of interpretation. Students of language and literature in different parts of the world, as well as the teachers designing their syllabuses, need to be able to discuss such matters in a systematic way. It is in the light of such concerns that Braj Kachru's contribution should be read. He, too, acknowledges the need for extensive further research particularly with reference to pedagogic practice. The clear implication in his paper that the interface of language and literature is a multi-faceted one involving 'reading' the languages of literatures in English as well as Language and Literature is therefore important and should be considered in conjunction with the kinds of ideological issues raised by Ngugi in his contribution to the literature and education section of this volume.

In order to prepare for the next half of our introduction, in which educational issues are more directly addressed, let us attempt to draw out some of the implications for teachers in the above discussion, where the main argument has been for fuller integration of language and literary studies.

It is unreasonable to expect non-native speakers to approach literary texts in English with the intuitions of a native speaker, but they can be encouraged to approach them with increasing command of different levels of language organization so that they can systematically check and work out *for themselves* the expressive purposes a writer might embrace in fulfilling or deviating from linguistic expectations. Such exploration can be overdone and can be operated mechanically, but objections to analysis *per se* are anti-intellectual. The processes which the teacher adopting this kind of stylistic approach can facilitate are essentially ones which are open and problem-solving, which complement intuitions about and responses to the context of the text and which lay a basis for fuller understanding, appreciation, and interpretation.

At the same time, we recognize that teachers need to contextualize such 'integration': (a) by recognizing the importance of linguistic and non-linguistic criteria in text selection; (b) by using 'language-based approaches' as prior to stylistic analysis where the needs of the learners require this; (c) by recognizing that some areas of language organization can create greater problems than others, especially in the case of foreign students (e.g. lexis with the many social and cultural associations it can convey); (d) by according a due contextualization to social, historical, biographical, and political background to text study, where appropriate, while at the same time recognizing the contrasting methodological problems this can produce, in that stylistics offers a basically heuristic, investigative learner-centred activity, whereas background studies often involve transmissive teacher-centred exposition.

The last two sections above explored the value which can accrue from studying varieties of language in conjunction, and from teaching response to literariness in language rather than to literary language as an exclusive domain. Seeing literature along a continuum of discourse styles can help students to develop sensitivity to all language use as well as foster acquisition of those kinds of sense-making procedures particularly but not exclusively relevant for the interpretation of literary discourse. However, teachers will recognize that the kinds of competence thus developed have to be located within a framework which incorporates culture-specific assumptions, relations between literature and ideology, notions of a 'canon' of texts, and the linguistic and other issues provoked by the existence of literatures in English alongside English literature—a framework, in other words, with direct implications for syllabus design and methodology in language *and* literature.

Literature and Education

Whatever view we take of the nature of literature, there is clearly some phenomenon which is recognized by educational administrators and by the general public as an appropriate object for study in schools and universities. Yet, perhaps because of the difficulties we have outlined in the first part of this Introduction, there seems to be far less clear thinking about the teaching of literature than about almost any other recognized 'subject'. In this part of the Introduction we propose to examine some of the problems raised by the teaching of literature (others will be explored in later papers). Many of these will apply equally to literature in the mother tongue and to literature in a foreign or second language. Other problems will be specific to non-native speakers and their teachers.

Is literature 'caught' or 'taught'?

If we see the teaching of literature as more than simply the use of literary texts in the classroom, we shall have to confront directly the implications of the notion of 'literary competence' as explored by our earlier discussion. If, in practice, reading a literary text involves some sort of engagement by the reader beyond simply being able to understand the meanings of the utterances in the text, then we need to ask how this engagement is acquired. Traditional practice has normally been to include discussion and analysis of literary texts in class, and to assume that learners will in some way 'catch' the ability to read appropriately from the process of discussion and analysis in a fairly random way. Some thought may go into the selection of texts, but the rest of the activity is frequently unplanned and random. And in many schools and colleges even the selection of texts is determined more by tradition or the interests of the teachers then by deliberate choice of those texts which are most suitable for the needs of the learners.

Now we need to recognize that random exposure is not necessarily a bad thing. We have already seen that literary texts are complex objects, and we can readily accept that their most important characteristics may be distorted or destroyed if a schematic and insensitive organization is imposed on a rich and subtle work of art. Good teachers have for many years selected works that they thought were accessible to their students and explored the implications of each work, without trying to impose a rigid syllabus on the activity. And few people would expect us to be able to 'teach' someone to like a particular book.

But we can help students to avoid disliking a book simply because they misunderstand the conventions being used, or because the language is too difficult, or because the cultural references are inaccessible. Even if we assume that the development of sensitive and committed appreciation of literature is not going to be explicitly taught, we can still be as systematic as possible about the principles with which we operate. Only then can we expect new, inexperienced, or overworked teachers to teach as effectively as their circumstances allow, for they will rely heavily on whatever publicly available help can be provided. Any successful teacher, therefore, has a responsibility to be as clear as possible about the principles—in so far as they can be publicly stated—on which that success has been based. At the same time, the process of making the bases of what we do as clear as possible will also help the private development and improvement of an individual teacher, for the more clearly problems and difficulties are stated, the more likely they are to be resolved.

In fact, the argument about what is caught and what is taught rests on a misunderstanding of the nature of teaching any complex subject. None of us teaches anything worthwhile directly to students: we simply create the conditions for successful learning. Only in a trivial sense will we be able to train specific responses by direct intervention, as with item-by-item question and answer. But we shall be able to demonstrate over a long period the process of responding to a varied range of works of literature and some of the infinite number of possible appropriate responses. In this sense, the teacher must provide the model towards which the students work—but only in general terms: we are not expecting students to replicate our responses in detail, only to develop their own, to move towards the kinds of responses we would expect of any sympathetic and reasonably knowledgeable adult reader. This is a model of behaviour which can only be caught; it certainly cannot be commanded or instructed.

As we have seen, the process of reading is a process of meaning-creation by integrating one's own needs, understanding, and expectations with a written text. Each student will have different needs, understanding, and expectations, so each student will derive slightly different messages from reading a particular book or poem. But the text itself will be constructed on the basis of conventions which may or may not be directly accessible to the student, and some of these conventions will, if misinterpreted, so distort the meaning that the text will be perceived as incomprehensible, or irrelevant. There is no point in leaving learners to grope their way towards understanding without direct intervention to clarify what might otherwise remain inaccessible for so long that they will abandon literature in frustration if they are not helped. Nor, conversely, is there any point in insisting on detailed examination of points which, while obscure, do not impede initial response. There is no need to demand from non-native speakers of English a closer understanding of Dickens than we would expect of native-speakers, at least at the early stages of learning.

In other words, we should think in terms of suiting the literary demands that are made of students to their stage of development. We should have some notion of grading our activities. In practice, of course, all experienced teachers do this. But, unlike language teaching for example, literature teaching does not seem to have had much serious discussion of the need to grade, or the nature of appropriate grading. Consequently, many literature teachers resent the idea that the subtlety of their work should be crudely schematized by some sort of rigid grading system.

Yet this is not what is being asked for. All that is expected is that some principles should be established for sorting out priorities in teaching, to enable teachers and learners to work together more effectively. This will involve the teacher working with a whole range of different procedures, with the overall aim of allowing students to catch the ability to respond enthusiastically and appropriately to works of literature, but with subsidiary aims which will help students to learn specific points which will assist the larger aim. (See 'Reading Skills and the Study of Literature in a Foreign Language' in this volume for development of some of these points.)

The nature of literature syllabuses

If we are to talk at all clearly about literary syllabuses, we need to distinguish between a number of different reasons for using literary works in the classroom. In second-language and foreign-language teaching there are at least three distinguishable major aims. Many teachers use literature to assist the development of competence in the language (for reasons that we ourselves have argued above). Although the texts being used are literary, and some of the responses of readers will be discussed in literary terms, the prime intention is to teach language, not literature, and the texts may be used as contexts for exemplification and discussion of linguistic items which have no bearing on the value of the work as literature. Sometimes, as Guy Cook's paper shows, there may be a major conflict in language pedagogy caused by the desire to use literary texts, and literary texts often carry potential danger if the reasons for their use are not clearly thought through. Good literary texts are not thereby 'good style' for non-literary purposes, and they may indeed be misleading as linguistic material for learners with non-literary learning intentions.

A second reason for including literary texts is in order to teach 'culture'. It is claimed that studying literature enables us to understand the foreign culture more clearly. McKay's paper partly adopts this position. Again, while we would accept this view, we would stress that there are dangers if the view of a syllabus for the teaching of culture is confused or blurred by an identification of literature with culture. As with a language syllabus, it is perfectly possible to conceive of a culture syllabus, for particular categories of learner, which would never include any pure literature at all. Certainly the role of literature in either language or culture courses should be a minor one, for there are many aspects of both language and culture which will be distorted by the process of literary creation.

The problem with using literary texts for non-literary purposes is that the status of the texts themselves is very difficult to define for most non-native speaking teachers, as well as for learners. Literature retains a self-consciousness about literary tradition which is often quite inappropriate for writing in other fields. We cannot entirely separate literature from the history of literature, and it is unhelpful to view literary texts as either naturalistic pictures of British or American life, for purposes of cultural study, or as examples of the best use of the English language, for language courses. The language and the content of literature is deliberately and creatively modified (even often distorted) for the needs of the writer. The kind of understanding we may expect to gain of Victorian London from Dickens's novels is at a far higher level of abstraction than that of the straight pictorial and descriptive, and it would be a strange view of Britain derived from the novels of Iris Murdoch, or of America from those of Malamud—or even from less obviously subjective novelists such as Margaret Drabble or John Updike.

Consider the following, for example (from Margaret Drabble's *Jerusalem the Golden*, 1967, Penguin edition, p. 61).

Victoria Station, when they arrived upon it, did not present a particularly exclusive aspect. It was crowded and swarming with school parties, hundreds of schools all gathered together, some in uniform, some not in uniform, some accompanied, some unaccompanied. Clara stared at them all hungrily, at the meek and the marshalled, at the loudly swearing, at the sophisticates, at the nervous and the panic-stricken ticket-mislayers. And she stared too at her own friends, who appeared to her suddenly in a new light, laughing and fiddling with their luggage labels, and casting their eyes around them as though unbalanced by the sudden variety of choice. The whole station was like some vast and awkward school dance, where need and constraint mingle in a heady, violent ferment of suppression. And Clara was glad that she was not accompanied by Walter Ash. She stood a better chance, she thought, upon her own: though a chance of what she would not have liked to have said.

This looks like a quite realistic description of Victoria Station, integrated with the subjective feelings of the heroine, Clara. Now consider the following (from Bernard Malamud's *The Natural*, 1952, Penguin edition, p. 180).

Judge Banner had a money-saving contract with a small maternity hospital near Knights Field (it was there Bump had died) to treat all player emergencies, so that was where they had rushed Roy. The flustered obstetrician on duty decided to deliver the hero of his appendix. However, he fought them deliriously and his strength was too much for the surgeon, anaesthetist, attendant, and two mild maternity nurses. They subdued him with a hypo only to uncover a scar snaking down his belly. Investigation showed he had no appendix—it had long ago been removed along with some other stuff. (All were surprised at his scarred and battered body.) The doctors considered cutting out the gall bladder or maybe part of the stomach but nobody wanted to be responsible for the effect of the operation upon the Knights and the general public. (The city was aghast. Crowds gathered outside the hospital, waiting for bulletins. The Japanese government issued an Edict of Sorrow.) So they used the stomach pump instead and dredged up unbelievable quantities of bilge. The patient moaned along with the ladies in labour on the floor, but the doctors adopted a policy of watchful waiting and held off anything drastic.

Even without the context of the rest of the book, there are features here that suggest something larger than life, an exaggerated picture which can scarcely be used as a source of information about real hospitals. Common sense, also, may suggest that baseball players are not typically treated in maternity hospitals. But how does this description differ from that in Margaret Drabble's book? Unless we know whether Victoria Station is a customary gathering point for school parties, whether uniforms are normal, or unusual, whether they mark the school off for social level, and without several other pieces of cultural information, we cannot tell whether we are dealing with something entirely conventional culturally, or something as distorted as the Malamud. Such judgements may not be crucial for understanding the novel as a novel—the significance of all this for Clara will emerge in the story—but they are important in interpreting this description as cultural information.

The problem is that unless you already know British or American life, you cannot use these writers as sources of realistic description, for you cannot recognize the nature of their artistic distortion. And similarly with language, for writers are by definition attempting to produce language which can be read independently of the situation of the reader, whereas most language learners, initially at least, are trying to learn language for their own practical needs.

This argument does not prevent us from making use of literary texts; nor does it stop us using them sometimes for linguistic or cultural purposes, as long as we are aware of the risks and feel competent to distinguish the typical native language or culture from the characteristic stylistic or reference features of the writers being used. Indeed, we may wish to benefit from the added interest of literary texts. But we cannot justify such material on the grounds that literature offers pictures of foreign life, or samples of typical excellent language. Both of these claims are based on false theoretical positions.

A good language syllabus, then, may include literary texts, but will not necessarily do so. A syllabus intended to provide valuable cultural information will probably include literary texts, but should include a great deal of other information and sources of stimulus, including historical and journalistic material, samples of other art forms, and accounts of scientific and technical and sociological factors.

But of course literature is one major aspect of culture, and many people wish to study it in its own right. In addition it is more cheaply and easily accessible than many other cultural phenomena, and—because it is often responsive to international movements—it may be easier to comprehend than other more locally-based art forms. It is this kind of argument which, for many people, justifies the inclusion of literary courses in education. We would not wish in any way to oppose those who argue in this way. Our only desire is to clarify the justifications for particular educational practices and traditions, so that inappropriate arguments are not advanced to defend and define particular practices.

Syllabuses for literature in its own right

The pure literature syllabus can be justified in its own right, educationally, but it should not be confused with syllabuses for the teaching of language or of culture. The criteria for the selection of texts to be used and the ordering most appropriate to the needs of students will vary, depending on which type of syllabus is being adopted.

Some literary syllabuses, usually at advanced levels, may be primarily informative in intention, and may legitimately be concerned with the history of English literature, or of part of it. Others may be concerned with relating aspects of the English-language literary tradition to particular local interests. There have, for example, been very interesting courses relating the American and Russian realist novel traditions. However, we would wish to argue that this kind of sophisticated language/literary discussion is best preceded by two independent stages of educational work. The first necessary preliminary is linguistic. There is a level of linguistic and cultural competence below which it is pointless trying to respond to works of literature.

Let us first of all modify this statement to the extent that we would accept that (for example) a German scholar, fully conversant with German, and perhaps some other literatures of the Romantic Period, might start studying English literature of the same period with scarcely any knowledge of English, and be able to go straight to Wordsworth, Keats, or Byron with the aid of a bilingual dictionary. Such a person would be able to profit directly from a clear understanding of many shared frames of reference, and there are many examples of language learners who have operated successfully in this way. But they are not, of course, typical, and we are concerned with the role of literary studies in conventional education. So let us ignore those with initially high motivation or aptitude, and concentrate on those whose motivation and aptitude can be developed through the educational experience.

For the typical secondary-school learner a literary response cannot be given by a teacher; it can only arise out of the reading of a text. The problem, for both native and non-native speaking readers, is that a literary response only really starts when fluent reading has already been established. (It will of course develop out of other aesthetic experiences, such as music, dance, listening to stories, and so on—but the adult literary response is in the last resort dependent on isolated reading for which certain preliminary abilities must have been developed.)

The first stage, then, is a minimum language competence. In the mother tongue, where there is a thriving literary tradition, this language competence will often develop side by side with story telling, nursery rhymes, word games, and personal narrative, so that the switch to written mode will not entail a switch to a completely different set of premises, for literary structures influence speech, as well as the other way round. In many parts of the world, where the mother tongue may be that of a primarily oral culture, the switch to written communication that comes with schooling may involve a much greater rhetorical shift. This is an aspect of literature teaching which has been little commented on, but it badly needs further study. We thus have three possible situations in school:

1 students working in their mother tongue on literature, with a

great deal of aesthetically structured speech and children's
writing behind them;

2 students working through a foreign or second language coming
from a culture with a well-developed literary tradition, with
which they are already slightly familiar (these will probably be a
little older than those in (1) above);

3 students working through a second language whose experience
of artistically organized language is primarily oral, and whose
culture may indeed have very different assumptions from those
of western Europe (and of the writers of this Introduction) about
aesthetics and language.

We should perhaps emphasize that major writers and critics within
the western European tradition have originated from all three of
these groups, though of course each bringing different perspectives
to bear.

These three positions are all relative to each other, and few
classes in schools will represent these in absolutely pure forms, but
the distinctions clearly have some validity, and each type will
require a slightly different syllabus. However, we would argue that
there are fewer differences between them than might appear at first
sight.

Even in the case of mother-tongue students, few will come from
homes where reading (in the sense that we are concerned with) is
customary or necessary—and this will apply as much to 'middle
class' or professional homes as to any others (see Pickett's
discussion of reading speed in this volume). Wide reading and
appreciation of literature is thinly spread in all groups of the
population. So we can assume that, in principle, we are developing
a capacity which nearly all students need help with. Where there
will be differences among the three groups is in the nature of their
previous linguistic experience. Those in the first group will be
developing greater linguistic and cultural (and cognitive) sophistication at the same time as they are being exposed to literature as a
teaching subject. Those in the second will probably (and perhaps
ideally should) meet the foreign literature when they have some
understanding of literature as a phenomenon in their own culture,
but with inevitably limited language, originally learnt with a more
instrumental intention (usually) before they turned to literary texts.
Those in the third group will have certainly learnt the language for
educational and instrumental purposes before they have looked at
sophisticated works of literature, but they will differ from the

second group in their lack of background in written literature of any kind.

For all of these, though, we must conceive of the reading of works of literature as primarily an *experience*. And this experience presupposes the ability to gain access to it, at least in some crude sense. A person who has not the reading or comprehension fluency to make sense in general of the words on the page is not in a position to respond to the literariness of the text, and—in our view—the response (however limited or unrefined it may be) must precede the analysis or description of that response.

In crude terms, then, a literary syllabus can start only when a certain level of language or reading competence is presupposed. That syllabus may take its cue from 'literary' elements in earlier reading or language work, but it can start only when considerations of literary significance can be directly apprehended by the learner. The literary syllabus itself (concerned primarily with enabling learners to respond to writing as literature rather than as instrumental, pragmatically useful discourse) should have two broad stages, with the second one an option for those who wish to go on to become self-conscious about the process.

The first stage will be concerned with enabling students to 'experience' literature; the second will enable them to describe, explain, or otherwise 'account for' the experience. (Our case study, discussed below, explores ways of developing this distinction.) But, in our view, the error of much literature teaching is that, in practice, it reverses this process. In other papers in this book some ways of enabling this experience to take place will be touched upon, but our concern here is to emphasize the autonomy of the literature syllabus in principle, and to suggest the basic requirements of a literature syllabus.

We shall not attempt at this stage to 'justify' the teaching of literature. Suffice it to say that for us, as for many teachers, the personal experience of reading major literature is sufficiently important for us to wish to communicate this need to our students and to help them develop the capacity to read for themselves in this way. Ultimately, perhaps, this is the only honest justification for any kind of teaching. Starting from this position, we can ask ourselves what particular groups of students need most if they are to become committed readers of serious literature. We are avowedly socializing students into a community of serious readers—not with any necessary assumptions about what texts must be read, but with an assumption that the best reading matter will be approached through a tradition, in the sense of the accumulated experience of thousands of readers in the past and present who have been committed to reading, thinking about, and discussing imaginative literature for the light it sheds on themselves and their position as human beings.

We do not start, then, with a programme of 'knowledge about' any particular literature, for we are not primarily concerned with external information. If students are to develop at some later date an understanding of particular historical traditions, they will be able to do that reliably only if they have already had some experience of genuine reading. We want to develop committed readers, who may read—say—Voltaire or Brecht or Solzhenitsyn or Greene or Achebe or Bellow. But we do not want to say to readers of novels that there are some of these writers that they should prefer. At a later stage there may be a place for arguments about which writers have most value in relation to particular philosophies or ideologies, but that argument should emerge from wide and varied reading. If our ambition is to produce as many students as possible who will read all these writers, and any others who could be included, we do not want to start with a course which relies on unnecessary limitation.

Consequently, the key criterion for a literature course is whether the books on the syllabus are accessible for serious discussion and personal experience to a particular group of students. Nor do we wish students to be 'taken' through the books. Discussion is not a way of learning to read a book; it is something which analyses an experience already achieved, at least in part. So we need to select texts to which students can respond immediately, without the mediation of the teacher. Only then can we guide the students' response, rather than impose it from the outside.

Issues of grading are discussed later in this book, so we shall not anticipate the discussion. For the moment it is enough to note that we need to be conscious of the intellectual level, the social and political expectations, the cultural presuppositions and the previous literary/aesthetic experience, as well as the linguistic level of each class of students. In practice, such matters are often intuitively raised by teachers' discussions of which books have been successful in the past, but it is possible to be clear about the implications of such discussion only if we have a fairly clear idea of where we are going in a literature course and of what qualities students will normally bring to the course at the beginning.

If we are to teach literature effectively, then, we need to have some specification of the characteristics of typical learners when they start our course, and of what we want them to be like when they finish. Particularly, we need to recognize that we cannot claim to be teaching specific books; rather we are teaching attitudes and abilities which will be relevant to the reading of any major works of literature. To do this we should in addition have some view of what being a good reader entails, and of how the various kinds of classroom activity available to us will promote effective response. Although many of the papers in this book begin to discuss such questions, the discussion can only be preliminary, for the traditional high status of literature has—paradoxically—prevented the degree of analysis of aims, methods, and objectives found in the discussion of other, less-favoured subjects.

'High' literature, literature, and reading

We have already suggested that the reading of literature is predicated upon a basic competence in general reading. In fact, many people, perhaps most people, even in highly literate cultures, do a certain amount of reading as part of their daily life, but do not read any kind of imaginative literature at all. Many others do read, but would never think of reading any of the writers who have so far been referred to in this discussion. One of the advantages of a concern with literature as an *attitude* to texts, rather than as a body of texts, is that it is unnecessary to become involved with a discussion of 'highbrow' writers versus others. The capacity to read so that one is 'inside' the story is as necessary for Fielding or Dostoyevsky as it is for Arthur Haley, Barbara Cartland, or Agatha Christie. The commitment for the literature teacher is to texts which can be discussed in such a way that the events, or characters, or anything else in the fictive world of the book are closely related to the personal needs of readers and learners as they attempt to define themselves and understand the human situation. The choice of books made by teachers, therefore, will reflect on profound and serious issues, and will draw upon the widely recognized tradition of 'serious' literature. But the methodology should encourage students to introduce into the discussion any books they read themselves which they themselves perceive to be relevant. Teachers of literature should not be concerned with the tradition because it is a tradition, but rather with books (which may or may not be part of the high tradition) that are directly needed by students at that stage of their literary development. These may be books which challenge assumptions, and should not normally be ones which merely reinforce local prejudices. But the issue of grading forces us to consider the relationship between colonial literatures and post-independence literature in Third World countries, or literatures of marginal groups and mainstream literature in most countries. Ultimately the aim must be that readers should be willing and able to read the literature of many traditions, for only thus will it be an educational and value-challenging activity. But there is a great deal of sense in moving outwards from what is fairly fully understood because it is based on local cultural assumptions to literature of another class, region, or period.

At the same time, it is dangerous to be too simplistic about what is accessible to whom. Shakespeare has been far more successful in Africa, where there is a strong tradition of oral rhetoric still alive, than in many urban centres in Britain, and students may find nineteenth-century literature closer to their own experience of how they live their lives than much contemporary work. The key question is how to provide students with a reading experience which to a greater degree than other available experiences enriches their perception of what it is to be human. It will be a long time before a more versatile piece of educational technology than the paperback book is invented, and there is no more easily available source for personal growth than serious literature. The tragedy is that, whether in mother tongue or foreign languages, literature remains inaccessible to so many people. It is our hope that the papers in this collection will enable us at least to start clarifying some of the many neglected problems in the development of effective literary education.

PART ONE

Literature and Language

Introduction

In this section we explore a variety of procedures and issues in considering a possible linking of language and literary studies in education. Michael Long finds links between the structural approach to language teaching and the relative neglect of the teaching of English literature to non-native speakers, in the fact that discrete-point teaching does not fit easily with literature, which allows differing interpretations and responses; and in the fact that from structural language teaching it appeared possible to postulate a highly systematized methodology, where the teaching of literature traditionally 'muddled by', with limited awareness of methodology. 'No methodology' is of course impossible. But teachers of literature often do not have a clear idea of what sort of response a non-native speaker might reasonably be expected to give. Michael Long investigates here the sorts of question to which the learner might be expected to respond, the frequency of such questions, and their range, and from this attempts to show that, properly arranged, such procedures might lead to a better undestanding of literary text, and offer definite advantages for language proficiency and language teaching generally. In fact, while literature teaching and study supplements language learning, a varied and slightly adventurous approach to language teaching (using literary text) aids the teaching of literature. This may not always correspond to a 'traditional' approach to the teaching of literature. Yet it is both defensible in itself and in line with current practice in the language teaching profession, where, from lower-intermediate levels upwards, a 'group dynamics' approach can involve both a considerable stimulus to learning, and a lessening of teacher-centredness. This article explores the teacher–learner/learner–learner relationship, but argues that the teacher needs to know how to set up the procedures, where and when to make a direct input, and when to rely on a learner-centred activity. The article does not examine the sorts of development which can occur through stylistic analysis. The issues raised by Michael Long are at a basic and introductory level of integration at the interface of literature and language study. Among the questions raised by this paper for our consideration are issues of the pros and cons of using children's literature in these circumstances, of the risk of 'preparatory questions' being found patronizing by learners, and of the difficulty of generating enough higher-order questions from this kind of text. Questions are liable to become 'content' questions, so that literary texts without heavy content (lyrical poems for example: cf. Widdowson's paper) will be neglected. Is this justifiable at the early stages of literary work? (Monica Vincent's paper in Part Two raises related questions with reference to simplified texts.)

Graham Trengove argues that awareness of language variety can be an important prerequisite for responding sensitively to literary language use. Writers will often exploit the capacities of a language to express shifts in social context, role relationships, attitude to subject matter, emotional association, and so on. Although literary language is not necessarily deviant, writers will often produce particular effects by subtly and strikingly deviating from expected contextual norms. Trengove argues that the development of awareness of varieties of English in use is crucial to an adequate teaching of literature in a foreign language, and that literature study should also enhance awareness of language functions. He concludes his paper with an examination and interpretation of how such uses of language are deployed in a poem by Robert Graves. This paper can be read within the framework of discussion of the continuum between literary and non-literary varieties in sections 2 and 3 of the first half of the Introduction to this book, but it also offers an example of stylistic analysis in action which complements discussion in Section 1 of the Introduction and in papers by Widdowson and Short and Candlin.

Walter Nash discusses some language-based activities which can lead to fruitful appreciation of literary uses of language and which can therefore run parallel or antecedent to close linguistic–stylistic examination of a text. The focus is on the technique of 'summary' or paraphrase (see also the first part of the paper by Carter for related discussion), a widely practised language teaching technique which Walter Nash argues can be notably productive in the teaching of literary idiom.

The paper attempts to define the possibilities of paraphrase, starting from the position that in so-called 'ordinary' language there are turns of phrase, common sayings, etc. which are *encapsulations* of literariness. We may paraphrase a proverb narrowly, translating instance into instance, or broadly, so as to display the scope of a generalized application. Such adaptability of 'scope', it is suggested, is a characteristic of literary language, and in poems is one of the primary obstacles to the writing of a paraphrase. Two styles of paraphrase are suggested: the explanatory, which summarizes or re-words, and the *mimetic*, which echoes or parodies. The value of both styles lies in their crass ability, through inadequacy or absurdity, to focus attention on details of grammatical structure, semantic patterning, and general qualities of 'literariness' in poetic and other texts. Some exercises and suggestions for development are appended. Walter Nash's paper can be usefully read in conjunction with discussions of literariness and language use in papers by Carter, and Short and Candlin, and in Section 2 of the first part of the book's Introduction.

The chapter by Short and Candlin describes in detail a course developed at the University of Lancaster specifically for the training of teachers of English as a foreign language and literature. Its focus is on the kinds of 'study skills' judged to be a prerequisite for both teachers and their students to effect an integration of language and literary study. Chris Candlin and Michael Short touch on a number of issues raised elsewhere in the book, notably the kinds of reading development appropriate to a progressive literary competence, the nature of the literary background needed by foreign students, and the usefulness of a stylistic approach to text studies. A particular feature of their course which is described in some detail in the chapter is the juxtaposition of 'literary' and 'non-literary' texts. This part of their paper links closely with the position argued in Sections 2 and 3 of the first part of the Introduction to this book. Candlin and Short pursue the principle that literary language is not exclusive from, but co-terminous with, general language use and that students of foreign literatures can derive heightened sensitivity to all texts, but especially literary texts, if they are given regular opportunities for textual analysis, comparison, and student-centred project-type investigation of literariness in language. We could well ask, though, whether evaluative considerations should not play a part in the selection of texts for such exercises—or would we expect all students to respond to all texts in the same way? Can we, indeed *should* we, teach foreign students to value some kinds of writing more highly than others? If we do not, are we actually concerned with literature at all, or simply with certain texts as stylistic artefacts? In Parts Two and Three of this book such issues emerge again, where the political and social values of literary texts are considered, as well as aesthetic value.

Ron Carter argues both for a greater integration of language and literature study and also for approaches which preserve the distinctiveness of each mode of study. To this end he proposes, with reference to a short story by Somerset Maugham, a number of language-based study strategies which can serve as useful activities preliminary to a fuller literary investigation. The activities can serve to promote defined language skills, as well as to develop a competence to recognize and respond to the literariness of a literary text. He then goes on to propose that linguistic models, such as those developed for narrative analysis, should be more widely used in literature teaching, since they can serve as heuristic enabling devices for appreciation and integrated study of narrative shaping for literary effects and of language use in narrative organization. The essay concludes with a recognition of both the strengths of systematic language study and of the need to see such language investigation both in a wider context of trans-linguistic investigation of literature and as preliminary to the kinds of stylistic analysis illustrated elsewhere in this book. Although interpretation of the 'meanings' of the Maugham story is not the main aim, a basis is laid on which those interested in this activity could usefully proceed. Carter, like Nash in his paper, argues for starting from the language, and with language activities, as a means of entry to literary texts. But other means have been attempted by teachers (for example starting through experiences—with photographs, music, and other stimuli). Are these procedures likely to be more motivating than linguistic ones? What could be gained, and what lost?

Widdowson considers the problem of addressing relatively 'content-less' lyrical poetry in class, and shows by close stylistic analysis how the essentially static effect of a lyric is achieved. As he says, 'the problem for pedagogy is how to persuade students, normally accustomed to recognize significance in terms of sequence in narrative and consequence in argument, to adopt a different perspective and see significance in the third-dimension associations represented in lyrical poems'. He is able to relate this problem to some conventional language teaching practices, such as using dictionaries for considering alternative lexical meanings avoided by the text. The role of alternative paraphrase, so that the meaning of a poem is seen as one of a number of semantic possibilities within a system of potential interpretations, each of which carries historical and social weight, deserves careful consideration. Such an approach demands considerable responsibility of the teacher, however.

In his paper on 'Non-Native Literatures as a Resource for Language Teaching', Braj Kachru examines the appropriateness of using in the language classroom writing in English by non-native users of English. He illustrates clearly a number of 'transcreational' issues of linguistic and cultural relevance to an appropriate reading of such literatures, and raises important questions concerning the degrees to which learners of English, here particularly in a South East Asian context, can achieve cultural identification with such material. In relation to what are more ethnocentrically-focused papers in this part of the book, this contribution provokes careful definition of just what is understood by literature, language, and learning contexts in English, and compares interestingly with the paper by Ngugi in Part Two.

Guy Cook examines the strengths and limitations of using extracts in the teaching of literature in a foreign language. He draws a useful distinction between 'text' and 'extract' and argues that, though often a pedagogical convenience, some kinds of extracts necessarily involve an artificial separation of sentences from a wider context of other sentences with which they more naturally cohere. He also points out that interpretative problems can result as much from difficulties of contextualization as from the kinds of linguistic deviation more usually associated with difficulty in literary text. Cook analyses an extract from the concluding sequence of the James Joyce story *The Dead*, and shows that interpretation of the language used, particularly in respect of cohesive ties, can be viable for the extract, but demonstrably false for our understanding of the whole story. He concludes with a set of suggested criteria for selecting passages for detailed study. The paper is an interesting study in applied linguistics, or 'applied stylistics', in that linguistic study is carefully balanced with pedagogical considerations relevant at all levels of literature teaching.

Finally, as we pointed out earlier, the chapters in Part One in particular, but also in Part Two, operate at different pedagogic levels. From Long's concern to develop a feeling for language among elementary-level students of English as a Foreign Language in the context in which he works in Thailand there is clearly a cline to the more sophisticated second- or even first-language learning contexts presupposed by Nash, Carter, and Short and Candlin. This is not to say, however, that basic issues of response, language awareness, and sequencing of learning tasks are not common to all the contexts. Paradoxically, many of the issues raised here arise in the next section on literature and education. The fact that papers by, for example, McKay or Cook could have appeared in either Part illustrates that some arbitrariness is inherent in 'sections' such as these. It also illustrates that language is always central to literature, but that literature is always more than language.

1 A Feeling for Language: The multiple values of teaching literature

Michael N. Long

Both literature and language teaching involve the development of a feeling for language, of *responses* to 'texts'—in the broadest sense of the word—in both written and spoken discourses. This is not the place to examine the histories of language and literature teaching, but I will do so briefly and crudely here in order to point out that some approaches in the past (in a period approximately 1960–1980) have not always served to develop responses to language or to isolate the different kinds of responses involved. I wish to make two basic points. First, that structural approaches to language learning, with their emphasis on discrete-point teaching, 'correctness' in grammatical form, and repetition of a range of graded structures, restricted lexis, etc., represent a methodology unsuited to literature teaching: it is no wonder that such approaches have been unable to accommodate literary texts. Second, that the teaching of literature has lacked a consistent methodology for presentation to non-native speakers. Too often texts have been presented with great enthusiasm but as if to native-speakers, with the result that learners are often too busy writing in translations of unfamiliar words to respond to the text. The teaching of literature is an arid business unless there is a response, and even negative responses can create an interesting classroom situation (as then the learner has to say *why* he or she dislikes the text). Teaching of literature to non-native speakers should seek to develop responses.

The notion of 'response' has, of course, been investigated before, and intensively, though it is clear that interpretations of the word differ widely. In an essay entitled 'Responses to language in poetry', Carter (1982a) questions the validity for *students* of literature of an article by F. R. Leavis (1969) where the latter refers to 'the delicate play of shifting tone' (and much more of the same kind) in a poem by T. S. Eliot. Leavis, of course, was recording *his own* response, refined almost to the point of being a separate and distinctive art form. Only vicariously does this sort of response concern students, though quotation from such writing has long been a feature of written assignments on text—even to the point of students learning by heart what somebody wrote about something, and reproducing it in examinations, a practice which, I think, has generally found approval among examiners. In the context of this article, however, this seems to be little more than second-hand response.

Carter, referring to the Leavis item, continues: 'It is my contention that criticism such as the above does not really help teachers and pupils to articulate responses to poetry' (op. cit.: 30). The key word here is 'criticism'; criticism is not the same as 'response', especially for non-native speakers. It follows from this that non-native speakers should not, at any but the most advanced levels, be asked to write 'critical essays', for which they do not have the necessary and lengthy training, or the background (which generally means wider reading). Thus when Carter talks of 'ways of integrating classroom study of English language and literature' (op. cit.: 30), any reaction on the part of the learner, whether spoken or written, would be 'response' rather than criticism. Even so, for Carter 'response', though a language-orientated procedure, is still something expected of the native speaker, as he points out in the conclusion to his article (op. cit.: 49), where he mentions having tried certain procedures with specific learners in a mother-tongue environment. For non-native speakers the procedure must necessarily be different again, to the extent that 'response' means basically 'classroom interaction between teacher and learners'. Such interaction might, of course, be everything or nothing; a suggestion as to the form it might take is presented in detail below.

One other 'response', also a native-speaker one, and perhaps a nineteenth-century survival, was to ask students to isolate similes, metaphors, and so on. Ironically, this not very rewarding technique was remarkably similar to what the structural devotees were doing with language teaching, in that it was a discrete-point approach which focused on the part at the expense of the whole, and could be neatly set up in textbooks for teachers who were not very imaginative or pedagogically creative. Moreover, as with the repeated 'over-learning' of a structural form, it was ruinous for motivation, though it had the advantage that it could be easily tested in written examinations.

Thus, while language teaching was going through a mechanistic phase, reducing itself to formulas, and forgetting its 'purpose as message', there was hardly a place for literature. But rather more surprisingly, literature was forgetting its origins as language. Teachers of literature were, of course, at a vast remove from the greater part of what language teaching had become; teaching language was like asking the great exponent of Chopin to practise scales in the concert hall. But the gulf had become even wider: literature for the humanist, language for the scientist—the two cultures—which, to say the least, was an unfortunate split when they could have been helping one another. And the literature specialists, faced with a scientific defeat, became more and more entrenched; delivering the same old lectures, 'Morality in *Macbeth*', or 'Donne's Imagery'. And while language teachers were a product of the new 'technology', literature teachers were becoming rarer and rarer, with the exception of the few enthusiasts, and in all this the learner was often forgotten. Will the current focus on communicative language teaching, with its emphasis on the human purposes and functions of language, bring about changes?

Consider now the following dialogue, which is typical of many current textbooks for language learning:

Mr. James   Will you have a look at my car please?
Mechanic   What's the matter with it?
Mr. James   Well, I'm not sure. But it's not running very well, and it won't start easily.
Mechanic   We'll check the engine for you and find out what the trouble is.

(Richards and Long, 1978)

This is a clear case of text-as-object. That is, the text itself contains one or more language items to be learnt. There is no information to be retrieved from the text, which is reproduced on the page not for any intrinsic interest, much less for any aesthetic reason, but because it contains something which we want the learner to acquire. It is not a concern to ask what response we expect from the learner. The answer is taking a part, whether in a group or as an individual or in response to a tape, to make 'What's the matter with it?' part of his or her active language store, and to be able to respond to it in a similar way in other situations; and while doing so to make improvements in all related features of learning English, by imitating a model which simulates authentic speech and which shows 'language in use'. Suppose I then continue with the line 'I wandered lonely as a cloud . . . '

The break indicates that we are not comparing like with like. Thus while a process of imitation and repetition may be *part* of the response, it will certainly not be the whole response. With the language-learning text it is possible to ask a series of low-order questions of the type 'what did the mechanic say?' or 'Why did Mr James take his car to the mechanic?', though there is little point in asking 'Who took his car to the mechanic?' Compare, using the line of Wordsworth quoted above, as text:

Who is the 'I' of the first line?
Why does he compare his wandering to a cloud?

which appear to be valid questions, because they require some sort of 'interpretation', in a way that the questions on the language text do not. This does not mean, however, that literary text invites 'high-order' questions while non-literary text presupposes 'low-order' questions.

But, while accepting that the two samples above, viz:

1 Will you have a look at my car, please?
2 I wandered lonely as a cloud

are scarcely sufficient evidence on which to base a hypothesis, it seems nevertheless legitimate to ask why the teacher asks questions about them at all, apart from following a general classroom procedure in which the teacher asks questions (to keep the students awake?). In the first example, there are two possible reasons for doing so, namely, to test comprehension, and, secondly, to allow learners some practice of language structures (and inevitably lexis) in formulating their answers. While it is possible to argue that these are a response to the teacher's questioning, they are scarcely a *response to the text* at all. This is not so with the two questions suggested by the first line of the Wordsworth poem. Moreover, while it is possible to make an answer to them without reading further, it seems very likely that a revision of the answer may be necessary after 'forward reference'. And even the first question, 'Who is the "I" of the first line?' invites other answers than simply 'the poet', for example, 'the writer's imagination', 'the human spirit', 'Everyman'. This, then, is 'response' which is individual and contestable. With a question like 'Why does he compare his wandering to a cloud?' it is, of course, possible to answer 'because he's drunk', 'because he's bonkers', 'because he's got his head in it', but this, though it may be humorous—according to the mood of the person to whom it is addressed—would not be literary.

It does not follow from this that literature is 'that which invites questions on it'. Nor does 'response'—in this case, a verbal response—depend solely on a question or series of questions. On the other hand, the questions are an *aid* to a response, leading the learner/reader to get an insight into the text which might not be possible otherwise. And at this point, there is—or should be—a difference between teaching literature to the native speaker and to the non-native speaker. With the former, many low-order questions would be unnecessary, and run the risk of seeming silly or even an insult to the student's intelligence; with the non-native speaker, they are a natural enough step, *because the student should come to expect that a higher-order question will follow.* In fact, students are submitting to a process not dissimilar to the formal learning of their own language, in a classroom context, with the difference that the 'first-form question' is immediately followed by (say) a 'fifth-form question', which may in turn be followed by (say) a 'fourth-form question', all with the purpose of helping them to respond to the text; because the questions are not random, and are not formulated merely to practise structure (though they do that too) but to assist the reader towards a simple evaluation of the reason for a particular combination of words, and an appreciation of their special quality.

Presentation of text

The types of question which might elicit response need exemplification, and, in some cases, a comment on the type of response the teacher might expect, and a few of the likely pitfalls. For this process I have selected an extract from A. A. Milne's well-known children's book *The House at Pooh Corner*. In case this appears a somewhat whimsical choice, let me say that there are at least two good reasons for doing so. The first is that incidents in it have a certain unity, and we do not need details of plot or characterization to understand the extract, while secondly it lends itself to what I called above 'the first-form question', which is perhaps never formulated at all with children who read the text (or have it read to them), but which leads on to 'higher-order' questions. What follows then, apart from being a delightful piece of prose and a clever insight into animal and human behaviour, might also be a primer in methodology for the teacher of literature to non-native speakers. The questions beneath which invite 'response' form a type of 'programme'; the experienced teacher may, however, prefer to improvise the questions, going more quickly in some sections which seem less interesting, and slowing and asking more questions in others, rather than accepting the controlled pace of a programme. There is, of course, no absolute reason why the questions should be in English if the teacher and group share a common language. What follows is a detailed lesson plan, in which my commentary is given in the left-hand column.

The House at Pooh Corner, first published in 1928, is the story of a small boy, Christopher Robin, and his animal friends. The animals, who of course behave like small boys too (or even like adults), are as follows in this scene:

A bear: Pooh, or Winnie-the-Pooh
A tiger: Tigger
A small pig: Piglet

At this point in the story Tigger arrives; none of the other animals has ever seen a tiger before.

Before learners read the text, it is generally helpful to ask a series of questions which attempt to create the right mental attitude for receptivity, a process known as 'set induction'. The level and type of question can be varied according to the level of language proficiency of the learner group, but the questions should be presented with a degree of informality. They are in no sense a test, even of general knowledge, and above all are designed to stimulate response, and a willingness to respond.

Set induction (1)

What animals do you like most when they are small?

What do you feel about a bear? a small bear? a koala bear?

What do you think of when you hear the word 'tiger'?

What about a baby tiger?

What would you do if you found a tiger in your garden?

What do each of these animals eat?

(etc.)

The teacher has various options for the presentation of the text, including silent reading, choral reading, etc., but where the text is short, as here, the use of a taped reading, of professional standard, can be a considerable stimulus as well as an aid to correct reading, and therefore comprehension.

Presentation of text (1)

a. Listen to this text and follow it on the page in front of you.
b. Read it again carefully.

'I'm Tigger,' said Tigger.
'Oh!' said Pooh, for he had never seen an animal like this before. 'Does Christopher Robin know about you?'
'Of course he does,' said Tigger.
'Well,' said Pooh, 'it's the middle of the night, which is a good time for going to sleep. And tomorrow morning we'll have some honey for breakfast. Do Tiggers like honey?'

'They like everything,' said Tigger cheerfully.

'Then if they like going to sleep on the floor, I'll go back to bed,' said Pooh, 'and we'll do things in the morning. Good night.' And he got back into bed and went fast asleep.

When he awoke in the morning, the first thing he saw was Tigger, sitting in front of the glass and looking at himself.

'Hallo!' said Pooh.

'Hȧllo!' said Tigger. 'I've found somebody who looks just like me. I thought I was the only one of them.'

These are low-order questions, with the possible exception of (2). They differ from the questions on the language-learning text above, however, in that (in conjunction with the other procedures used) they create an involvement with the text. An alternative is to ask the group to make a summary in (say) twenty words.

Let us give the above section a title. We'll call it 'Arrival of Tigger'. You will be asked to give a title to the sections which follow. Now answer these questions:

1 When did Tigger arrive?
2 Was Pooh pleased to see him? How do you know?
3 Where did Tigger sleep?
4 What was Tigger doing when Pooh woke up?
5 What did Pooh give Tigger for breakfast?

This exercise may appear at first sight to be little more than dialogue-building. It is also a useful and practical method of differentiating literary and non-literary text, while at the same time introducing a simple dramatic component into the study of text. In this task, response should amount to total group involvement.

Work with your neighbour

Imagine that Pooh and Christopher Robin are having a conversation. Continue the conversation, telling of Tigger's arrival.

Pooh: I suddenly heard somebody knocking at my door in the middle of the night.

C.R.: Who was it?

Pooh: It was an animal I'd never seen before. He said his name was Tigger.

C.R.: ....

This activity presupposes familiarity with group work, and that the class can form groups in seconds and with the minimum of disruption. Discussion is then unstructured and unmonitored. It is at an opposite extreme from the questions above. The only 'rule' is that it should not go on for too long. In any single session of this type, the teacher should not expect great success, but over a period of time, learners will express their own private responses to text in this type of work. Such responses might be more original than those elicited by formal questioning.

Discuss in groups

What would you do if somebody knocked at your door in the middle of the night?

Set induction (2)

Do you think tigers are clever animals or stupid animals?

Do you think bears are clever animals or stupid animals?

Which animals are intelligent? Which are stupid?

Presentation of text (2)

a. Listen to this text and follow it on the page in front of you.
b. Read it again carefully.

Pooh got out of bed, and began to explain what a looking-glass was, but just as he was getting to the interesting part, Tigger said:

'Excuse me a moment, but there's something climbing up your table,' and with one loud WORRAWORRAWORRA-WORRAWORRA he jumped at the end of the tablecloth, pulled it to the ground, wrapped himself up in it three times, rolled to the other end of the room, and, after a terrible struggle, got his head into the daylight again, and said cheerfully, 'Have I won?'

'That's my tablecloth,' said Pooh, as he began to unwind Tigger.

'I wondered what it was,' said Tigger.

'It goes on the table and you put things on it.'

'Then why did it try to bite me when I wasn't looking?'

'I don't THINK it did,' said Pooh.

'It tried,' said Tigger, 'but I was too quick for it.'

This is a more demanding exercise than it may seem. The process for selecting a title is similar to that for making a summary, and requires consideration of the whole. Until this has been practised several times, almost certainly some learners will select details which do not cover the whole. Judging the suitability of words for a title constitutes a first but important step in acquiring a 'feeling for language'. Invite learners to shout out their titles, and reject the least appropriate. The next stage then constitutes a change of pace.

Question 6 is of a much higher order than the rest, and could be demanding at any level. It leads on, however, from Question 4, which is deceptive: by boasting that he was 'too quick for it', Tigger is only showing his 'tigerness'. But a complete answer would indicate that the learner has penetrated the delights of the text—the essential human-ness of the nursery animals. If the questions have helped in this, then the process seems justified as a teaching method for non-native speakers. Of course, the questioning must not become boring, in order to ensure a lively and informal response.

Think of a title for this extract.

Now answer these questions:

1 Why did Pooh explain what a looking-glass was? (Look back at the first extract.)
2 Why did Tigger jump at the tablecloth?
3 Why was there a 'terrible struggle'?
4 Why is Tigger pleased with himself?
5 Imagine yourself to be Pooh, and prepare a short talk describing this incident. Begin: 'I was just going to lay the table for breakfast. I put the cloth on and . . . '.
6 Explain how in this incident Tigger behaves like a tiger, but Pooh behaves like a human.

Set induction (3)

What do bears eat? What do tigers eat?

Tigers, like all cats, spend a lot of time sleeping. What do they do the rest of the time? What do you understand if I say that tigers are 'bouncy'?

It may be preferable to introduce a different mode of presentation here. Variation of presentation and questioning is important in holding interest.

Presentation of text (3)

a. Listen to this text and follow it on the page in front of you.

b. Read it again carefully.

Pooh put the cloth back on the table, and he put a large honey-pot on the cloth, and they sat down to breakfast. And as soon as they sat down, Tigger took a large mouthful of honey . . . and he looked up at the ceiling with his head on one side, and made exploring noises with his tongue, and considering noises, and what-have-we-got-here-noises . . . and then he said in a very decided voice:

'Tiggers don't like honey.'

'Oh!' said Pooh, and tried to make it sound Sad and Regretful. 'I thought they liked everything.'

'Everything except honey,' said Tigger. Pooh felt rather pleased about this, and said that, as soon as he had finished his own breakfast, he would take Tigger round to Piglet's house, and Tigger could try some of Piglet's haycorns.

'Thank you, Pooh,' said Tigger, 'because haycorns is really what Tiggers like best.'

So after breakfast they went round to see Piglet, and Pooh explained as they went that Piglet was a Very Small Animal who didn't like bouncing, and asked Tigger not to be too Bouncy just at first. And Tigger, who had been hiding behind trees and jumping out on Pooh's shadow when it wasn't looking, said that Tiggers were only bouncy before breakfast, and that as soon as they had had a few haycorns they became Quiet and Refined. So by-and-by they knocked at the door of Piglet's house.

Think of a title for this extract.

Note that Questions 4 and 5 are a focusing process, rather than real questions. They require the learner to look at the part, not the whole, and are thus the reverse of the questions asking students to provide titles. Both of course are valid for the literature teacher, whatever the type of text.

Now answer these questions:

1 Why do you think Tigger 'looked up at the ceiling'?
2 Why did Pooh feel pleased when Tigger said he liked 'everything except honey'?
3 Why did Pooh take Tigger to see Piglet?
4 Which sentence suggests that Piglet would be afraid of Tigger?
5 Which sentence suggests that Tigger was very playful?

Work with your neighbour

In the last paragraph of this section, Pooh and Tigger have a conversation, which is reported (that is, it is not in direct speech). Reconstruct the dialogue, working with your neighbour. Begin:

Pooh: OK, Tigger, let's go and see Piglet.
Tigger: That's a good idea.
Pooh: Piglet, you know, is very small.
Tigger: ......

Then act out your dialogue in front of the class. The person who is Tigger must remember to bounce!

This is only very loosely related to the text. It is exploitation of the text, rather than questioning on it. But as a topic for discussion, it arises naturally at this point, and the experienced teacher will detect the difference between this, and announcing to a class (even a quite proficient class) 'We're going to talk about food'. Response to the latter will almost certainly be artificial and restrained. Work based on literature can lead to discussion or written work in related areas.

Work in groups

Discuss in English your likes and dislikes in food.

What do you like especially? Dislike?

What would you miss most if you were living in England or America?

What food from your country do you think foreigners might dislike?

The remainder of this scene (in which Tigger, having said that first haycorns, and then thistles, are 'really what Tiggers like best', and is then forced to the conclusion that 'Tiggers like everything except honey, haycorns and thistles') lends itself perfectly to questioning on the pattern exemplified above. The wider issues which arise are to what extent the learner's response is greater than the purely linguistic control required to formulate answers; is there any general principle involved for the teaching of literature to non-native speakers? and is response synonymous with evaluation of 'why this combination of words'?

These are, of course, debating points, and as such do not invite answers which might form a code for all seasons and circumstances of teaching literature. In fact, it is clearly impossible to *quantify* 'response' in the sense in which it has been used in this article. On the other hand, there is every likelihood that it will be *different* from the type of response required for language-learning text, if only because of a greater intrinsic interest. At the beginning of this section I referred to the extracts from *The House at Pooh Corner* as 'a delightful piece of prose'. That is a value judgement, and it does not follow that by taking learners through this series of questions they will come to a similar assessment. They are, nevertheless, likely to observe that the exercise is not just to see how many questions it is possible to generate on the text, first with 'yes/no' questions, then with 'wh' questions, etc. Learners should be able to see that the interest is in the text, and that the questions are only a means to better observation of that interest factor; in other words, that a single reading, supposing they know both the range of structures and the lexis, and the procedures for decoding them, does not do it justice. A 'good' response to the questions, in their varied types, will be a fair indication of recognizing the extra something which I termed 'a delightful piece of prose', though there is no need for the reader/learner to agree with that phrase.

The general principles for the teaching of literature to non-native speakers are, if they exist, not easy to isolate. It is worth noting, however, that the classroom activity indicated is a close study of the *language* of the text, to unveil some as yet undefined quality of 'literariness' in the same text; but as it is also literature which is being studied, so the questions serve to extend the reader's control of and interpretation of language. This suggests a diagrammatic representation as in Figure 1.1.

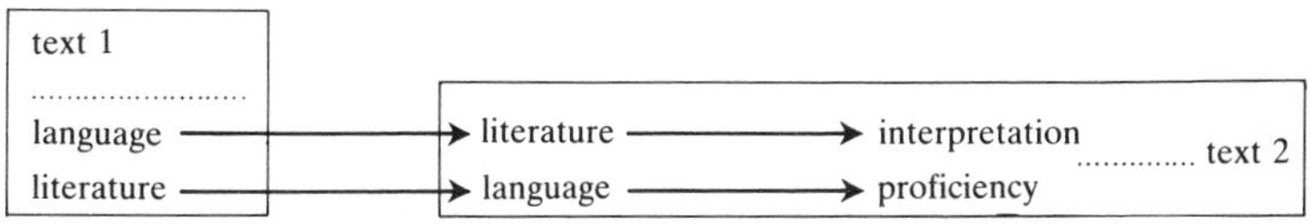

Figure 1.1

These 'programme' details are one way of presenting text. It is by no means the only way. Yet there is little doubt that an 'only way' has dominated literature teaching much more than, or much longer than, any single procedure in language teaching. The 'only way' I refer to is the lecture, or, anyway, 'extended teacher-controlled presentation' in which there was little interaction between teacher and learners. The historical basis was perhaps that literature was not something to be treated in a 'knockabout' way in the classroom, since it has a universal message to be expounded only by the master, who emulated the priest and the pulpit to do so. And, once established, traditions of this sort die hard, although there have no doubt been some very brilliant lecturers, and some students have profited from them.

An analysis of the shortcomings of the lecture is not, however, a very productive exercise. At the end of such an analysis one is invariably left with the same participants, namely teacher and learners, and while both these have a part to play, the part of the former has often been too restricted and that of the latter seriously under-developed. Diagrammatically the lecture may be represented as in Figure 1.2.

Figure 1.2

It is a uni-directional process, and response is not normally invited, because it constitutes an interruption. Response may, however, occur in the form of written assignments, in an ideal situation with a 'research' component added. Such assignments are always presented after a considerable time interval, and do not affect the initial presentation. As a substitute for the above, I suggest a multi-directional mode of presentation as in Figure 1.3. While there may be an element of idealism in this, too (it presupposes the availability of suitable textbooks, among other things), it does seem that it opens up a necessary 'varied approach' to the teaching of literature, where the text, rather than the author, or the period, or something else, determines how it should be presented.

I have indicated three input channels running from teacher to learners at the top of the diagram. I have labelled these (1) activity preparation; (2) linguistic investigation; (3) background. To take the third of these first: there are occasions when some additional information is either useful or essential in understanding a text. Ironically, the most efficient way of transferring this information is by lecture. Then let there be a lecture, short and relevant, and with close

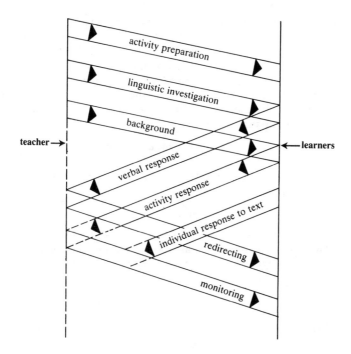

Figure 1.3

reference to text, in terms which the learners can understand. It is assumed, however, that the lecture will be combined with some other mode of presentation during the same hour or lesson.

The second channel is marked 'linguistic investigation'. This is a complex area, but to me it implies teaching rather than lecturing; that is, that text is always interposed between teacher and learner (see Figure 1.4), so that the process is investigative and analytic (and this will be at word level, at sentence level, and at discourse level), rather than simply one of information transfer. The process will certainly involve classroom questions, ideally in both directions, and lead the

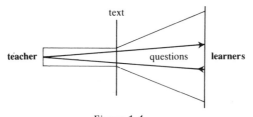

Figure 1.4

learner to a better understanding of how message is conveyed in literature, and the special standpoint of the 'sender'/writer to the 'receiver'/reader (see Widdowson, 1975: 50–54 and chapter 6), as well as relevant features of either syntax or lexis which contribute to the 'literariness' of the text. In case this seems indistinguishable from the discrete-point teaching which I have elsewhere criticized, it is necessary to give an example, and I would point the reader to the special use of pronouns without antecedent in:

> She was sitting on the verandah waiting for her husband to come in for luncheon.
>
> (Somerset Maugham: *The Force of Circumstance*)

> It was an eighty-cow dairy, and the troop of milkers, regular and supernumerary, were all at work.
>
> (Hardy: *The Withered Arm*)

> He was an inch, perhaps two, under six feet, powerfully built, and he advanced straight at you with a slight stoop of the shoulders, head forward, and a fixed from-under stare which made you think of a charging bull.
>
> (Conrad: *Lord Jim*, chapter 1)

(The first two are quoted by Widdowson (op. cit.) in examples taken from *The Penguin Book of English Short Stories*.) These may not be peculiar to literature, but they occur naturally enough there, and uncomfortably elsewhere.

Both the above channels are teacher-centred. That means that they depend on the teacher and the teacher controls the response, either largely or entirely. Though not exemplified here, it should, nevertheless, be pointed out that the channel designated 'linguistic investigation' allows for a great deal of variety both in what is investigated and how it is done. This is not so of 'background', where, largely, only the information will change. The third channel, which I have marked, somewhat unobtrusively, as 'activity preparation' is, however, entirely learner-centred, and the teacher, having established what has to be done, can then hand over to the learners themselves, usually working in groups, and act as monitor of the on-going proceedings, which are as much a form of learning, perhaps far more so, as those which are under full teacher-control. In fact, though marked as a single channel, this would be better illustrated by a dual response channel, as in Figure 1.5.

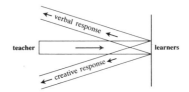

Figure 1.5

The role of the teacher is virtually the same for both, but there is a response channel which is intellectual, and 'text-related', and another which is creative. In short, in the former the text governs the 'answer', while in the latter it does not. The programme on *The House at Pooh Corner* above is text-related, and belongs to the former. So does any 'Readers' Theatre' which requires reading aloud or dramatizing of a text, which is itself a varied and rewarding task. On the other hand, exercises which require learners to predict what follows in a text ('prediction'), to create a scenario for a text, or which lead to creative writing, belong to the category which I have labelled as 'creative' (for fuller illustration of these activities see Carter and Long, forthcoming). There is, of course, a considerable number of possibilities already opening up for the presentation of text, but the point to be added is that one text is seldom, if ever, exhausted by the application of one technique. It is then up to the teacher to 're-cycle' it; that is, bring it to the attention of the class again for further treatment in a different way—I deliberately avoided the word 'teach' there, to indicate that the second attempt is just as likely to be learner-orientated as teacher-orientated. As a methodological point (not the primary concern of this article) it often pays to consider the text a second time after an interval of at least a few weeks from the first attempt.

Presentation implies response, and the diagrammatic form of this is given in Figure 1.3 above. There are here three learner channels of response, and these overlap and integrate with the teacher-input channels, and *do not have a one-to-one correspondence with them*. The first of these I have marked 'verbal response', where the learner makes an answer to a direct text-related question from the teacher, or, alternatively, asks a direct question. The second channel is marked 'activity response'. This is the learner's involvement in the task, which may be verbal, or creative, or both. Note that this channel is marked with a broken line before reaching the teacher; that is, the teacher may or may not hear what is said, or see what is done. Some of it is certain to escape if there are several groups working simultaneously, and the teacher is monitoring one of them. The third channel is quite separate and individual and, indeed, I have marked it 'individual response to text'. This is the area where the learners, as a result of the stimuli they have received (which for convenience I will classify as 'teaching', though some of them may have come from peers), begin to make their own value judgements of liking or disliking a certain work, or liking more than or less than. This probably never reaches the teacher at all, or if so, only indirectly, by the quality of response elsewhere. But some of the three learner channels will certainly reach the teacher, from these varied modes of presentation, and this in turn opens up further channels from left to right, which I have marked 'monitoring/redirecting'. Traditionally, this was done by the conscientious teacher in the comment at the end of an essay, which was often too late, when the iron had cooled, and the immediate interest was no longer there, especially if there had been a great deal more reading on the part of the learners since they read the original text. This is, of course, the opening up of a discussion process; and few things occasion discussion better than literature, when you know it. And knowing it, for the non-native speaker, must mean tackling it from various angles and differing techniques, and developing his or her linguistic competence in the process, to the point where discussion is not inhibited by some defects of articulation and expression.

I mentioned above the 'extended teacher-controlled presentation', a deliberately clumsy phrase to describe the lecture, which I then indicated was not recommended in teaching literature to non-native speakers. In fact, the whole emphasis of my procedure, and this article, is on the response channels; that is, on the learning rather than the teaching. As outlined above, I have offered a detailed programme for elicitation of response, adaptable to any text, but in the case of a longer work almost certainly to be applied to some pivotal point of the whole. There will still no doubt be many people concerned with language teaching in general who see the teaching of literature as a luxury.

Where this is argued there can, of course, be no definitive answer. There are, nevertheless, numerous points to recommend the teaching of literature. Doubtless these have been argued before, though I would like to review them in association with the response channels I have listed. Thus, literature is by definition authentic text, and both verbal response and activity response are genuine language activities, not ones contrived around a fabricated text. Moreover, current methodology—for 'communicative' language teaching—favours group activities and learner–learner interaction. Prediction, creating a scenario, debating topics on or around a text (see Carter and Long, forthcoming) all seem to develop naturally out of literary text, while they are either difficult or impossible with the type of text favoured by 'English for Specific Purposes'. Note that literature is not classified under that heading, though it is otherwise considered too specific for general study. Meanwhile, linguistic investigation is every bit as practicable with literary text as any other, though generally more interesting, or at least having a wider general appeal than any other type of text. From this it would seem to follow that a literature course which incorporates activities is of value in a language-learning course.

The latter point could clearly be argued from several angles (for example, vocabulary acquisition), and though probably accepted in a general way would fail to convince opponents of the teaching of literature, who I can foresee might object to the arbitrariness of such learning, or the incidence of low-frequency items of vocabulary. Literature does, however, allow the development of techniques for finding meaning from context, for distinguishing between the important and the unimportant (which the native speaker is able to do without trouble), and for discovery of those items of lexis which one expects to be known, but which are not. Examples of these categories were recently revealed to me when teaching a text experimentally in a Teachers' College in Thailand, where standards were reasonable but where students were very remote from exposure to English. The text was the poem 'The Dark-Eyed Gentleman' by Hardy, which begins:

I pitched my day's leazings in Crimmercrock Lane

where 'leazings', an obvious target for those opposed to the teaching of literature (or certainly in the situation in which I was teaching this poem), elicited good guesses (meaning from context) and was then used as an example of a word which a native speaker would not know for certain, but is unlikely to look up in the dictionary. Why? Surely this discriminatory technique has to be learned like any other? The third stanza of the same poem begins:

Yet now I've beside me a fine lissom lad

which revealed that the group did not know the word 'lad', and were much more hesitant to guess because of the unknown 'lissom'.

It is, however, the creative response channel which seems to be the strongest justification for the teaching of literature. It is here that opportunities for language use occur most naturally and in most varied form—with suitably inventive presentation by the teacher—and the results effectively combine the behavioural goals of both literature teaching and language teaching. Moreover, it is here that the language of literature, adapted for group and interaction activities, overcomes the restrictive element (perhaps necessarily so) of language teaching, and encourages the learner to test the dimensions of words. In short, it creates a feeling for language.

2   What is Robert Graves Playing At?

Graham Trengove

Dear Maria

I hope very much this finds you well, as it leaves me. I expect you are surprised to find yourself reading this letter at a moment when you thought you were busy with self-improvement, keeping up with your subject. Don't be alarmed; all will become clear, and self-improvement remains a possibility. The same goes for those others of you who are reading this letter, despite its being so clearly addressed to Maria and not to you, Mario, Marek, or Mahendra. I feel sure that, unless you are a censor or a secret policeman, you don't often do this kind of thing, though the temptation to eavesdrop on the personal communications of others isn't necessarily confined to these professionals. But those who succumb to it can't expect social approval. Certainly, I wouldn't readily admit to it myself. Except, that is, when the letters I am reading have been brought into the public domain by posthumous publication, like Evelyn Waugh's correspondence, or by literary invention, like Samuel Richardson's epistolary novels. However, to avoid disappointing you, I have to make it clear that no appeal of that kind can be made to excuse your reading these presents: I am not dead, and, as a correspondent, I am no Byron.

Given the informal nature of our developing relationship, perhaps you will let me make some parenthetical remarks on the phrase I have just used, 'these presents'. If you are not familiar with this usage, you won't for once find help in A. S. Hornby's *Oxford Advanced Learner's Dictionary of Current English*. You will need an authority as comprehensive as the *Oxford English Dictionary* to inform you that I use it quite properly to mean 'the present document or writing; these words or statements', because it is 'used in a document to denote the document itself'. The entry continues, 'chiefly, now only, in legal use'. So why am I using it in a non-legal context, you may reasonably ask? Thinking it through as I write, I suppose it can be explained as an attempt to lighten the tone of what I am saying by introducing what is, for a personal letter, an inappropriately ponderous and therefore slightly comic note. You may not enjoy facetious pedantry of this kind, in which case you can rebuke me in your reply. But I would like to point out that such a judgement in itself depends on your having recognized that the expression is one that you might find in a will, say, or a contract, but not one that you expect to meet in a personal letter. This you will have been able to do only if your experience of English has embraced both the variety appropriate to legal documents and that of informal letter writing. Having recognized the mixture of styles, varieties, or registers, as they are variously called in linguists' accounts of English, you need then to be aware of the potential function of that mixture, of the general communicative tactic which I am engaged in (the word 'strategy' seems disproportionate here).

So it now turns out that what I described in the last paragraph as parenthetical remarks are less of an aside than I thought they might be. Nevertheless, let's go back to where I left at least the non-Marias, with imputed bad consciences. From which I must now arrange your release.

If you have read this far, it will have been because your curiosity was, quite properly, aroused by linguistic inconsistencies between this and other chapters of this book, and indeed of most academic books. What are they exactly?

Most obvious is the presence of 'Dear Maria'. You would not have expected to come upon an initial personal salutation in this context, carrying the implication that what followed was addressed to some known individual, rather than a class of readers identified by a shared professional interest in teaching English as a foreign literature.

A more pervasive and probably more powerful suggestion to you that this is a letter derives from the selection and incidence of personal pronouns. However, I do not refer to the first-person forms, as you might have supposed. Writers using the impersonal style traditionally seen to be appropriate to academic writing shun first- and second-person forms comprehensively, a practice ascribed to a fear of being thought egotistic.[1] This requires recourse to 'editorial we', the indefinite pronoun 'one', third-person self-references like 'the present writer', and even sentence structures which allow avoidance of human subjects. But in contemporary academic writing this coyness has given way to the liberal and liberated use of 'I'. Evidence for this is to be found, for example, in the recent collection of essays *Language and Literature*[2] in which all ten contributors deliver observations in the first-person without, as it seems to me, undue egotism. There are, it is true, marked differences in the frequency with which 'I' and its derivatives appear from these different hands, and this reminds us usefully that the linguistic habits of all members of even so narrowly defined a community do not change at a uniform rate. But the central fact is that 'I' now figures regularly in formal writing.

Not so the second-person. 'You' and 'your' have bespattered my pages so far, but in *Language and Literature* they appear infrequently and only in restricted circumstances. In so far as it is necessary to mention those reading the book, this is normally done by using 'inclusive we' ('we should now try to see how . . . ' (p. 133)), passive constructions ('it can be seen that the foregoing analysis . . . ' (p. 60)), or some third-person locution ('since most readers who use this book . . . ' (p. 4)). My own recent scanning of other books directed at mature readers who are either advanced students or academic peers of the author confirms an impression derived from experience of them over the years and reassures me that *Language and Literature* is in this respect typical of its class. I feel confident that most of you could make appeal to similar experience of this language variety to account for your feeling that I am not behaving as the context suggests that I might, or even should.

Having detected these inconsistencies or anomalies, comparable in essence though not in extent to the case of 'these presents' discussed earlier, you will again ask yourself why I have engaged in them. As practised readers you will be looking to me to provide reasons, overtly or otherwise. But before responding to this very reasonable wish, I want to comment on those aspects of the distribution of 'you' which (unfairly, you may have thought) I buried under the phrase 'only in restricted circumstances'.

At the end of each chapter of *Language and Literature* the editor suggests ways in which his readers might apply or pursue ideas introduced by his contributors. In doing so, he employs forms typical of direct address, including many imperatives and second-person pronouns, as in for example, 'try to relate your linguistic observations to the presentation of character and setting'. This contrasts not only with his contributors' practice, but also with his own when writing his introductory editorial essay. In behaving thus he is not being arbitrarily inconsistent. When I look at other books at hand which in some measure deal with the same topic and similarly indicate further activities for their readers,[3] I see that the distribution of 'you' is precisely the same there; that is, it is found exclusively in the post-chapter suggestions. Though there is no necessity that this should be so (Leech proposes similar exercises after each chapter of his *Linguistic Guide to English Poetry*[4] without once using a second-person pronoun), it is evidently a widely accepted convention for such publications. It is equally clearly a voluntarily observed convention, and one which users acquire familiarity with through experience rather than through instruction or reference to style books,[5] which make no mention of these discriminated usages. I would suggest that the purpose of the convention is to mark a shift in the role proposed for the reader by the writer; he or she is now the target for overt instruction. In Hallidayan terms, the convention has interpersonal function.[6]

Similar appeal to the Hallidayan framework seems appropriate to account for those instances of 'you' which occur in the even more narrowly defined circumstances of the opening paragraph of Chapter 11 of *Language and Literature.*

> And where do you go from here? You've taken some poem or conveniently sized piece of prose. You've spent time and effort mastering a sensible descriptive grammar of English. You've meshed understanding and knowledge of both to produce a rigorous analysis of the language used to construct your text, together with a 'relevant' sensitive interpretation. You have talked about 'effects', 'foregrounded features', 'overall impressions', and so on. Very nice. Very satisfying. But what are you going to *do* with it? What now?

Here, and nowhere else in the body of this chapter or of any other, I find an academic writer employing second-person pronouns, and in a way which at once reminds me of vigorous, even attacking, face-to-face, oral argumentation. This linguistic choice and the associations it calls up for me induce in me an unfamiliar stance towards the book. I no longer feel allowed to be an anonymous reader; instead, I am personally challenged. I read what follows with livelier attention, shocked into this state by an assault on my linguistic expectations. This use of 'you', unlike that cited in the previous paragraph, is not in accordance with a convention of formal written English hitherto undescribed. Instead, this is an instance of an individual writer idiosyncratically borrowing a linguistic feature from one accustomed context of use and installing it in new surroundings with rhetorical purpose.

Within this chapter, you have now experienced three applications of this tactic of discourse; the trivial example of 'these presents', the more readily justifiable paragraph just discussed, and the extended example of the pages by which you arrived at this point. You ask, 'Why? What relevance has all this to the interests of teachers of English literature?' As I believe, a great deal.

Any one instance of the tactic of variety switching gives rise to English unfamiliar in some degree even to native speakers; it must, if it is to achieve the desired effect. But as a rhetorical device, the principle of switching is familiar, because widely employed in both the written and the spoken English of everyday circumstance.[7] It is one which all advanced learners and their teachers should be aware of, though probably not attempt to use, because it may carry important information about an addresser's view of his own or his addressee's respective roles, or about his attitude towards his message.

In so far as teachers of language and teachers of literature may be separately identified overseas, the latter cannot resign to the former responsibility for raising their students' consciousness of this feature of English. Whether or not we agree that literature can be defined by its being written in deviant language, there is no escaping the fact that linguistic deviance of many kinds is a prominent feature of much literary writing, not least the one I have been discussing. Alertness to the characteristic features and normal contexts of use of varieties of English may be crucial in the understanding of literary writing.

This is a claim best sustained by illustration, and I choose for this purpose a short poem by Robert Graves, which means that I can discuss a unity rather than an extract. It is a poem which, in my experience, is accessible and appealing to those who do not have English as their first language, both students and their teachers, particularly when approached in the fashion now to be described.

The Persian Version

Truth-loving Persians do not dwell upon
The trivial skirmish fought near Marathon.
As for the Greek theatrical tradition
Which represents that summer's expedition
Not as a mere reconnaissance in force
By three brigades of foot and one of horse
(Their left flank covered by some obsolete
Light craft detached from the main Persian fleet)
But as a grandiose, ill-starred attempt
To conquer Greece—they treat it with contempt;
And only incidentally refute
Major Greek claims, by stressing what repute
The Persian monarch and the Persian nation
Won by this salutary demonstration:
Despite a strong defence and adverse weather
All arms combined magnificently together.

The need for some historical background information will be apparent. Many readers will already have it at their command. Others, even though nationals of states with an inherited cultural connection with classical Greece, may themselves be ignorant of it and its relevance to this poem. Or they may belong to states which have much slenderer cultural links with Hellenic civilization than those enjoyed by some. But no great instructional apparatus is required to prepare the ground for the poem. The essential facts about the battle of Marathon, transmitted in the Western tradition and taken by Graves to be at his readers' command, can be quickly and economically supplied.

In 495 BC a mainly Athenian army some ten thousand strong met in battle an enormously larger Persian army charged with the suppression of a Greek revolt against the hegemony of Darius, King of the Persians. At a cost of fewer than two hundred men, the Greeks resoundingly defeated the Persians, who left six thousand dead upon the field. They thereby established that a small, democratic nation could successfully challenge the might of an empire. The popular tradition to this day has rejoiced in concord with those Athenians who first heard of their army's victory from Pheidippides.

Armed with this knowledge, the reader is surprised by the poem's apparent challenge to this traditional account of the battle and its significance in offering, as its title puts it, the Persian version of the episode. A first reading may well leave the impression that Robert Graves is presenting an unusually sympathetic assessment of the Persian involvement. We may wonder why he should bother to adopt such a revisionist, not to say perverse, view of events almost two thousand years distant from us.

I hope to show that the poem is most successfully understood if we distinguish Robert Graves from a persona whose voice we hear in the poem. Though this strategy of reading will be familiar to teachers of English literature, its application to this particular poem has to be justified by close examination of its language. We need to identify the linguistic cues which encourage us to proceed in this way.

The very title of 'The Persian Version' should warn us that poet is not persona. That its adjoining component words should rhyme so obtrusively, on two syllables, undercuts the dignity of the account which follows, and should excite doubt about its validity. Similarly, the first word of the poem proper should discourage us from accepting the proffered historical corrective too readily. There is an ambiguity here, which language teachers will be quick to notice. What is the relation of 'truth-loving' to 'Persians'; is it restrictive or non-restrictive? Reading it as restrictive, we would infer that there is a category of Persians who are not truth-loving and who presumably *do* dwell on the battle of Marathon. But we discover soon enough that this reading does not cohere with the development of the poem, in which no such contrast is drawn. The alternative, non-restrictive, analysis leaves us with the large claim on behalf of the Persians that they have a love of truth as an inalienable national characteristic. This runs so counter to our real-life experience of any national group that we are effectively warned to question the objectivity of the speaker.

We might at first read this as irony coming directly from the poet speaking in his own voice, as a suggestion that Persians are anything but truth-loving. However, a better explanation emerges from later lines once the normal context of much of the vocabulary is recognized. Phrases like 'reconnaissance in force', 'three brigades of foot and two of horse', 'left flank', and 'light craft detached from the main fleet' do not frequently occur in the English of everyday life. They belong to the specialized vocabulary of military historians, the official chroniclers of battles and campaigns on land and sea. They exemplify the precise, technical, dispassionate terminology found in descriptions of military engagements written by men who seek to present themselves as detached, professional, and trustworthy. People who are adepts in any vocabulary specially associated with an area of human competence, whether it be sport, trade, engineering, or scholarship, are thereby enabled to invest their remarks on relevant matters with great apparent authority. Of course, outsiders may then take the appearance of authority for the reality, a fact which confidence tricksters exploit to their advantage. For the speaker in this poem, his employment of these terms of art has the function of persuading us that he is dispassionate, seeking to be objective, perhaps even regulated in his judgements by an institution or by his peers, and therefore reliable.

If we accept his assessment of the nature and significance of the Greek victory, very different from the traditional view, it is because we are impressed by his apparently finely discriminated choice of phrase. The passage of arms known to history as the battle of Marathon he categorizes as a 'skirmish'; what the Greeks regarded as an attempt at re-conquest, he calls 'a reconnaissance in force'; what is normally recorded as a crushing defeat for the Persians, he presents as a 'salutary demonstration', presumably of the might of the Persian power, though he is not explicit on this point. Diminishing further the magnitude of the Greek success, he speaks of 'that summer's expedition', where the demonstrative suggests that this was only one of a series of perhaps annual campaigns. The battle is described as 'near' rather than 'of' Marathon, a preposition indicating a wish to define the locale of the battle rather than to impute strategic or historic importance to it. His delineation of the Persian force in terms of naval and military units reminds us that the Greeks met not simply 'the Persians' or the Persian host, but brigades rather than divisions or armies, and a number of small vessels rather than fleets. We are persuasively invited to accept this unemotional, considered, scientific description in preference to the 'Greek theatrical tradition', that is, the account received down the ages from Greek dramatizations of the events.

This is to read 'theatrical tradition' as a neutral, objective label; equally possible, for this context as for others, is to read both its elements as connoting 'removed from reality'. It then becomes evaluative, even abusive. If there is room for doubt here, there is none about other evaluative words in the poem. Marathon is not simply down-graded in the hierarchy of military encounters by being called a 'skirmish'; it is also described as 'trivial' of its kind. In similar fashion, the importance of the 'reconnaissance' is diminished by its modification by the intensifying adjective 'mere'. We accept the evaluations these words record because we are impressed by his professional use of neutral vocabulary elsewhere. He is, as it were, drawing on credit.

In my view, if we are to read the poem aright, we must recognize that he is bankrupt, and is operating as a confidence trickster. One possible cue to this insight is his use of the word 'refute'. In an age when an ever-increasing number of native speakers use 'refute' as though it were synonymous with 'reject', we must be careful not to lose sight of its more nicely discriminated sense, 'to prove an argument wrong'. The speaker, who has up to this point appeared fastidious and orthodox in his choice of word, says here that the Persians have proved wrong the Greeks' claims to have won a famous victory. In reality, he offers no proof but merely a counter-claim that Persian prestige had somehow been enhanced, in ways which he does not specify. His modification of the verb by 'only incidentally', at first simply condescending to the Greeks, can now be seen as an evasion of the requirement for argument, which alone can legitimize the use of 'refute'.

It may be at this point that we start to wonder if we should uncritically accept the speaker's version, or it may be the final couplet which provides the spur. 'Despite a strong defence and adverse weather/ All arms combined magnificently together.' Couched in the same specialized variety, with the same addition of evaluation (this time, in 'magnificently', it is positive) this sentence reveals the speaker's true stance. Not only does he continue to suppress the undeniable, historically received fact that the Persians were defeated in battle, nowhere acknowledged in the poem; he now so constructs the sentence that an uninformed reader would naturally conclude that the Persians were victorious. The 'despite x, y' construction would normally mean that the condition 'x' did not prevent the successful outcome of 'y', and the observation that 'all arms combined magnificently' is more consistent with success than failure. The expectation of Persian victory could only be cancelled by a following clause beginning with 'nevertheless' or its equivalent.[8]

It is impossible to reconcile his use of this stratagem with our earlier conception of the speaker. We should now recognize not the voice of a detached historian, of an impartial seeker after truth, of a man whose judgement we can reasonably trust, but rather that of a manipulator of language who is practised in deceit. Retrospectively we now reinterpret all the linguistic choices embodied in the poem as flowing not from a desire for genuine precision and balance, but from a wish to conceal bias and distortion. The poem demonstrates the perversion of a variety of English more often employed for honourable purposes. We should recognize in it the voice of an official spokesman, someone accustomed to issuing emollient communiqués in the aftermath of military disaster. In particular, we should hear a clear echo from the 1914–18 war, when Robert Graves, then an infantry officer, observed for himself that there was a grotesque disparity between the experience of the men in the front line and the official, 'sanitized' reports of the actions in which they fought.

We can now be confident that Graves is not perversely siding with an overdog. Nor is 'The Persian Version' a genuine attempt to redress an injustice done to the Persians by history, or an implicit commentary on the unreliability of the received accounts of historical events. Instead, the poem reminds us that events can be cosmetically presented, facts can be obscured, news can be managed by public relations officers, official spokesmen, anonymous compilers of anodyne communiqués. By taking on the linguistic cloak of such a person, Graves points to the propensity of authorities to 'doctor' the presentation of information which in its raw state is unpalatable to them. By doing so in poetic form, he implicitly generalizes from the particular case.

Few modern readers, no matter what their nation, have to search far in their experience to find parallel cases, and in consequence most can readily perceive in this poem the universality of reference which makes for easy engagement with it as literature. This in itself makes the poem attractive to teachers seeking to arouse interest in literature in English. But, as I have tried to demonstrate, discussion of the process of interpretative reading requires reference to many features of the English language as a system. It thus provides both a cue for investigation of, and a focus for application of aspects of the linguistic competence which teachers seek to develop in their students. This it does simultaneously or alternatively, as the teacher chooses. It is especially appropriate when the teacher wishes to sharpen awareness of the links between language varieties and the normal contexts of their use.[9] Beyond this, and importantly for their understanding of everyday English as much as of English in literature, it points to the possibility of original, creative extension of elements of these varieties to unfamiliar contexts.

Yours sincerely,

Graham Trengove

Notes

1 See note [a](ii), Quirk *et al.* (1972: 208).

2 Carter (1982b).

3 Leech and Short (1981), Quirk (1962).

4 Leech (1969).

5 Maney and Smallwood (1971), MLA (1970).

6 See e.g. Halliday (1973: 106): 'In the second place language serves what we may call an interpersonal function. This is quite different from the expression of content. Here the speaker is using language as the means of his own intrusion into the speech event: the expression of his comments, his attitudes and evaluations, and also of the relationship that he sets up between himself and the listener—in particular, the communication role that he adopts, of informing, questioning, greeting, persuading and the like'.

7 In spoken English, stylistic discontinuity in vocabulary or syntax is often reinforced by some phonological marker; the speaker may adopt a 'funny voice' to emphasize that he has somehow changed his role.

8 Leech (1974: 318–23).

9 For discussion of the theory of language varieties and examples of its application, see Crystal and Davy (1969); Gregory and Carroll (1978); O'Donnell and Todd (1980); Quirk *et al.* (1972: 13–32).

3   The Possibilities of Paraphrase in the Teaching of Literary Idiom

Walter Nash

An idle procedure?

The *heresy of paraphrase*, it used to be called, by sage and serious critics; 'heresy', because the language and content of a literary work, being conceived as one, are indivisible, and there is no separable quantum of 'meaning' that can be made more readily accessible by altering the words in which meaning is couched. Richard Wilbur, speaking up for poets, puts the case thus:

> It does not upset me to hear poetry paraphrased and its 'subject matter' stated. But I don't usually care for the sort of poem which too readily submits to paraphrase. A poem ought not to be fissionable. It ought to be impossible satisfactorily to separate 'ideas' from their poetic 'embodiment'. When this can be done to a poem, it is a sign that the poem began with a prose 'idea'—i.e. began wrongly—and that the writer was not a poet but a phrase-maker.[1]

With this reasonable statement, made from the insider's point of view, no teacher of English could quarrel. To accept it, however, is to invite the awkward inference that qualities in language characterized as 'poetic' or 'literary' are not isolable or definable, hence perhaps not even teachable; that indeed there is no 'poetic language', but only the language of particular poems, indissociable from their unique status as acts and artefacts. The awkwardness is felt especially by the language teacher, to whom paraphrase—a discredited procedure for literary critics—is a customary tool. In the widest sense—of reformulating, defining, expanding, expatiating, mimicking, making parodies, transposing and translating, seeking parallels—we use paraphrase as a method of teaching the idiom and usage of English. And as we affect to teach the whole language, it is hard for us to accept that there is a privileged domain from which our methods are debarred; that literary utterance cannot be fairly characterized as 'usage' or 'idiom'. Our position is that there is an element of 'literariness' in language, a deposit of practice, as it were, that invites analysis by any means at our disposal. So we may ask of paraphrase—is it inevitably heretical, or may it not sometimes serve a heuristic purpose?

Absurdity is the mother of insight

By way of general discussion, and to make an apparent case *against* paraphrase, let us take a few lines of verse, one of the most familiar passages in the Romantic canon, the opening of Keats's 'Ode to a Nightingale':

> My heart aches, and a drowsy numbness pains
> My sense, as though of hemlock I had drunk,
> Or emptied some dull opiate to the drains
> One minute past, and Lethe-wards had sunk . . .

An attempt to paraphrase these lines will reveal difficulties possibly unsuspected by the reader who knows them well and who may consequently take them for granted as comfortable old exponents of the Romantic death-wish. There is a perverse intricacy in the passage, and any effort of reformulation is simply inadequate to the text, e.g.:

> I feel great grief and weariness, as though I had just drunk poison or a drug, and were drifting into the sleep of death.

or:

> Poignant sadness fills me, and an aching sleepiness, as though I had just taken a toxic substance or a narcotic drug, and were sinking into oblivion.

The most careful attempt to express accurately and adequately the 'meaning' of the poetic text founders in absurdity. Paraphrases of the kind suggested here do not bring a poem more firmly into our possession, and may even mislead us if we rely on them as a form of explanation and commentary. Their necessary tendency, indeed, is to omit, or 'filter out', things essential to the communicative art of the text. Taking Keats's lines, consider—the consideration is inevitably somewhat ponderous—what features are lost in the proposed attempts at paraphrase:

1 In the poetic text there is a lexical pattern (and concomitantly a syntactic design) involving the nouns *heart, sense,* and the verbs *ache, pain.* These items somewhat resemble the casual collocates of 'ordinary' language (e.g. 'heart and soul', 'body and soul', 'sense and feeling', 'aches and pains'), and we may therefore be lulled into a careless reading;[2] but they invite scrutiny, as terms elevated into precise significance. The reader must assume that for Keats *heart* and *sense* have particular values—e.g. that *heart* = 'psychological state or event'

and *sense* = 'physiological correlate', or that *heart* = 'emanation of feeling' and *sense* = 'recipience of sensation'. At all events, there is here a duality and complementation of meaning that evades the blurring paraphrase of 'I feel grief' or 'Sadness fills me'. Paraphrase might eventually discover adequate equivalents for *heart* and *sense*, but what is really required, and is hardly available, is some expression tantamount to 'heartsense'.

2 The pairing of *heart* and *sense* involves the companion pairing of *aches* and *pains*. As noted above, there is in ordinary language a banal collocation of nouns ('We all have our aches and pains to put up with'); but in this poetic text the collocates happen to be verbs, each coloured by distinctive properties of semantics and syntax. One (*aches*) is intransitive, the other (*pains*) is transitive; one is 'stative', the other 'dynamic';[3] in one case the verb in relationship to its subject suggests energy proceeding from an endogenous source (cf. *my head reels, my foot hurts, my hand itches*); in the other the relationship is that of an agent and a recipient (*the whisky turned my head, a stone bruised my foot, the nettles stung my hand*).[4] The poetic relevance of all this is that it confirms a design in the lexicon, a design that presents *heart* as the active principle, *sense* as the receptive principle; feelings come *from* the heart, sensations come *to* or operate *on* the sense. But the agent of experience operating on the sense in Keats's lines is extraordinary—no object or instrument, but a *-ness*, abstract and vague. We cannot paraphrase *a drowsy numbness pains my sense*, or arrive at its meaning by diligently seeking out word-by-word equivalences. To grasp it we must respond sensitively to the paradoxical teasing of the text.

3 The fact is that paraphrase can do no more than fumble at what is a profound and significant ambiguity in these lines, an ambiguity well expressed in the oxymoron of *numbness* (subject/agent) and *pains* (verb). How can a 'numbness' (absence of sensation) cause 'pain' (presence of sensation)? Is the experience through which the poet is passing pleasant or unpleasant? Certain words (*dull, drowsy* = the agreeable onset of sleep) suggest pleasant experiences, while others in the immediate context (*aches, pains*) unmistakably denote suffering. Does the hemlock starkly kill, or does the opiate agreeably coddle? What is the poet saying by means of these extraordinarily well-matched mismatchings? 'This hurts, and is desirable'? 'This is pleasant, yet hurtful'? The opening of 'Ode to a Nightingale' displays a curious shiftiness, an elaboration of defining that postpones definition until the poem's fruitful contradiction is overtly formulated in its fifth and sixth lines:

'Tis not through envy of thy happy lot,
But being too happy in thine happiness . . .

4 Some literary language is designedly vague—in no bad sense of fudging accuracy, but in its prudent avoidance of specific terms, its reliance on the competence of the reader to recognize time-honoured generalities. Thus *hemlock* has respectable status as a literary word for 'poison'—reminding us, quite possibly, of Socrates' resigned and stately death—and *opiate*, or rather *some opiate*, is a dignified abstraction that avoids the necessity of going into grim chemical details. Undoubtedly there are moments in the life of literary language when specification would be disastrous:

> My heart aches, and a drowsy numbness pains
> My sense, as though of Brasso I had drunk,
> Or emptied all my Valium to the drains
> One minute past, and Lethe-wards had sunk.

Absurd, and grievously unKeatsian. We may struggle in paraphrase with words like 'poison', 'drug', 'toxic', 'narcotic', etc., but the struggle is vain, because Keats's lines do not really imply these things; the poetic vocabulary makes symbolic *resonances*, not precise references to the pharmacopoeia. Of course any person of literary competence understands this, and only a fool would want to ask Keats (a medical student, after all!) what particular opiate he had in mind. Reference may be paraphrased; 'resonance' cannot.

5 Nor can paraphrase capture the localized symbolism of literary allusion. Keats alludes to *Lethe*—the river of forgetfulness which all travellers must pass on their way to the underworld; supposedly, then, a symbol for death. But there are two components here: oblivion and extinction. Is it so certain that Keats implies the latter with the former? Does he wish for a truly *lethal* administration of hemlock? Does he really mean the blank discontinuity of death, or is his *Lethe* a way of *forgetting* and *transcending*, rather than dying into non-existence? Forgetting appears to be the keynote of the poem ('Fade far away, dissolve, and quite forget . . . '). It develops the theme of escaping from the cheerless present; an escape which the poet effects not by opiates, or even by alcohol ('not charioted', he tells us 'by Bacchus and his pards'), but by the power of the poetic imagination, a power that will not lead him into the blackness beyond Lethe but, for one brilliant moment, into the moon-world of the nightingale. It is worth noting that Keats refers to Lethe in a coined word *Lethe-wards*, a formation obviously based on or analogous to 'towards', 'downwards', 'homewards'. The suggested movement or transition is *towards* Lethe, not into or across the fatal river; it is *downwards*—as the verb *sink* confirms; and we may suppose that it is a gradual or drifting movement rather than a sudden descent.

So, after all this, what are we to say of paraphrase? Having pointed out its manifold imperfections, can we improve it in a version expanded to accommodate all the noted points?

> I feel poignant emotions, while a desensitizing lethargy disagreeably attacks my nervous system, as though I had just taken poison of that noble kind so movingly associated with the death of Socrates, or had ingested a powerfully hypnogogic drug and had begun to drift slowly, vaguely, downward towards oblivion, if not actually into death.
>
> ???

Well, says the questing spirit, forget the paraphrase, let us take the easy option and read the poem. And not surprisingly, for all we have done here is provide detailed attestation to the truth of Richard Wilbur's words: 'It ought to be impossible satisfactorily to separate "ideas" from their "embodiment".'

Yet there is something interesting and quite important to add. If there is any merit in these observations on Keats's lines, if these deliberations express any insight into the language of the poetic text, the value derives ultimately from those limping, inadequate, foolish attempts at paraphrase. The consciousness—sometimes embarrassed, sometimes humorous—of what is defective and awry in paraphrase creates a sharp focus on the text. The paraphrase is a vain attempt to reflect what is in the poem; the vanity becomes apparent to us, and we set about trying to identify and explain what we have missed. So a process of discovery begins. We discover patterns, couplings, networks in the 'literary' vocabulary; we note how the 'ordinary' word is thereby endowed with complex poetic significance; we observe the presence in the text of accredited 'literary' words and traditional symbols; we note the nonce-item and the special coinage; the figurative and generalizing power of the literary text declares itself in specific and intermeshing details. Paraphrase may have no critical status, may be utterly ludicrous as an account of what the poem is and does, but it can still be the step that initiates a sophisticated response to language. In this, as in so many fields of study, absurdity is often the mother of insight.

Paraphrasing 'ordinary' language

For foreign students especially, the paraphrase of quite a small part of a poetic text may prove a daunting task, since the crudest essay in reformulation requires a refined linguistic competence that the learner does not always possess. It is obviously a self-defeating exercise if, before students can attempt a paraphrase or use one, they must have continual recourse to a dictionary. (One of the more depressing experiences of the poetry class is to observe the frantic paginal whirring of *Duden, Larousse,* and *The Oxford Advanced Learner's Dictionary of Current English.*) Some teachers, in any case, seem to regard the comprehension of literary language as God-given, and therefore none of their instructive business: 'Either you have the sensitivity or you don't'; 'If people don't respond to poetry in their own language, they obviously won't respond to it in English'. From which assurances we may turn, relieved, to teaching language of the dear old 'Hi-there-Hans-good-morning-my-Dad-has-come-down-with-a-fever-and-is-temporarily-indisposed' variety.

But such a retreat from the problem is both vain and unnecessary, for 'ordinary' language (however one might define that concept) is full of the seeds and weeds of literariness. Everyday speech includes turns of phrase, idioms (for which foreign students have a bottomless appetite), folk-sayings, proverbs, encapsulations of the common experience, the accredited thought, the conventional wisdom, miniature acts of literary creativeness. These 'encapsulations' invite paraphrase, and the invitation does not overawe foreign learners. Ask them to paraphrase a sonnet, a passage from a story, a speech from a play, and they may look askance, but require of them something straightforward and banal like the rewriting of a proverb—for instance, *It's the early bird that catches the worm*—and they will cheerfully oblige, with many comments, applications, and striking international instances. It may not occur to them that in the simple, routine paraphrasing of 'ordinary' language, they are beginning to learn something about 'literary' language and English manifestations of 'literariness'.

Take the proverb suggested above: *It's the early bird that catches the worm.* Asked to explain this, each student will produce a rendering, as competence and temperament dicate, and the versions will range from something like this:

If you get up early in the morning you will achieve your task

to something like this:

When we are promptly attentive to our business, we are rewarded with success

(two actual instances recorded in my class notes). Of such exercises two things may be observed. The first is that nobody, not even the most inept and linguistically incompetent student, ever supposes that he is dealing with a purely factual statement, i.e. that when we say *It's the early bird that catches the worm* we are talking about birds as such and worms *per se*. This is perhaps an obvious point, inasmuch as when a teacher says to a class 'Here is a *proverb*' they understand that they are being invited to consider a non-literal category of utterance. However, it is observable that if one presents an example *without* the predisposing stimulus of a label such as 'proverb', 'popular saying', 'motto', etc.,—if, for example, one should quote *Blood is thicker than water*—students will still respond with a non-literal (transferred, generalized, metaphorical) interpretation. Possibly all folk-sayings and gnomic utterances have tell-tale characteristics of form and structure that key the appropriate response. A profounder possibility, however, is that when we encounter a piece of language that seems far too obvious to make much sense, we try to render it sensible by putting it into a non-literal frame. Blood is undeniably thicker than water, as a matter of physical fact, but there seems little point in saying so unless we mean blood figuratively and water metaphorically. Taken that way—not *literally* but *literarily*—the saying becomes more meaningful. The willingness to construct a viable meaning in this way is surely an index to the literary competence that we all possess in some measure.

A second interesting aspect of the attempt to paraphrase proverbs is that the versions offered can usually be arranged in a progression running from the most specific, or *narrow* paraphrase, to the most general, or *broad*; from a particular or local interpretation (perhaps making birds into students and worms into examination results) to the account that transcends particularities of person, time, and place (birds as general agent, worm as a gratifying general consequence of action). Presented with a narrow and a broad paraphrase, and asked to assess their acceptability, students will generally reply that both are acceptable, and indeed that both might apply simultaneously to the test-proverb; perhaps some will add, on reflection, that the interpretation of the latter will of course depend on contexts and circumstances of usage. In saying this, they acknowledge the essentially *literary* nature of proverbial utterances. The proverb lives as a poem lives, both by specifying and generalizing. And its language, therefore, is the language of literary discourse—patterned and multivalent. *It's the early bird that catches the worm* and *My heart aches, and a drowsy numbness pains my sense* are types of literary statement, differing in scope and complexity, but affined in their deliberate arrangement of words and their implication of meanings that transcend brute literality.

Students are amused if one makes the simple point that many proverbs are not, so to speak, reversible. We say *It's the early bird that catches the worm*, but no one is inclined to consider the vermicular viewpoint of *It's the tardy worm that cops the bird*. This rewriting would not be accepted, other than as a Woosterish sort of joke. The reason for this is surely that the proverb *It's the early bird that catches the worm* is a particular realization of the paradigm, or archetype, of hunter and quarry, pursuer and pursued. The paradigm implies a psychological sequence: the hunter or pursuer or agent comes first in the natural order of things. Now many folk-sayings, perhaps the greater number, can be referred to such archetypes of the perceived 'natural' order: working, playing, hunting (or trading), preparing and consuming food, providing shelter, forming relationships and alliances, maintaining social hierarchies, making war and keeping the peace—all the primary provinces of human activity and organization create the 'paradigms' from which proverbs are derived, *and also* the complexes of fact and feeling which enter into poems and stories. Proverbial encapsulation and free poetic elaboration have the same cultural sources. Sometimes the two coincide, as in a poem by Robert Frost called 'Mending Wall', which is constructed round the saying *Good fences make good neighbours*. The poem makes a commentary on the proverb, criticizes its application, and might be described as a protest against the literal interpretation or the excessively narrow paraphrase.

Though paraphrase is a general term, covering a variety of techniques and practices, two styles are commonly apparent. One is the *explanatory/interpretative* type, that tries to express something 'in other words', possibly with complementary illustrations. The other is a *mimetic/parodic* type, depending on a technique of word-for-word substitution that often has comic results: *It's the auroral avian that mugs the maggot*. These also are 'other words', but they explain nothing; rather, they laugh at literariness, or possibly, through their manifest absurdity, pay subtle tribute. One curious effect of the comic substitution technique is to destroy all figurative scope. *Early* may imply 'early in the morning', 'punctually', 'promptly', 'opportunely', 'before others can act', 'with a proper sense of urgency', etc., adjusting its meaning to changeable contexts of application; *auroral* is a funny way of saying 'at dawn'. The scope of the paraphrase narrows to zero; the true literariness of the proverb is reduced to the falsity of a pseudo-literary gesture. But this kind of game is not without its uses.

The scope of the literary utterance

The scope, i.e. the breadth of application, of literary utterances is worth a moment's consideration. One well-known feature (indeed a diagnostic symptom) of literary texts is that while they may intensively state a case, they also have the inherent power to illuminate a universe of parallels, analogies, and variants. They become emblems of general and continuing experience. If, quoting Samuel Johnson, I declare *Slow rises worth by poverty depress'd* (and we may remind ourselves that Johnson himself was paraphrasing Juvenal) I may mean, specifically, that poor Bloggs has had a raw deal in life, or my remark may be a contribution to a general discussion on the difficulty of making one's way in the learned professions. The classic line provides us with a saying of fairly wide scope.

In common usage we exploit the scope of literary language as it occurs in tags and adages, well-known quotations, and the genial patchwork of the anonymous folk-tradition. A personal example: when my daughter was very small, I would sometimes play with her a game requiring the accompaniment of a familiar nursery rhyme:

> Rock-a-bye-baby on the tree top,
> When the wind blows the cradle will rock,
> When the bough bends the cradle will fall,
> Down comes the baby, cradle and all.[5]

To play our game, the child would lie in my lap, along the cleft between my legs. I would begin by moving my legs gently from side to side (*Rock-a-bye-baby*). Then I would begin a slow alternate tramping of my knees (*When the wind blows . . .*). This would be followed by a slow parting of the legs (*When the bough bends . . .*), and a hysterically gleeful pantomime of dropping and catching on the word *down*, the focus of the game.

This fairly typical piece of parent-and-child play represents a practical application—one might say an *action-paraphrase*—of a piece of verse with much wider scope. 'Rock-a-bye-baby' invites interpretation as a paradigm of false security in any form: complacency in politics, false optimism in business, self-satisfaction in the performance of work, failure to read the obvious signs of rift in personal relationships—to all such situations the old rhyme might provide a fitting commentary. To use it as a sort of timing-device for a child-distracting game is to narrow its scope considerably.

Taking this one step further, suppose that in the course of these amusements I had devised a verbal paraphrase to match the action. I was never rash enough to propose any such heretical procedure, but had I done so, I might possibly have produced something like this:

> Rock-a-bye-daughter, here in my lap,
> When I waggle my knees you may take a wee nap,
> When I open my legs you will take a big drop,
> And your lapping and napping will come to a stop.

Having narrowed the scope of the original text with an action-paraphrase, I now suggest a verbal paraphrase that is concomitantly narrow. This could be applied *only* in direct connection with the rocking game, the successive phases of which it specifies. The relationship of this verbal paraphrase to the original text is tenuous; the expression *Rock-a-bye* and the familiar metre serve to invite comparison with an underlying model. The removal of these props would destroy all suggestion of mimetic paraphrase, and with it all allusive power. What we then make is just another action rhyme:

> Swingaroo, kiddo, so deep,
> While I wiggle my knees, you can sleep;
> When I open them—PHEW!
> You're going to drop THROUGH!
> And land in a horrible HEAP!

This, like 'Rock-a-bye-daughter' (and unlike 'Rock-a-bye-baby'), may be bad verse, but such spoofings are not *unliterary*. We may still find in them a literariness of structure that allots significance to certain items of vocabulary or conveys, at particular points, a sense of gesture. What is lost is the power to generate many meanings—or, as we have put it earlier, to create the *resonance* of literary language.

The message of mimicry

The point of the mimetic paraphrase may be to have fun at the expense of the original—i.e. it may be frankly parodic, an exercise in literary vandalism. This is not the whole point, however. The explanatory paraphrase, through its inadequacy, directs us to the fullness of the text; comparably, a mimetic paraphrase, act of hooligan mockery though it be, pays tribute to the refinement of the original—if, that is, the original has real merits. Here is a poem that is often used as a text for foreign students, because of its ostensible (but in fact quite deceptive) simplicity.

Richard Cory

Whenever Richard Cory went down town,
  We people on the pavement looked at him:
He was a gentleman from sole to crown,
  Clean favoured, and imperially slim.

And he was always quietly arrayed,
  And he was always human when he talked;
But still he fluttered pulses when he said
  'Good morning', and he glittered when he walked.

And he was rich—yes, richer than a king,
  And admirably schooled in every grace:
In fine, we thought that he was everything
  To make us wish that we were in his place.

So on we worked, and waited for the light,
  And went without the meat, and cursed the bread;
And Richard Cory, one calm summer night,
  Went home, and put a bullet through his head.

(Edwin Arlington Robinson)

This poem seems readily susceptible to explanatory paraphrase, encapsulating as it does some kind of moral or 'wisdom'. When students are asked to state the meaning of the text, their answers range from the laconic 'Wealth doesn't make you happy' to somewhat fuller explanations, e.g. 'Rich persons may seem to enjoy every advantage in life, yet still have some despair not seen by those who envy them'. Occasionally these summaries have an ideological ring, suggesting that the material sufferings of the proletariat do not impair their moral soundness, whereas the well-to-do are corrupted by their possessions and become spiritually dead. Those who are thus disposed to interpret the poem antithetically—'we, the strong ones, survived, but he, the moral weakling, perished'—are not as a rule deterred when a teacher asks them to consider that the conjunction introducing the final couplet is not the adversative *but*, but the continuative *and*, suggesting something slightly subtler than a crude adversarial reading. There is certainly a predisposition to read the text as some form of moral injunction; yet it could be argued that the dramatic—indeed, melo-dramatic—final stanza is an existentialist statement, or a comment to which we may attribute a morality or not, as we please. ('We unaccountably went on living and he inexplicably chose to die.')[6]

Discussion of the paraphrasable meaning or 'moral' of this poem nearly always reveals that it is not, after all, so simple. It is when one begins to discuss its vocabulary and its lexical patterning, however, that one is reminded how the plainest texts often seem to be the most impenetrable. For some foreign students the vocabulary of 'Richard Cory' may have cultural and social overtones that are not easy to interpret. I once read this poem with a group that included a pupil from one of the poorer Third World countries. He found *imperially slim* unconvincing as an image of class ascendancy, since most of the wealthy and powerful people in his society were distinguished by the portliness of the well fed; and his interpretation of *he glittered when he walked* was that the sweat shone on Cory's forehead (Richard being intrinsically a fat cat, whatever the poem might say to the contrary). We may smile at these misconstructions, but they should make us ask how often, from our own cultural presuppositions, we might go astray in attempting to read an exotic literature.

The central difficulty of the language used in this poem, however, is not primarily cultural; even native students can go astray, merely by taking the poem for granted as an exercise in the mimicry of the naïve. If it is indeed naïve in its diction and idiom, the naïvety is oddly complicated, not to say troubled. There is a speaker-in-the-poem, a 'person on the pavement', behind whom lurks (like some ventriloquist or puppeteer) the poet, Edwin Arlington Robinson. Robinson makes his speaker-on-the-inside construct the kind of text one might well imagine to be the production of a literary man-in-the-street—clichés, posh phrases, proper words and all. (Thus it is in the character of the *narrator* to describe Cory as *quietly arrayed, richer than a king*, and *admirably schooled*.) At the same time, the poet Robinson exploits this mimetic vocabulary as an idiom for the creation of ambiguities, ironies, and fine implications of lexical patterning. The last two lines of the first stanza exemplify this. The phrase from *sole to crown* clearly imitates *from top to toe*, and might be regarded as the narrator's conscious 'literary' striving to improve on a common phrase. Validly so—but there is something more; by reversing the perspective of the phrase (i.e. *top to toe* = 'downwards', but from *sole to crown* = 'upwards'), Robinson adds to the figurative intimations of the text. The people on the pavement 'look' at Cory, and the 'looking' is that of subjects contemplating a ruler who is in some way placed above them. (*To look up to someone*, we may recall at this point, implies respect and admiration.) *Crown*, furthermore, connotes regal attributes, and this suggestion of royal eminence is further reflected in *imperially*. Through his speaker's blunderingly earnest attempts at literary description, i.e. through one act of mimesis, Robinson constructs a parallel act, contriving the semantic links and overlaps that build the image of Cory as an inaccessible, aristocratic, indeed regal personage. That one word *crown* quite effectively illustrates how the poem speaks with two voices. The simple insider means only 'top of the head'; the artful outsider, the poet, means us also to think of the conventional symbol of monarchy.

To get at these manipulations of meaning by discussing each in turn takes a long time, and in the end may leave a class bemused and unconvinced. There is another way of drawing attention to the lexical peculiarities of a poem like 'Richard Cory', and that is to make a mimetic paraphrase. Here is an instance of a rival text, a bad poem created in order to suggest how the real poem works:

Roger Crotty

If Roger Crotty went down town some day,
  We ordinary folk would stand and gape;
He was a gentleman in every way—
  Clean-shaven, smart, and such a lovely shape.

His suits were always tasteful, never loud,
  And when he talked, he sounded just like you,
But he'd this way of moving through a crowd
  And dazzling one and all with his 'How do?'

He'd all the earmarks of a millionaire,
  The style, the education—oh, the lot;
Put it like this, if he'd have said 'Hi there!
  Change places?' we'd have done it like a shot.

Still, there it was. We struggled to get by,
  And ate some awful meals, which made us grouse,
But Roger Crotty, one night in July,
  Committed suicide—in his own house.

This has the merit of being so awful that it makes the students laugh.

They feel superior to the silly act, and can be made to realize that this feeling stems from some competence to recognize qualitative differences between the deft original and the banal imitation, the language of which certainly resembles the style of the street but is far removed from the studied idiom of poetry. Then every line of the paraphrase evokes comparison with the original. We may, for example, contrast *gape* with the oddly inert *look at*, asking what is present in one and notably absent from the other. (*Look at* is difficult to paraphrase; as, indeed, it is in the proverb *A cat may look at a king*.) Or, a slightly more complex task, we may try to explain how and why *clean favoured* means a great deal more than *clean-shaven*—more, perhaps, than a portmanteau packing of *clean-shaven* and *well-favoured* ('handsome'). These are random instances indicating the general thesis that systematic comparison of the two texts would define the literary peculiarities and procedures of the true poem.

Perhaps in token of an analysis we may take up just two points. First, as to titles. Names are not paraphrasable (proper nouns, the philosophers tell us, have unique reference), but in the world of myth, names are regarded as having peculiar efficacy in consubstantiating the person they denote (whence the common taboo prohibiting the naming of the godhead or the devil). This mythic view of language is reflected in poetry, which often posits a quasi-magic relationship between words and things. Thus, if we change the name *Richard Cory*, we seemingly change or dislocate the relationship between the title and its poetic expansion. Could the poem—the original poem—be called *Ricco Corti*?; no, too Italinate and even gangsterish. *Rory Coonan* then? *Reuben Cohen*? *Rudi Kafka*? No, clearly, such inventions could never be considered in connection with the original poem. We feel a decorum in the association of the name *Richard Cory* and the 'quietly arrayed', 'admirably schooled' personality it denotes. Then change the name to *Roger Crotty* and in effect a new poem must be designed, bespeaking Crotty-like attributes.[7] The whole subject of titles, particularly name-titles, is interesting and fruitful, because it has much to reveal about literary resonances, those associative waves that ripple through a text.

For a second point of general interest, consider the final stanza of the poem. The original text, like so many in this moralizing, punch-lining genre, is *focused*, all its rays of meaning converging on a point.[8] We may compare it with nursery rhymes like 'Rock-a-bye-baby' in which there are one or two words (*fall*, *down*) that attract emphasis and are spoken with peculiar energy in performance. In 'Richard Cory' there is a brutally exact emphasis on the word *bullet*, which we read against the background of *light*, *meat*, and especially *bread*. ('We got bread; he got a bullet'; the emphasis is even supported by alliteration.) The precise act of self-destruction figures suddenly and surprisingly (largely because of those designedly drifting conjunctions, *so . . . and . . . and . . . and*) against the dull doggedness of working, waiting, going without, cursing. In 'Roger Crotty' there is (a) no surprise, and (b) a ludicrous change of focus; no shock effect but 'how shocking—*in his own house!*' 'Roger Crotty' is trivially blurred; 'Richard Cory' is most precisely focused. Here is a notion worth wider exploration, and the mimetic paraphrase is one way of exploring it.

The possibilities of paraphrase

In summary, the following points emerge:

1 'Paraphrase' may be understood in a broad sense, to include techniques of explaining, summarizing, imitating, rewriting. (The latter has scarcely been touched on here, but see below, under 'Notions and exercises'.) A distinction is made between 'explanatory' and 'mimetic' paraphrase.

2 In the teaching and study of 'ordinary' language we have constant recourse to paraphrase; any attempt to answer such questions as 'What do we mean when we say . . . ?' involves paraphrasing. Thus language teaches language, one usage amplifies another, one style comments on another. This is in effect the case for paraphrase, and for extending its use to the exploration of 'literary' language.

3 Paraphrase, however, will not reveal all the secrets of literariness. Some literary works are more obviously amenable to paraphrase than others. It seems notably applicable to work that presents an argument, defines a condition, or points a moral.

4 Explanatory paraphrase should fall within the competence of the student, representing his or her attempt to 'engage' with the text and account for its language. Such paraphrases provide the basis for discussion and elaboration of the concept of literary language. They are at least a useful language drill; at their best they are a step towards the comprehension of literary values.

5 Mimetic paraphrase should be the teacher's province (unless the students volunteer to attempt it). Strictly speaking, it requires native competence, some gift for parody and burlesque, and a sensitivity to the humorous nuances in language: specifically, an awareness of the difference between tbe ordinary and the banal, the original and the bizarre. Any competent teacher should have the sense of fun and the skill required to contrive the entertainment that is also a form of instruction. The teacher who cannot use language to inform, inspire, and amuse is a dead duck—i.e. a dolorous bird that neither flies nor quacks.

Notions and exercises

There must come a point at which a theme, especially a pedagogic theme, loses theoretical impetus and calls for development in practice. Here, then, are one or two suggestions for the kind of work that might be done, using explanatory paraphrase, mimetic paraphrase, and rewriting.

1 *Proverbs re-phrased.* Here are some English proverbs, randomly interspersed with paraphrases. Some of the latter are more or less serious attempts at explanatory paraphrase; others exploit a vein of burlesque mimicry. Attempt (i) to identify the proverbs and match each one with its paraphrase, and (ii) to discuss the adequacy of the paraphrase and the light it sheds on the literariness of the proverb:

a When you really need to, you can find ways of solving your problems.
b Don't cross your bridges before you come to them.
c Frequent lapses divert the drinking vessel from the labial protrusion.
d A little effort to repair a defect will forestall subsequent requirement for more extensive labours.
e Take care of the pennies and the pounds will take care of themselves.
f Necessity is the mother of invention.
g Pride goeth before a fall.
h God's anointed is the legitimate object of feline contemplation.
i There's many a slip 'twixt cup and lip.
j A stitch in time saves nine.
k Self-esteem precedes catastrophe.
l The reward of prudence in minor expenditures is relative ease in the management of major financial matters.
m A cat may look at a king.
n It is pointless to worry about any difficulty in life before you actually have to deal with it.

2 *Explanatory and mimetic paraphrase.* Here is the text of a well-known poem by Robert Frost:

Dust of Snow

The way a crow
Shook down on me
The dust of snow
From a hemlock tree

Has given my heart
A change of mood
And saved some part
Of a day I had rued.

First, let students attempt an explanatory paraphrase of this, and see how the paraphrase relates to the syntactic and lexical pattern of this poem. (They should not overlook the title.) Then ask them to consider what insights are created by one or two exercises in mimetic paraphrase, e.g.:

Epigram Upon An Impertinent Fowl

A crow, impertinently, from his bough
Cast snow on me, deject; I know not how,
But this erratic blessing, in strange way,
Lifted my spirits up, and sav'd the day.

or this:

Crow Jive

Crow, you're a clown
Dashing snow down

From that old hemlock tree;
Are you mocking me?

I'm feeling so blue,
Then here's you

Doing your dashes,
Saying 'ashes to ashes,

Likewise, if you must,
Dust to dust'—

Man, that makes me smile!
I feel better by a mile!

So I say to you, crow,
Before you go,

As you fly away,
Have a nice day,

And when you ride the air,
Take care.

3 *Rewriting prose passages*. This topic is not explored in my paper. Here is a possible exercise. One of the passages below is the opening of a classic novel (no prizes for identifying it). The other is a rewriting· which conveys substantially the same message, but effectively destroys the texture of the literary language used in the original. Let the students compare the two texts closely, making a point-by-point commentary. (If by any chance none of them can identify the original text, let them try to do so on stylistic grounds.)

a In front of me is this tract of flat country where the River Floss, getting wider all the time, rolls seaward between its green banks, and where the tide comes up to meet it with all the impetuosity of a lover hastening to a tryst. That powerful tidal insurge carries along to St Ogg's the black ships laden with timber, linseed, and coal. St Ogg's is here in the foreground; we see its fluted red roofs and the broad gables of its wharves, with the river on one hand, and on the other, behind the town, the low wooded hill. Caught in the light of the February sun, the little town makes colourful reflections in the water.

On either side, as far as the eye can see, stretch the farmlands, some of them newly ploughed, others just showing the first shoots of spring corn. We can see the remains of the haystacks made last autumn, and everywhere, all along the hedges, we see trees—why, even the masts and sails of distant ships seem to merge into the branches and foliage! Not far from the town, with its red roofs, is the swift-flowing River Ripple, a tributary of the Floss and a most attractive watercourse. For me its sound is like the voice of a real person, a companion in my rambles round charming old-world St Ogg's. Everywhere I turn I meet well-remembered topographical features—those willows, for example, and that stone bridge.

b A wide plain, where the broadening Floss hurries on between its green banks to the sea, and the loving tide, rushing to meet it, checks its passage in an impetuous embrace. On this mighty tide the black ships laden with the fresh-scented fir-planks, with rounded sacks of oil-bearing seed, or with the dark glitter of coal—are borne along to the town of St Ogg's, which shows its aged, fluted red roofs and the broad gables of its wharves between the low wooded hill and the river-brink, tinging the water with a soft purple hue under the transient glance of this February sun. Far away on each hand stretch the rich pastures, and the patches of dark earth, made ready for the seed of broad-leaved green crops, or touched already with the tint of the tender bladed autumn-sown corn. There is a remnant still of the last year's golden clusters of beehive ricks rising at intervals beyond the hedgerows; and everywhere the hedgerows are studded with trees: the distant ships seem to be lifting their masts and stretching their red brown sails close among the branches of the spreading ash. Just by the red-roofed town the tributary Ripple flows with a lively current into the Floss. How lovely the little river is, with its dark

> changing wavelets! It seems to me like a living companion while I wander along the bank and listen to its low placid voice as the voice of one who is deaf and loving. I remember those large dipping willows. I remember the stone bridge.

4 *Text paraphrases text.* It is an old classroom stratagem—a device of 'Comp. and Crit.'—to explore texts similar in theme. Not infrequently we find that texts paraphrase or provide a commentary on each other. These 'natural' manifestations of paraphrase can be used in the same way as any artificial contrivance. A passage from Walt Whitman's *Specimen Days*, for example, makes interesting comparison with *Richard Cory*, in language as well as in theme.

> Ten thousand vehicles careering through the Park this perfect afternoon. Such a show! and I have seen all—watch'd it narrowly, and at my leisure. Private barouches, cabs and coupés, some fine horseflesh—lapdogs, footmen, fashions, foreigners, cockades on hats, crests on panels—the full oceanic tide of New York's wealth and 'gentility'. It was an impressive, rich, interminable circus on a grand scale, full of action and color in the beauty of the day, under the clear sun and moderate breeze ... Yet what I saw those hours (I took two other occasions, two other afternoons to watch the same scene,) confirms a thought that haunts me every additional glimpse I get of our top-loftical general or rather exceptional phases of wealth and fashion in this country—namely, that they are ill at ease, much too conscious, cased in too many cerements, and far from happy—that there is nothing in them which we who are poor and plain need at all envy, and that instead of the perennial smell of the grass and woods and shores, their typical redolence is of soaps and essences, very rare may be, but suggesting the barber shop—something that turns stale and musty in a few hours anyhow.
>
> (Walt Whitman, *Specimen Days*; in *Prose Works*, 1892, Volume 1, ed. Floyd Stovall, New York University Press 1963, pp. 198–9.)

Notes

1 Quoted from *The Genie in the Bottle*, an essay by Richard Wilbur prefacing a selection of his poems in the collection *Mid-Century*

American Poets, ed. John Ciardi, Twayne Publishers Inc., New York, 1950, p. 6.

2 At first, transcribing the all-too-famous lines from memory, I wrote 'My heart aches, and a drowsy numbness pains my *soul*'. The error is an instance of being 'lulled into a careless reading'—in this case, one dominated by the cliché-collocation *heart and soul.*

3 On these terms, see Randolph Quirk and Sidney Greenbaum, *A University Grammar of English*, Longman, London 1973, p. 46.

4 The distinction perhaps somewhat impressionistically formulated here could be made more precisely in terms of 'case' grammar; but the question is whether it is worth embarking on a fairly long grammatical preamble in order to make the stylistic point.

5 The text of this rhyme, as printed here, is commonly attributed to one Charles Dupee Blake (1846–1903). However, *The Oxford Dictionary of Nursery Rhymes* indicates an earlier history.

6 I do not argue that this is the 'correct' interpretation; only that the syntax of the poem makes it possible. The pattern of conjunctions is of course important in leading to the shock of the last line.

7 An acquaintance who was a schoolboy at Christ's Hospital during the 1930s has informed me that in those days the word *crotty*, in school slang, was a noun meaning a foolish or inept person. His explanation, that the word derived from the name of a Mr Crotty, a clergyman, who had delivered to the boys a sermon of appalling banality, has the ring of folk-myth—eponymy raised on onomatopoeia, so to speak. But my telephone directory tells me that the name Crotty does exist.

8 I am not using the term *focus* in its grammatical sense (see Quirk and Greenbaum pp. 406 ff.). There are, however, discernible relationships between grammatical focus and the semantic marshalling of a literary text.

sophisticated response to minute details of language, and culture-specific background knowledge and literary structure. Non-native teachers of English or specialist language teachers have felt uneasy when expected to provide guided responses based on these factors. They have frequently retreated into teaching *about* literature (for instance, giving students biographical facts about authors, descriptions of literary movements and critical schools, synopses of novels and plays) instead of teaching the literature *itself*. A similar impetus has led to courses on English culture and literary background. The theory underpinning such courses was that they provided the necessary information for a non-native speaker to understand a text. In practice, the background course tended to displace the texts—not surprisingly, as background is easier to teach. We can link this preoccupation with fact with a generally transmissive mode of teaching, characteristic of many language and literature classrooms throughout the world.

If literature is worth teaching *qua* literature, then it seems axiomatic that it is the response to literature itself which is important. There has been much critical debate in the twentieth century (cf. discussions of 'The Intentional Fallacy') about how much knowledge of the author, if any, one needs in order to understand a literary text. But whatever stand one takes on the minutiae of this debate, it is obvious that one can proceed a fair distance with no knowledge of the author at all. Indeed, some texts have no known authors, for example, ballads developed in the oral tradition, while others (for instance, the canon of George Eliot) are read by people who do not know the true identity of the writer. Of course, sometimes knowledge of the author is helpful. Often, however, it can be dispensed with. We would also wish to argue that the role of background cultural knowledge has often been overstressed and mistaught. Courses on cultural background of necessity lean towards statements of general, large-scale 'facts' about a culture. They are prone to trite judgements and sweeping remarks. But the background knowledge needed to interpret particular linguistic events (inside and outside literature) is often of a much more specific kind:

a Knowledge of the particular social situation and the particular participants involved. This is only a part of what ethnographers of speaking regard as the context of events deemed to be essential to the understanding of linguistic messages in general, and which teachers of literature implicitly draw upon in their commentary upon texts.

b Small-scale social facts. For example, in David Lodge's recent novel *How Far Can You Go?*, the following sentence appears: 'It was necessarily a Registry Office Wedding.' In order to understand this sentence you have to know that divorced couples in England cannot (usually) be married again in church. It is difficult to imagine this fact, among a myriad of other conceivably relevant facts, turning up in a course on cultural background, very relevant though such information is in this particular case.

It was as a result of these considerations that we decided to teach texts and provide specific background as it was 'prompted' by the texts themselves.

2 *Literature and language teaching should be linked and made mutually reinforcing.*

Early in this century the teaching of English literature to non-native students involved, in large measure, a concentration on the classics of English literature. The assumption was that if the students were continually exposed to the best uses of the English language, it would in some sense 'rub off' on their own performance in the language. The difficulty with this position was that many literary texts of a high calibre were difficult and inaccessible to these non-native English-speaking students. Much, after all, of what is best in English literature derives from ages linguistically very distinct from Modern English, and even modern writers present problems of comprehension, as they often break both writing conventions and the rules of English in the service of literary artifice. As a consequence, literature teaching began to disappear from the 'language' classroom, to be replaced by a surrogate literature, commonly in the form of textbook dialogues and short tales, where learners were presented with the appearance of literature in the form of text devised to carry structure, but with none of its literary effect. The significant complementarity of patterning in both form and function, characteristic of genuine text, whether literary or non-literary, was replaced by a patterning of form only, free from any significance. This move is in our view unfortunate, for reasons other than that of the interest intrinsic in studying literature:

a Contrary to much received opinion, it is difficult to make a *linguistic* distinction between literature and other kinds of language (see Werth 1976, Pratt 1977). If this is the case, there is no *a priori* reason for banishing literature from the language curriculum (although there may well be a need to grade literary texts in terms of difficulty and accessibility).

b Although language and literature may appear to be distinct from the point of view of the teacher, they do not, necessarily, appear so to the learner, for whom literature is also language.

c Many students enjoy reading literature. As enjoyment plays an important factor in any learning process, literature is a potentially useful aid to the language teacher.

d Literary texts often contain within them a number of different varieties of English. They can thus be extremely useful in sensitizing more advanced learners of English to linguistic variation and the values associated with different varieties (see Widdowson 1975).

e If a student is taught language and literature by the same person, it is possible for the lessons to be mutually reinforcing. Literary texts, or extracts from them, can be used to break up language classes and used to identify difficulties that students experience in reading in general and reading imaginative texts in particular. Similarly, there is no reason whatsoever why time should not be taken in a literature lesson to focus for a moment on a portion of text relevant to a previous language class.

3 *The participants (and also, eventually, their students) should be made sensitive to the processes involved in reading.*

Reference to, and study of, the reading process is an area of common ground for literary criticism, linguistic approaches to literature (stylistics), and also for psycholinguistic studies in language learning. It was likely, then, that course participants would bring with them a wide range of expertise in the understanding of the reading process (as, indeed, would the teachers on the course) and this could be drawn upon during the course itself.

4 *The course should seek to relate the development of an integrated language and literature curriculum at the school level with that of the post-school tertiary institutions.*

The implications for the curriculum of much of the foregoing are that non-native school-leavers are rarely equipped for the demands made upon them by the literary departments of universities and colleges. They come with an impoverished command of the language, in many cases, and little exposure to the reading of complex, connected text, whether literary or non-literary. Yet, once within the tertiary institution, they frequently receive neither instruction in language nor activities designed to improve their reading skills. They are doubly disadvantaged. One way in which this situation might be improved, we felt, was to consider the planning of a connected and integrated curriculum covering both levels of instruction.

The 1980 course

The participants for this course were all teachers of English as a Foreign Language. Most of them were teachers at university or college level. A minority were secondary school teachers. They came from a variety of countries, including European (Greece, Italy), African (Algeria, Senegal), and Latin American (Brazil, Mexico). As this was the first course of its kind at Lancaster, we tried to devise an approach which would not be so pre-planned that we could not react to needs which might emerge during the course itself. Questionnaires were sent to the participants before the course began, in order to determine their felt needs. The initial plan for the course was devised partly from the results of these questionnaires and partly from the general background philosophy for the course described above. The four-week course was planned, accordingly, one week at a time, in the light of comments and end-of-week questionnaires completed by the participants. This procedure enabled us, within the general design features of the course, to respond to comments, criticisms, and requests from the participants, as well as to accommodate developing ideas of the teaching staff.

As all the participants were experienced teachers of literature, we made an early decision not to have a strand within the course concerned with traditional approaches to English literature and/or practical criticism. We felt that to do so would in large measure replicate the skills and approaches which the participants already possessed or were familiar with. Instead, we chose to give the students three course units operating in parallel throughout the four-week course:

Stylistic analysis

Stylistics is a linguistic approach to the study of literary texts. It thus embodies one essential part of the general course philosophy: that of combining language and literary study. The first part of the unit dealt with introductory materials and techniques for the analysis of poetry (see Leech 1969); the second part with prose (see Leech and Short 1981); the third part with discourse analysis and drama (see Short 1981). At first sight, it might seem that such a technical approach to literature might not have been appropriate to non-native teachers and learners of English. In some ways, however, such non-native learners have advantages over native speakers. The chief advantage is that, unlike English undergraduates, for example, foreign students have learned how to analyse sentences grammatically and frequently have a considerable awareness of English phonological structure. They are thus often more consciously aware of linguistic structure and better equipped to analyse it and its relationship to meaning than, say, today's average native-speaking undergraduate student of English. They may, in addition, have a more consciously accessible awareness of larger-scale patterns of written and spoken discourse than do native speakers.

One particular matter, relevant to the other course strands, but especially so for this unit, should be mentioned at this point. The course we had designed was specifically for teachers. It was stressed throughout that the techniques being taught ought to be useful for teachers in their understanding of language and literature; it was also stressed that this does not necessarily mean that such methods of analysis should be automatically passed on unfiltered (or even at all!) to the pupils of the teachers concerned. Sometimes it would be appropriate to do so, and sometimes not, depending upon the level of linguistic and analytical skills of the students concerned. However, even if the level of a particular teacher's students was below that needed for a stylistic approach to be successful in class, the teacher would often be able to use his or her stylistic expertise to inform more general and/or less technical discussion.

Reading in a foreign language

This unit focused on three main areas: the product of reading, the process of reading, and difficulties experienced by foreign-language readers in and with texts (see Alderson and Urquhart 1984). The first part of the unit examined the notion of levels of meaning that can be 'extracted' from texts, and related these levels to reading skills. The second part examined attempts to characterize the reading process and reading strategies, while the third part related what had been learned from research into the teaching of reading (including the reading of literary texts) and the development of appropriate exercises and tasks for the EFL learner. The unit as a whole was concerned to make a point of using literary texts for discussion wherever possible, and related the processes involved in reading literature to those involved in reading non-literary texts. In addition to the link established between the Stylistics and Reading units through the joint use of the same texts (the reading unit followed the genre order established by the stylistics unit), it was also the case that the teachers of the two strands found themselves adopting similar language to describe the phenomena they were examining, and a similar approach to the teaching of reading strategies and processes, especially when texts were examined in practical detail.

Curriculum development/discourse analysis

In this unit general procedures for curriculum development were applied to literary studies at both macro and micro levels. Stress was laid on the need to integrate the curriculum components of purpose, content/methodology, and evaluation in an interdependent scheme (see Breen and Candlin 1981). In particular, emphasis was laid on relating course design to learners' needs in terms of eventual target and learning process, paying special attention to the level of overall linguistic competence and foreign-language reading skill of the learner. At this macro-level there was, accordingly, greater focus on the learner as determiner of content choice than on the inclusion of a particular writer merely because he or she was a 'good' representative of the eighteenth century or could not be reasonably excluded from any representative course in English literature. At the micro-level, the unit examined a variety of strategies for teaching literature in the EFL classroom, emphasizing in particular variation across text-types and instructional mode (see Candlin and Edelhoff 1982). This aspect of the unit made a connection with the workshops (see below) and the Stylistics unit's treatment of style variation in poetry.

This strand also examined new approaches to the analysis of spoken discourse, and an explicit link was made with the Stylistics unit in its analysis of drama and the presentation of character speech and thought in the novel. And there was some discussion of the expectations by tertiary level teachers of secondary level teachers, and vice versa, in respect of giving students adequate introduction to and development of textual study skills in the context of an overall national educational system.

Figure 4.1 represents an attempt to capture the integration of the three course components, with the central focus on the description, interpretation, and evaluation of texts. The diagram formed the basis of initial discussion with the course participants on course content and organization.

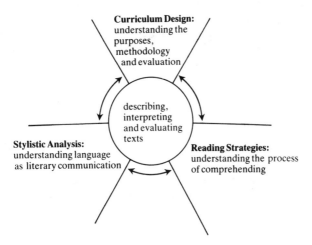

Figure 4.1: Course Components

Workshops

The detail of the workshops is dealt with separately. It will, however, be helpful to know here that they were conceived as being central to the course. They took place at the end of each week, and a considerable amount of time was set aside for the participants to work in small groups, developing their own suggestions and materials. These teaching materials, textual analyses, and general comments were then offered to the other course participants in workshop presentations. Each such workshop was designed to link literature and language study by comparing literary texts, or parts of texts, with their non-literary equivalents, with the aim of encouraging participants to explore similarities and differences in the texts in terms of form and function. We gave considerable attention to the implications for practical teaching: how particular texts might be taught to particular students (or indeed, if it was appropriate to teach such texts at all).

When the participants first arrived at Lancaster, it was clear that there was a considerable range of differing assumptions about the likely course content. Participants expressed interest in the selection of literary texts, techniques of teaching literature (generally and in relation to specific countries and audiences), current critical theory and its application to the teaching of literature, practical performance, the linguistic study of literary texts, the application of linguistic theory to the language of literature, especially in the bilingual context, creative writing, and translation theory. No short course could hope to deal adequately with a minority, let alone all, of these topics. What it could do, and our description is intended to make this clear, was to provide a coherent approach to the teaching of literature, linked to the learning of language, within which at least some of these concerns could find a place. In the event, feedback from the participants was very enthusiastic, although they suggested that they would have welcomed the addition of a fourth course strand concerned with more traditional literary criticism.

The 1981 course

The general philosophy of the course remained the same as that lying behind the previous year's prograame. However, we took up the participants' suggestion from 1980 that we introduce a separate strand concerned with literary criticism. Unfortunately, however, the 1981 course could be of only three, rather than four, weeks' duration, thus raising the major problem of an expansion of course content coinciding with a reduction in available time. Once again, participants were drawn from a variety of countries (including Nigeria, Brazil, Argentina, Indonesia, Sudan, Finland, Turkey, Senegal, Algeria, Greece), with Nigeria and Brazil being particularly well represented. In addition, our feeling that the interests of a very small minority of secondary school teachers had not been sufficiently well catered for in the 1980 course led us to restrict the 1981 course to teachers in tertiary education.

The inclusion of a new unit on Literary Criticism made for greater course cohesion, in that it was scheduled to parallel the Stylistics unit in its movement through the genres. The unit itself was appreciated during the course by the participants, yet in their end-of-course report an overwhelming majority suggested that it be dropped in any future year, on the grounds that the techniques involved were sufficiently familiar to them. Moreover, its absence would allow them to spend more time in studying those new techniques and content areas which the course also provided. Ironically, then, the view of the second group of students directly opposed that of the first group and coincided with our original reasons in 1980 for not including it as a separate unit. Once again, feedback was extremely positive; indeed, one of the 1981 participants has since used the techniques developed in the drama section of the Stylistics unit as the basis for an article in a Brazilian scholarly journal, and one of the 1980 participants has introduced the general approach of the course to Greek teachers via conference presentation and publication.

The Nanjing course

Within the same overall philosophy, this course differed from the others in a number of important respects. The participants were all Chinese teachers of English language and literature in Chinese universities and colleges with a strong interest in English literature. Accordingly, the course tutors (J. C. Alderson, D. R. Carroll, and M. H. Short) introduced a strand on Post-War British Literature, taking up a third of the available course time. The Literature and the Stylistics units were organized in parallel in terms of treatment of genre. Necessarily in this course, given that C. N. Candlin was not a member of the teaching team, the aspect of curriculum development was touched upon only incidentally. The post-course feedback was good, especially from the more able participants. In its earlier stages, however, the course suffered for reasons unconnected with course content. Firstly, there was a large disparity of expectations between teachers and students in terms of teaching style. The students expected to be informed of facts which could be committed to memory; the teachers, on the other hand, expected them to take a much more active role in analysis and interpretation. It took some time for an amicable accommodation to be reached. Those who have taught in China will recognize this lack of fit between students' expectations and Western teaching styles as a general problem. Secondly, the students were far from homogeneous in terms of ability and background. This did not, however, lead to any major alteration in the approach developed in the two previous Lancaster courses, and it seemed from student feedback to offer an experience to the Chinese students which was relevant to their classroom needs.

The workshops

As we have indicated above, the workshops, although only one part of the overall course provision, did represent a significant opportunity for the participants to work in detail on a range of issues treated in outline in the other course strands. Accordingly, we list below the activities that took place during the half-day periods at the end of each week which were devoted to the Workshops. It should also be pointed out that these sessions were preceded by up to a day's preparation by the students. The outcome of the small-group activities usually took the form of a group report examining the relationships between similar text-types chosen from literary and non-literary sources. The comparison typically involved the students in searching for both similarities and differences between the texts, initially in terms of formal linguistic differences. These formal characteristics had then to be explained in terms of particular functional relevance in both the texts in question. In addition, workshop participants were asked consistently to reflect on the pedagogic implications of the analyses they were engaged in, or the materials they were proposing for student use. In this way, analytical and descriptive discussion was firmly linked with practical teaching procedure. In summary, then, the workshops had three main aims:

a to encourage links between language and literature studies;
b to clarify the connection between linguistic form and pragmatic function;
c to design usable teaching materials for piloting in participants' home situations.

For the purpose of illustration we list below a selection of workshop titles and topics. The participants on each of the courses described above made their own selection from this 'bank' of possible activities:

—the language of poetry and the language of advertising;

—the language of instruction (e.g. on how to operate a tape-recorder) and poems making use of this particular variety (e.g. Ted Hughes's 'To Paint a Water Lily', Henry Reed's 'Naming of Parts');

—passport descriptions and character descriptions (e.g. Leonard Cohen's 'All There Is To Know About Adolph Eichmann'; Charles Dickens's initial description of Mr Bounderby in *Hard Times*);

—place descriptions (e.g. a travel guide to Chester and Charles Dickens's initial description of Coketown in *Hard Times*);

—a nineteenth-century sermon and Mr Chadband's speech of thanks for the meal provided by Mrs Snagsby in *Bleak House* by Charles Dickens;

—dramatic texts and authentic, tape-recorded dialogue.

Occasionally, workshops were used to discuss more general matters of interest; for example, the interface between secondary and tertiary education, in order to examine what each sector expected from the other in terms of the teaching of language and literature; discussion of a set of proposals for a new-style examination for literature within the set of Cambridge Proficiency Level examinations in English, focusing on the connections that can be made between literary and non-literary language.

It should be emphasized that the workshops offered the opportunity for open-ended, flexible, and free discussion. At times the participants found themselves stressing similarities between literary and non-literary texts, at times maintaining their distinctiveness. On occasion, as with Mr Chadband, the description of Coketown, and 'To Paint a Water Lily', a writer could be seen to be using an established variety of English in special ways, thus using the variety concerned as a 'backboard' against which to create new meanings and effects. Whatever the outcome, the exercise was always found to be fruitful. Of course, these sessions and the activities of the main course strands were not intended to replace more traditional forms of literary discussion. None the less, at the end of the courses, participants declared that they had on the one hand developed new and exciting ways to help non-native speakers of English appreciate English literature more fully, and, on the other, that they could now integrate more fully the teaching of language and the teaching of literature.

A workshop in detail

We have chosen the third item on the above list as an illustration of the kind of workshop task which the course participants were involved in. In this particular case the group were asked to compare three texts, (a) a passport description from a British passport, (b) a poem by Leonard Cohen called 'All There Is To Know About Adolph Eichmann', and (c) the description of Mr Bounderby from chapter 4 of *Hard Times*. Readers who are familiar with chapter 6 of Widdowson (1975) will recognize some similarities between this workshop task and the discussion of literary and non-literary descriptions there. The generally comparative (literary v. non-literary) nature of the tasks which the course members were often set owes much to Widdowson's pioneering work, and we would like to acknowledge that fact here. We pick a task maximally similar to that presented by Widdowson, however, in order to be able to use it to highlight some different assumptions between his approach and ours. This matter will be taken up later.

The participants were asked to work together in small groups in order to:

1 examine the linguistic features which the texts had. in common, if any;
2 examine the linguistic features which differentiated the texts from one another;
3 examine the similarities and differences in pragmatic function which could be said to give rise to the linguistic features noted, and
4 consider how these passages might be used interestingly in their various teaching situations.

For ease of reference, the three texts are reproduced below:

(A)	**Bearer** Titulaire	**Wife** Femme
Occupation Profession	*University Teacher*	*Housewife*
Place of birth Lieu de naissance	*Heathfield*	*Stockport*
Date of birth Date de naissance	*10·4·47*	*13·9·46*
Residence Résidence	*England*	
Height Taille	*5* ft. *5* in.	*5* ft. $2\frac{1}{2}$ in.

Distinguishing marks *Scars on right wrist*
Signes particuliers *and left knee. Mole on right cheek.*

CHILDREN   ENFANTS

Name Nom	**Date of birth** Date de naissance	**Sex** Sexe
Hiroko E.	*16·4·72*	*F*
Benjamin W.	*16·1·74*	*M*

Usual signature of bearer
Signature du titulaire   *M.H. Short*

Usual signature of wife
Signature de sa femme   *Hilary Short*

(B)

ALL THERE IS TO KNOW
ABOUT ADOLPH EICHMANN

EYES: .... Medium
HAIR: .... Medium
WEIGHT: .... Medium
HEIGHT: .... Medium
DISTINGUISHING FEATURES: .... None
NUMBER OF FINGERS: .... Ten
NUMBER OF TOES: .... Ten
INTELLIGENCE: .... Medium

What did you expect?

Talons?

Oversize incisors?

Green saliva?

Madness?

(Leonard Cohen)

(C)

Mr Bounderby

NOT being Mrs Grundy, who *was* Mr Bounderby?

Why, Mr Bounderby was as near being Mr Gradgrind's bosom friend, as a man perfectly devoid of sentiment can approach that spiritual relationship towards another man perfectly devoid of sentiment. So near was Mr Bounderby—or, if the reader should prefer it, so far-off.

He was a rich man: banker, merchant, manufacturer, and what not. A big, loud man, with a stare and a metallic laugh. A man made out of a coarse material, which seemed to have been stretched to make so much of him. A man with a great puffed head and forehead, swelled veins in his temples, and such a strained skin to his face that it seemed to hold his eyes open and lift his eyebrows up. A man with a pervading appearance on him of being inflated like a balloon, and ready to start. A man who could never sufficiently vaunt himself a self-made man. A man who was always proclaiming, through that brassy speaking-trumpet of a voice of his, his old ignorance and his old poverty. A man who was the Bully of humility.

A year or two younger than his eminently practical friend, Mr Bounderby looked older; his seven or eight and forty might have had the seven or eight added to it again, without surprising anybody. He had not much hair. One might have fancied he had talked it off; and that what was left, all standing up in disorder, was in that condition from being constantly blown about by his windy boastfulness.

(Charles Dickens, *Hard Times*)

Text (A): the passport text

The most obvious features associated with this text are its layout as a form, the use of two languages, English and French, and the fact that the text is composed entirely of noun phrases. In addition, the categories and features referred to by the noun phrases are either permanent or semi-permanent. All of these characteristics are a function of the fact that passports are used to identify individuals quickly and unambiguously. It is interesting to note that the printed noun phrases have a dual function, depending upon whether you are the individual filling in the form in the first place or an official reading the passport at a border post. In the first situation the phrases will be interpreted as questions (What is your profession? What was your place of birth? etc.); in the second they will be informatives. In other words, the text can be seen as having a basic question-plus-answer or topic-plus-comment form, depending upon situational context. For the individual filling in the form, the dominant linguistic structure of the document to be completed and knowledge of its intended function constrain the linguistic form of the information supplied. Hence, in this particular case, the person filling in the form could have written 'I have a şcar on my right wrist and my left knee and I also have a mole on my right cheek'. He did not do so because he was aware, presumably, of both linguistic patterning in the document and its future function. The layout and the use of short noun phrases mean that the text can be read rapidly and easily. Features like height and distinguishing marks are permanent, and in addition to the inevitable photograph they aid identification. In a sense, the most interesting thing about this text is the absence of the sorts of features which we would normally associate with a text. The 'sentences' do not have inter-sentential links of any kind, or any variety in the kinds of construction used. One consequence of all this is that it is more or less impossible to make inferential links of any real significance between one sentence and another. As a result, the text is straightforward, not just in layout but by virtue of the fact that it is difficult to read underlying meaning into it. In other words, it could be deemed to count as an obvious example of what would traditionally be thought to be objective, non-literary language. And indeed, it is difficult to imagine a complete text with these features and these alone turning up in a book of poems. But of course such a form could turn up as part of a novel, and with not many changes, at least the beginnings of literary interest can be achieved, as text (B) shows.

Text (B): *the poem by Leonard Cohen*

The first thing to notice about the Cohen poem is that it alludes to the notion of a passport, an identity card, or some such thing. It does this most obviously by virtue of the fact that the first part of the poem, like the passport, is not normal running text, but is laid out as a form and consists of a series of pairs of noun phrases which can be seen as questions and answers or minimal topics plus minimal comments adding up to the description of an individual. Participants felt that they would be able to teach this poem because it was not very difficult (they did not always feel that they would be able to teach the texts we confronted them with, for reasons like linguistic difficulty or lack of background cultural understanding on the part of their students). They also felt that by examining the passport text before or along with the poem they would be able to sensitize their students to the way in which the poem depended upon knowledge of the form and function of identity cards for its meaning and effect. It was suggested that students could be asked to write passport descriptions of themselves. This would produce effective language work as it would mean that the students would have to write in appropriate linguistic forms, thus sensitizing them to the inter-relation between form and function. The writing could also be used as the basis for interesting class discussion about this relation and about topics to do with identity, identity cards, and so on. Language work of this kind would then help the students to see the allusive properties of the poem and the role that such allusion plays in understanding the text as a whole.

The reason that it is important to notice the 'identity card' form of the Cohen poem is precisely because the information given does not help us to identify the individual concerned. If we look at the right-hand column of the form, we see that for all gradable characteristics Eichmann is described as 'medium'. He does not, therefore, stand out. The answers which do not use the word 'medium' supply the most normal, and therefore the least distinguishing, comment. If we look at the left-hand column of topics, we find some features which one might reasonably expect to find in a passport, but some we would definitely not find. The number of fingers or toes would not appear, because it is very unusual indeed to find people with more or fewer than ten of each. From the point of view of an official reading an identity card, then, information about the number of fingers would be so redundant as to waste his time. Any deviation from the norm would be so surprising that it would be bound to turn up under 'distinguishing features'. From all of this, it is plain to see that we as readers are meant to deduce that Adolph Eichmann, well known as an individual involved in the Nazi massacre of Jews during World War II, despite his notoriety, was an ordinary man in all other respects. So much so, that we might well, in our minds, go on to think of other, parallel, possible characteristics—presumably he loved his family, for example. If the poem ended at this point, we would have a text which consisted of an identity card format with not an enormous amount extra in purely linguistic terms. It would still be an interesting text, however, and to arrive at its meaning the reader would have to make inferences based upon textual pattern. The natural assumption is that someone who looks ordinary is ordinary, and that someone who is evil should appear evil. Cohen demonstrates that this is not necessarily the case. The participants on our course noted that a simple poem such as this could thus be used to help students become aware of the processes of inference which readers use in order to understand texts. In terms of literary merit, what we have just outlined is not particularly complex or fine. But in pedagogic terms it was felt that what we had noticed so far was most certainly of use in getting students to understand how texts (and therefore literary texts) worked.

If we now move on to the second half of the poem, the first thing to note in terms of linguistic features is what stylisticians usually call 'internal deviation' (cf. Levin 1965). The identity-card format is broken by the line 'What did you expect?' This line thus stands out. It is not a noun phrase, but a fully-fledged sentence; it is typographically distinct from the previous items on the left-hand side of the page, and it is the first question. The question suggests that the reader, who in effect has been put in the same position as an official might be in examining Eichmann's passport, must have expected some other description of Eichmann than the one which he has just read. From this and the following questions we can infer that Cohen is suggesting that the reader (and therefore people in general) expect people who are labelled metaphorically as 'monsters' to exhibit all of the characteristics commonly associated with the class, an assumption which is obviously untrue. In other words, the contribution of the second half of the poem is to reinforce the message seen in the first half by approaching the issue from the opposite end. In the first half of the poem we are surprised at first that Eichmann appears so unexceptional, because we expect (unreasonably, we soon realize) people who appear ordinary to be ordinary. Now what is being challenged is the unthinking assumption that people who act extraordinarily (in this case monstrously) should look extraordinary too.

Like the first half of the poem, this part turns out to be interesting in that it reveals processes of inference at work in the reader. Given the parallelism between 'Talons?', 'Oversize incisors?' and 'Green saliva?', we look for a way of connecting them together. They are all noun phrases functioning as questions, they successively occupy whole lines of the poem, and they all refer to physical objects. Talons could belong to eagles as well as monsters; large dogs could have large incisors, as well as Dracula figures, and people who are ill could have green saliva as well as monsters from the late-night movies. But it is only the second kind of interpretation in each case which allows us to connect the items together into a satisfying pattern. The last item in the list, 'Madness?', deviates from the rest of the list in that madness is an abstract quality, not a physical thing. This last item in the list is thus emphasized (as it is by being the last word of the poem). And it is this question which brings with it the unthinking assumption (which, like the others, we now have to reject) that people who do abnormal things must be mad. A typical reaction to the mass murderer is to remove him from normal societal status by labelling him as insane. The eventual point, then, of the Cohen poem is to make us question this automatic assumption for Eichmann, and therefore, by extrapolation, for others who might be deemed to be similar in some way.

By discussing linguistic form in considerable detail, the workshop group were able to come to a detailed understanding not just of the poem itself but also of how they as readers arrived via inferencing strategies at the interpretation that they discovered. One part of that process of inference was a set of inferences based upon knowledge of the linguistic form of passports and identity cards and the typical functions which such documents served. An understanding of this fact itself then prompted pedagogical strategies designed to help their own students to understand (a) the poem and (b) the procedures involved in arriving at that understanding. Whether this was to be carried out at an explicit or an implicit level depended upon the students concerned. But in any such case, the belief was that in establishing solidly what was involved in understanding this relatively simple poem, students would be able to go on more confidently to tackle more complex pieces of writing.

Text (C): Mr Bounderby

If we compare the description of Mr Bounderby with the other two descriptions, we can see that this one is very different in type, both linguistically and functionally. There are some surface similarities; for example this text also has a series of noun phrases which constitute whole sentences. But this time the passage has an obviously rhetorical function. This is reflected in the structure of the noun phrases already alluded to by the repetition of 'a man who . . . ' and 'a man with . . . ' at the beginning of most of the NP-sentences, a repetition which helps to ensure that the reader notices the parallelism between the sentences. This rhetorical quality is also to be found in the presence of tropes like metaphor ('metallic laugh', 'brassy speaking-trumpet of a voice', 'windy boastfulness') and paradox ('the Bully of humility'). Another obvious characteristic of the passage which marks it off from the passport description is the direct textual involvement of the reader by reference to him or her ('or, if the reader should prefer it, so far off'), and a question and answer sequence along with discoursal features normally associated with conversation ('Not being Mrs Grundy, who was Mr Bounderby? Why, Mr Bounderby was . . . '). This involvement of the reader is one of the things which suggests that this description, unlike the passport, is not objective, but subjective and value-laden. Dickens makes it appear as if the reader, like the writer, has a choice over wording, for example. He also uses a number of non-factive constructions, which thus reduce objectivity ('*seemed* to have been stretched', '*seemed* to hold his eyes open', 'a pervading *appearance* on him of being inflated like a balloon', 'Mr Bounderby *looked* older', 'one might have *fancied* he had talked it off'). Mr Bounderby's description contains one or two features one would expect to find in a passport description (for example, we know his profession and his size), but there are also features of physical description which we would not expect to find, for example those which are impermanent ('he had not much hair'), or which are much too specific in type to count as general physical descriptive categories ('great puffed head and forehead, swelled veins in his temples'). The metaphors noted earlier assist this particular aspect of the description. The metaphors often refer to non-physical aspects of his character, and because they have to be interpreted non-literally they give a much more specific descriptive impression than any passport.

These individual features are not there just to give a detailed sense of the individual, however. From their presence we are able to get a series of insights into Mr Bounderby's character and his likely behaviour. The fact that he has a metallic laugh, for example, and that he is made out of a coarse material will lead us to suppose that he is a rather vulgar man who may well not care very much for the feelings of others. The fact that he looks like an inflated balloon will lead us to think that he is rather pompous, and so on. Dickens thus makes use of the automatic connections that we make between physical appearance and character that Leonard Cohen was at pains to point out as unreasonable assumptions in the final analysis. The participants in the workshop were able to see that the reason for the marked differences between this text and the other two lay in its very different function, that of giving an account of Mr Bounderby's general character, and ensuring that the reader disapproves of him and laughs at him. One obvious strategy to achieve such an end is to resort to exaggerated and comic description and to invite the reader to take on the stance of the writer. This strategy in turn leads to the employment of the linguistic features in the particular functional settings that were pointed out above.

When discussing how they might teach this text in class, the participants noted that the contrast between this text and the others would provide useful material for discussion. It was also suggested that an interesting task for students to do would be to write a passport description of Mr Bounderby and then compare it with Dickens's own description. The examination of literary text could thus be used to foster linguistic production on the part of the students. Discussion of the more simple texts examined in the first part of the workshop would help the students to cope with the more difficult description of Mr Bounderby.

This account of the results of a particular workshop cannot adequately describe the process of small-group discussion and debate which we have referred to earlier and which are essential to this particular teaching methodology. Our description also does not focus except in general terms on classroom applications. We hope, none the less, that it offers some insight into the nature of the workshop activity and that from it readers can themselves construct similar tasks and recognize how the study of literary and non-literary texts can be mutually reinforcing and of reciprocal benefit for the teaching of language and literature at different levels.

Concluding remarks—literary and non-literary language?

We stated at the outset that it is difficult to make a *linguistic* distinction between literature and the rest of language. By this we mean that, despite a widespread assumption to the contrary, we know of no particular linguistic feature or set of linguistic features which are found in literature but not in other kinds of text. This became particularly clear to the course participants and ourselves when, in another workshop, we compared the language of poetry with the language of advertising. We quickly discovered that the sorts of features which we traditionally associate with poetry (e.g. rhyme, metre, ambiguity, metaphor, parallelism, linguistic deviation) and which certainly turn up in literary texts also appeared in abundance in advertising language. So much so, that in this particular workshop the course participants began to analyse the advertisements in the kind of way that we would traditionally reserve for literature, talking, for example, of the effectiveness, strikingness, and freshness of the language involved. In a sense, we were discovering nothing new here. Leech (1966) devotes a whole chapter (chapter 20) to the presence of literary tropes, etc. in television advertising. Once we examine the functions of advertising and poetry, we discover that the two 'genres' have much in common. It is a common factor in both kinds of text, for example, that they are designed to be memorable and have an emotional effect on the reader or hearer. Given functional similarity, it is surely unsurprising that we find similarity in terms of linguistic features.

One possible objection to this attack on the notion of a special literary language is that advertising is marginally a linguistic art form in any case. But such linguistic features also turn up in text-types which traditional critics would be less happy to accept as aesthetic objects. Gläser (1975) examined scientific texts for the presence of what she called 'emotive features' and concluded that 'Even in scientific and technical English, emotive elements do occur. In the given context they have a communicative function. Emotive features are justified whenever they help in conveying information and in facilitating the communicative effect on the part of the recipient of the message . . . ' Short (forthcoming) demonstrates that a particular deviant structure, the polysyndetic list construction, occurs regularly in a corpus of non-literary texts as well as in a series of literary ones.

It is as a result of accumulating evidence of this kind that we wish to agree with linguists like Fowler (1971) and reject the traditional notion that there is a separate literary language. If there is a distinct corpus of texts which can be called 'literature', it would appear that the corpus will have to be defined at least partly in socio-cultural rather than in linguistic terms. In turn, it is for these reasons that although we wish to endorse Widdowson's (1975) advocacy of a comparative approach to literature teaching involving extracts from literature and extracts from other texts, we would not want to encourage the use of the comparative approach, as he explicitly does, to develop in the learner 'an awareness of the nature of literary writing as a type of discourse'. It may be that there is a quantitative difference between the occurrence of certain linguistic features in literary as opposed to other kinds of text, and this could be determined by empirical research. But even if such a quantitative difference were found, it would only be a quantitative and not a qualitative one. Another possibility, and to our minds a much more likely one, is that if we assume a particular text to be literature, we as readers may well attempt to process it in ways partially different from texts we assume not to be literature. Evidence of this kind of procedure can be found in our earlier examination of the character descriptions. For example, our attempt to make sense of 'Talons?/Oversize incisors?/Green saliva?/Madness?' in the Cohen poem involved not only the search for a meaning for each of the lines which connected them together in a sensible way (a strategy based on relating parallel and contiguous items together so that they are related semantically to one another, which, it should be noted, is used in the processing of all kinds of English text), but also an assumption that the meaning we arrived at should fit in with the rest of the text so that it formed an organic and patterned interpretative whole. The more we are successful in interpretative strategies of this kind, the more likely it is that we will perceive the text not so much as a literary one in the non-honorific sense (good or bad) but as an *interesting* (and therefore at least to some extent good) text, particularly if the text is seen to have other interesting features like density of meaning and a high degree of inferability.

What is being suggested here, then, is that if a reader feels some need to process a text as a literary artefact (perhaps because he or she has been told that it is literature on the jacket of the book or by a friend, perhaps because it contains a high degree of linguistic features traditionally associated with poetry or some other literary genre, and so on), he or she will attempt to apply a set of special interpretative conventions. The more the reader succeeds in doing this while at the same time arriving at a consistent interpretation, the more likely it is that the text will be seen as valuable in some way. In other words, the strategy set may be applied to literally any text, but the more successful the application of that set is, the more valuable the text will be perceived to be. This suggestion is only a tentative one, but it has the merits of (a) taking into account the available evidence about the linguistic structure of literary and other texts, and (b) providing the outline of an account of the relationship between the honorific and non-honorific definitions of literature. It may be, of course, that similar interpretative strategies are employed by readers when processing texts which they do not perceive as being literature, but it is not obvious that they do, and so the processing approach looks like a fruitful one to pursue in academic terms. This is also why our course in general, and the workshop sessions in particular, were not just used to examine similarities and differences between the structure of the different texts concerned, but also involved the examination of how we as readers built up meaning in our interaction with the text. Like the assumption that literature is linguistically distinct from the rest of language, the suggestion that readers process texts which they perceive as literary in different ways from other texts is verifiable, and we would welcome attempts to demonstrate or refute our suggestions. In so doing, others will contribute to the debate over the nature of literature and language and also, in the long run, help to discover more effective ways of teaching them in the classroom.

5 Linguistic Models, Language, and Literariness: Study strategies in the teaching of literature to foreign students

Ronald Carter

Introduction

The main aim of this chapter is to argue that in the teaching of a foreign language, opportunities should be sought for more extensive and integrated study of language and literature than is commonly the case at present. The first half of the paper discusses some language-based *study skills* which I consider important preliminary activities to reading literature. Although the study skills I discuss are language-based, I am not claiming that understanding the language is the same as understanding the literature. For this reason, I stress that these skills/activities are preliminary and pre-literary. In the second half of the paper I discuss the use of a linguistically-based model in application to a literary narrative. I claim that models like this can contribute much to the development of literary competence. Such linguistic–stylistic analysis can have considerable benefits for the study of the language and thus aids the integration of language and literary study; again, however, we must exercise caution, since language and literature are separate *systems* or phenomena, although literature is made from language which is its medium and is, therefore, of considerable significance in our reading of literature. For this reason, I consider that the use of linguistic models enables us to work on the *literariness* of texts rather than on texts as literature. Recognition of literariness is one of the most fundamental components in literary competence.

Other related aims of this chapter are as follows. It is suggested that for students of a foreign literature linguistic models and pre-literary linguistic activities can:

a aid recognition of and sensitivity to the nature of *language organization* in related discourse types in the target language;

b lay a basis for *interpretation* of texts by analysing closely key structural features of the language of that text;

c explain the literary *character* of particular texts (in this instance, narrative style in a short story);

d point to features of *literariness* in texts by simultaneous application of relevant models to non-literary texts *and* to texts conventionally considered literary;

e promote *learner-centred language activities* which are useful in their own right.

Language teaching strategies

In this section a number of teaching strategies are proposed. They have no special claim to originality; indeed, language teachers will probably recognize them as part of their everyday tools of the trade. They are employed in the belief that they can assist the preliminary or pre-literary process of understanding and appreciating the text in question. It is clear that another text may require different strategies and also that any adequate teaching of a literary text goes beyond language teaching techniques, however widely used and principled they may be. However, it is claimed in the case of short narratives like Somerset Maugham's 'The Man with the Scar' that the strategies are broadly generalizable. The text is printed at the end of the chapter.

Prediction: What comes next?

This requires careful preparation before the story is read in class. The technique is for the teacher to stop the reading at key points and to elicit predictions of how the narrative will develop. In the case of 'The Man with the Scar' a number of 'stopping places' can be suggested.

a. The title can be omitted and, after the story has been read, students can be invited to predict what it should be.

b. At the end of the first paragraph, students might be asked to predict, on the basis of the information supplied about the man, what the story is going to be about. This can be an important stage in sensitizing students to the function of the opening of the story in an interpretation of the whole. This opening bears an interestingly oblique relation to the rest of the text.

c. In the second narrator's narrative a cut-off could occur at lines 105–7: 'She flung herself into his arms and with a hoarse cry of passion . . . , he pressed his lips to hers'; or at the question of the general in line 124; and/or at a point which elicits a prediction of the reaction of the general to the action of the man in slitting the throat of his wife (lines 127–871): 'the general stared at him for a while in silence'.

d. The end of the story also allows an interesting predictive focus at
the point where a question is asked about the man's scar in line 141:
'"But how then did he get the scar?" I asked at length.'

These are all key points in the development of the plot.

This is not the place to discuss in detail the nature of predictions
made. Each class will produce its own varied responses. The teaching
point to underline is that a heightened degree of attentiveness to the
story can be brought about by prediction. There is increased
involvement from the natural desire of seeing one's own expectations
fulfilled or contravened.

Features of the structure of the story can be highlighted for
subsequent discussion. A firm basis is laid for exploring such questions
as: why did the man do what he did?; was he right or wrong in so
doing?; did the general torture him more by allowing him to live?
Prediction exercises lend themselves particularly to work in pairs or
small groups, with individuals being invited to justify their own or the
group's verbal prediction by close reference to the foregoing text and to
their own individual experiences of human behaviour. Some groups
persist in their preferences for outcomes alternative to those given by
the writer, and they can be encouraged in this so long as evidence and
support is forthcoming. Such activities can be a basis for stimulating
and motivating class oral work and discussion. There is no reason why
in some cases this should not be done in the students' own language,
but the target language should be used wherever feasible.

In the face of 'gaps' (see Rimmon-Kenan 1983: 125–7) in the
narrative, such as some conclusion or evaluation of the behaviour of
the man with the scar on the part of the first narrator, then prediction
serves the function of allowing that gap to be filled by the reader.
However, it must be said that prediction activities should be used
sparingly. Not all texts lend themselves to this kind of macro-stylistic
work. Most lyric poems, for example, or texts where descriptive states
are evoked do not benefit. But texts with a strong plot component,
where the next step in the action can be significant, do force readers to
predict. And the best narratives will contain the seeds of their own
development, so that readers have to read back as well as project
forward. This is the case, I want to assert, with 'The Man with the
Scar', where an additional advantage of prediction exercises is that
they draw attention to the dual narrative structure of the story.

Cloze procedure

This is, as many language teachers know, a form of prediction. The
focus is on individual words or sequences of words, rather than on
stretches of text. There is also an inevitable concentration on micro-
stylistic effects which can be of a subtle and complex kind in some

stories. Teachers will need to give careful attention to the number of words deleted, to the relative multivalency of the chosen items, to the linguistic competence of a group, and, perhaps, to preparatory activities on non-literary texts in order to give practice in contexts where a greater degree of predictability may obtain (though predictability is not the exclusive preserve of the non-literary text—indeed, 'literary' effects can be produced by predictable *and* unpredictable elements). Items which might be deleted from this story include:

a. line 125. 'I — her.'

b. line 129 'It was a — gesture,' he said at last.

c. from the title: 'The Man with — — ' (e.g. *a* scar; lottery tickets; a grudge?).

d. line 13 '. . . strolling leisurely round the bar offer — for sale'

and so on.

Lexical prediction can be made during a reading or after the story has been read, and preferably after some preliminary discussion. It can be used as well as, or instead of, structural prediction. Reasonable and supportable predictions require students to be alert both to the overall pattern of the story and to the immediate verbal context in which the deleted word occurs. Some students are assisted if the first letter of the word is given or if a list of words—from which an appropriate choice is to be made—is supplied by the teacher. For example, with reference to (b) above, if students are asked to choose from a list of words as follows:

'It was a — gesture,' he said at last.
brave noble foolhardy futile ignoble

then they are being asked to focus on words which have resonances across the whole story. To justify and account for their decisions they are being asked to demonstrate careful and close reading of the story.

As with structural prediction, such 'lexical' prediction can lead to the kind of individual and group involvement with the text as well as to the kind of oral language practice which are not usually engendered by exposition from the teacher. Structural and lexical prediction can be employed jointly, and interesting oral and group language can emerge from asking students to delete words for other classes to predict. (For an interesting history of cloze methods in language teaching (some with obvious possibilities of transfer to the literature class), see Soudek and Soudek 1983.)

Summary: What's it all about?

A strategy designed to focus attention on the overall point or meaning of the story is to ask students to produce summaries of the text.

Indiscriminate use of summary has its dangers, and instructions need to be fairly precisely formulated, because otherwise there is a danger of committing the heresy of paraphrase by suggesting that there *is* a paraphrasable meaning to the story. The technique should be seen rather as an enabling device for students in their personal process of interpretation or engagement with the text.

It is useful to impose a word limit for the summary (in a range say, 25–40 words, in the case of a story as short as 'The Man with the Scar'), and too ask initially for a summary which is not an interpretation of the story but rather an account of *what happens*. The reasons for this are mainly threefold:

a An imposed word limit makes the exercise a useful one linguistically. Much syntactic re-structuring, deletion, and lexical re-shaping goes into meeting the word limit. The teacher can do much here to foster integrated language and literature work.

b A word limit enforces selection of what is significant. Does the summary, for example, include reference to the 'scar' or to the man's run of bad luck at cards prior to the execution? Is the story's political background brought into the foreground? Students learn that even a summary of what happens is in one sense an interpretative act.

c Students come to see that a summary of what happens is not a reason for valuing our reading of short stories by writers such as Maugham. There is, of course, more to it than this. But they should also come to understand the difference between plot and theme, evaluate the role of plot in a story like this, discuss why there appears to be no clear indication that we are to read this as any more than an account of what happens. That is, the title (in one sense a summary) is strangely oblique and there is minimal thematic pointing by the two narrators—especially in their dialogue at the close of the story. Summarizing the story means that attention can be focused on *how* it is narrated as well as on what is narrated, and questions can be generated about the structure and shape of this kind of narrative. Such work points to an introduction of the kind of linguistic model for narrative *structure* described below.

A related linguistic and literary exercise is to invite students to compare and criticize alternative summaries. Here are three recently produced in my own class (structured limits were not always met, but the effort to conform is valuable for all):

A man with a scar now lives a life of misery because, when facing an execution, he killed the woman he loved and was pardoned.

A man received a scar from a burst ginger-beer bottle. He was a general and was to be executed but is now a lottery ticket seller.

A political exile from Nicaragua ensures his own survival by murdering his wife in a sufficiently 'noble' way. He impresses his executioners but becomes emotionally scarred.

Note that summaries can also be supplied by the teacher for comparison. (See also discussion by Nash and Widdowson in this volume.)

Forum: debating opposing viewpoints

One advantage of a story such as 'The Man with the Scar' is that it is a relatively open text, sufficiently inexplicit in its meanings to allow for students to be asked to debate opposing propositions.

A. *The man calculated that to murder his wife was the only way he could survive execution. He deserved the scar he got, but life is a lottery.*

B. *The man was so devoted to his wife that he knew their life could not be lived alone. He thought they should both die together. The scar is the surface sign of a deep emotional wounding at his loss. He did not deserve this kind of scar, but life is a lottery.*

'Forum' is not a technical term but suggests the inherent potentiality of literature to mobilize among students discussion and debate with each other. The exercise is one which lends itself to small group-based activity with groups being allocated to defence of either one of the propositions, even if this may not be their own personal view. The group (and then its spokesman/woman) adduces evidence from a combination of world knowledge and the text in question to support points relevant to the 'argument'. The other groups listen and try to provide counter-examples. Either the whole class can participate or a section of the class can be assigned the task of judging and then voting for which propositions they consider to have been most persuasively argued. The whole exercise is a stimulus to oral language work through role play and can be prepared for accordingly; from a specifically literary–textual viewpoint students learn that texts *of any kind* do not easily allow of singular or unitary interpretation.

Guided re-writing

Guided re-writing is another widely employed language teaching strategy. It is aimed at helping students to recognize the broader discoursal patterns of texts and the styles appropriate to them. It involves the student in re-writing stretches of discourse to change its communicative value. As Johnson (1983) puts it:

In such an approach, the starting point for a production exercise is pieces of discourse which the student is asked to do operations on.

In the case of communicative language teaching this can involve re-writing a set of instructions as a description, or turning a lecture transcript into academic prose. The basis for the strategy is to provide practice at expressing intents within contexts according to clearly specified information about audiences and purposes. In the case of a literary text it is, of course, much less easy to specify such parameters, but it is claimed that, as a general rule, it can be productive to focus re-writing exercises at the beginnings of texts, since it is here that the kind of 'information' conveyed can have most impact on readers. It is also claimed that the re-writing of one style into another should help students to get inside a writer's intended communicative effects and to explore the connections between styles and meanings: furthermore, such investigation can be especially illuminating when openings to literary and non-literary texts are juxtaposed.

An illustration of this is provided if we examine the following newspaper narrative report together with the opening to 'The Man with the Scar':

'DINGO' APPEAL REJECTED

By DENIS WARNER
in Melbourne

THREE Federal Court judges in Sydney yesterday dismissed Mrs Lindy Chamberlain's appeal against her conviction in the 'dingo baby' case.

They ordered 35-year-old Mrs Chamberlain to be delivered to the Berrinah Jail in Darwin as soon as convenient to resume her sentence of life imprisonment with hard labour for the murder of her infant daughter Azaria at Ayers Rock in Central Australia.

As soon as the appeal was dismissed, Mrs Chamberlain's lawyers applied for a stay of the imprisonment order, but this was refused. The lawyers later sought leave to appeal to the High Court

What is a dingo? Why inverted commas?
The reader assumes it is an appeal against conviction in a court. But conviction for what?

The place names indicate that the case and presumably the crime took place in Australia.

But what is the 'dingo baby' case?

which may hear her application for renewed bail on Monday.

Background begins.

The case began with the disappearance of Azaria from a tent in a holiday park near Ayers Rock in August, 1980. Mrs Chamberlain maintained that the baby had been taken by a dingo (Australian wild dog).

We are told what a 'dingo' is, and what happened. We can now explain the inverted commas in the heading.

New baby

After two inquests she was found guilty of murder at a trial in Darwin but was released on bail after the birth three weeks later of her fourth child, Kahlia.

Mrs Chamberlain maintained her composure throughout yesterday's brief court session. Her husband Michael, a 38-year-old Seventh Day Adventist minister, also appeared calm after hearing the court dismiss his appeal against his conviction for disposing of nine-week-old Azaria's body.

Further background is provided.

The husband, under a suspended sentence as an accessory after the fact, left court with Kahlia and church officials for his living quarters at an Adventist college.

At the Darwin trial, the jury unanimously decided Mrs Chamberlain slit her daughter's throat in the family car at Ayers Rock. But the prosecution never found the body or a murder weapon.

From *The Daily Telegraph* (London) 30 April 1983

Here the teacher uses the newspaper report to generate questions which are not immediately answered by the text (see marginal comments to the text). It is a particular case of a report in which the reader is presumed to know certain information. If the reader does not have access to this information, then it is not until the background is supplied that it begins to make sense. The following re-writing exercises would be designed to sensitize students to the different ways in which information is structured for readers in different texts:

1 Re-write the text '"Dingo" Appeal Rejected', deleting all references to the background in the case and all information concerning the 'characters' in the case (including the definition of a 'dingo').

2 Re-write the same text, bringing as much background as possible to the first two paragraphs of the report.

3 Re-write the opening paragraph of 'The Man with the Scar', including as many details as you can invent about the man, his name, age, where he is from, how he got his scar, why he is selling lottery tickets in this bar, and so on.

Teachers will doubtless be able to construct for themselves numerous related activities. A more technical linguistic discussion can be found in Harweg (1980).

What can students and teachers hope to gain from this kind of examination? It is to be hoped that the following learning takes place:

1 Students begin to manipulate or, at least, practise manipulating bits of English text. This is a linguistically-based, language improvement exercise, but it is useful to consider such activities in the light of an article by Brazil (1983) where he concludes:

> Possibly the best way of fostering a pupil's sensitivity to literature is not by feeding him more and more literature but by encouraging him to see literary language as continuous with, and deriving its power to move from, his total language experience.

For example, here is an 'alternative' re-written opening to 'The Man with the Scar', produced by a small group of German students of English. It is based on Exercise 3, above:

> Emmanuel Montes was always noticed on account of a broad, red scar which ran in a great crescent from his temple to his chin. He was forty-two years of age and widowed. He frequented the 'Palace Hotel' in Guatemala City where he tried to sell lottery tickets to the guests although he was an exile from Nicaragua and not really at home here. He often looked miserable and indeed his life had been a sad one. He had been subjected to the kind of absurd quirks of fate that made the selling of lottery tickets somehow appropriate. For example, his scar was caused when a ginger beer bottle accidentally burst open at the bar. However, he was a noble and dignified figure and I learned from an acquaintance of mine a story which well illustrated both his loving devotion to his former wife and his sense of self-sacrifice if fate demanded it.

2 Students learn that different texts have different communicative values based, in part at least, on the different ways in which readers are

expected to go about making sense of what information they are given.

In a literary text the only place the reader can turn for the resolution of background information is the text itself, or at the very least to the other texts to which this text might allude. Such allusiveness or 'intertextuality' takes two main forms: either there is reference to other works which the reader may be expected to know, or the writer assumes that the reader is conversant with certain literary conventions which govern how the story is to be read (for example, in a 'whodunnit' we do not know the motivation for the murder, but we know that the immediate suspect is unlikely to be the person named as the killer in the final act of the drama). It is predominantly the case, therefore, that unlike other sources, *literariness* is marked by the extent to which the material is read as largely self-referential. Seeking the reason why the man is selling lottery tickets or has the kind of scar he has is an active interpretative process which involves the reader in constructing the necessary 'information' from the story itself.

However, another significant mark of literariness can be the way in which the omission of certain expected propositions or background information is assigned thematic significance. For example, we consider a number of ways to interpret 'scar' when the 'normal' explanation is not forthcoming, or we start to equate the absence of names and defined places in the text with an anonymous, featureless scenario for the story. We begin to question the constant repetition of the word 'lottery' and the references to the man's luck. This text, in particular, seems to require to be read with an additional semantic overlay in these sorts of key places. The author does not allow his narrators much overt comment and the reader is made to infer more. Literary texts differ in the degree of information supplied to a reader. In a non-literary text, however, information omitted is not generally assumed to be relevant.

A linguistic model for narrative structure

This model is one developed by William Labov and his associates (Labov 1972) working on Black English Vernacular (BEV) in New York. Oral narratives (whose skilled execution is highly prized in Black communities) were collected. Initially, they were examined in the context of a study set up to investigate the notion of linguistic 'deprivation' in such communities and its educational implications. It was discovered not only that the collected narratives regularly exhibited evidence of considerable facility in the use of English (though according to the rules of BEV and not standard American English), but also that the narratives most highly prized had structural properties in common. The structural features extrapolated by Labov were not, however, highlighted by intuition but were observed to correlate with particular linguistic forms and stylistic patterns. Such observations make it easier to work with Labov's model. Unlike some narrative models where it is difficult to retrieve the analyst's decision to assign a part of the narrative to one category rather than to another, Labov's model is generally more attestable. The marking of structural properties in terms of defined language forms also has, as I hope to show, considerable advantages for integrated language and literature study.

The structural properties isolated by Labov can be described as follows (see also Figure 5.1):

1 *Abstract.* This is a short summary of the story that narrators generally provide before the narrative commences. It 'encapsulates the *point* of the story'. Not all, but most, natural narratives have an abstract.

2 *Orientation* is an essential constituent in helping the reader/listener 'to identify in some way the time, place, persons, and their activity or situation'. It can include 'an elaborate portrait of the main character'. Orientation can be marked by *many past progressive verbs*, and, obviously, *adverbial phrases of time/manner and place*.

3 *Complicating action* contains *narrative clauses*. Such clauses have a verb which is simple past or simple present. They are the minimal units of the narrative and are temporally ordered, in that 'a change in their order will result in a change in the temporal sequence of the original semantic organization'. For example, 'The girl got pregnant. The girl married' is a very different story if the sentences are reversed.

4 *Evaluation.* Like the basic narrative clause, this is a most important element in narrative. Culler (1981: 170) argues that narrative clause and evaluation correspond to the *fabula* and *sjuzhet* of early Russian and Czech formalist analyses, but he omits to point out that Labov's definitions help to eliminate much critical fuzziness. Evaluation can take many shapes and be marked by a number of different linguistic forms:

A. *Evaluation: Commentary*

1 *External*: comments by the narrator external to the action and addressed directly to the interlocutor.

2 *Internal*: comment is embedded:
   a the evaluative comment occurs to the narrator or character at a specific moment of the action;
   b comment is addressed to another character;
   c evaluative remarks are attributed to a third party.

B. Sentence-Internal Evaluation Devices

1 *Intensifiers*: e.g. gestures, expressive phonology, repetition, interjection, etc. In other words, a host of available stylistic-expressive-rhetorical means.

2 *Comparators*: generally speaking, a 'comparator moves away from the line of narrative events to consider unrealized possibilities and compare them with events that did not occur'. Realized linguistically by *inter alii* negatives, futures, modals, comparatives, questions.

5 *Resolution*: this contains the last of the narrative or free clauses which begin the complicating action.

6 *Coda*: the coda should provide a sense of completeness, signalling that the story has ended and has been evaluated by bringing 'the narrator and the listener back to the point at which they entered the narrative'.

a

1	Abstract............................	What was this about?
2	Orientation	Who, when, what, where?
3	Complicating action..........	Then what happened?
4	Evaluation.........................	So what?
5	Result or resolution..........	What finally happened?
6	Coda.................................	

b

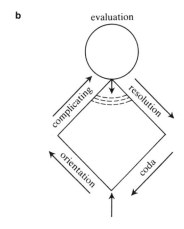

Figure 5.1: Narrative Structure (From Labov 1972)

It is clear that to satisfy the demands of a full literary analysis which accounts for as many features of narrative organization as possible requires considerable refinement. For example, the category of *evaluation* might be studied further to investigate the notion of embedded comment and how this is stylistically realized; or the range of 'stylistic-expressive-rhetorical' means available as 'intensifiers' might be explored; or the kinds of features which might make up a reader's 'orientation' to a main character (e.g. the *omitted* information here).[1]

However, we should also be alert to the dangers of relying too heavily on a model. Teachers will, of course, decide for themselves the extent to which such a model needs to develop according to the aims of a particular lesson or syllabus. In any case, it is often not until a model is seen in relation to the working of a particular text that areas for refinement can be isolated. Indeed, it is a key principle of working with models in such contexts that they should not be seen as finite or self-complete but rather as hypotheses to be tested against data. This gives a distinctly *investigative* edge to their pedagogic application.

It is interesting to attempt to characterize the structure of this story in terms of Labov's model and to explore the extent to which such a structure might embody or correlate with the themes of the story, and to ask whether it can account for the nature of readers' experience of the story. Such a description is a challenging one, since a number of readers of this story have commented that it produces a feeling of 'so what?'. This is reported as connected with their feeling that the story does not have a proper ending, that the title is odd, and that overall it seems difficult to work out the point of it all. (For example, why does the story end with reference to 'ginger ale'?) It is clear, then, that the meanings of the story are not easily or overtly extractable but rather communicated in an embedded or indirect way to the reader. In this respect, the story is typical of many modern—even modernist— short stories. (Hemingway, Gertrude Stein, Saki provide many comparable examples.)

The structure of the story may be best analysed by working chronologically through Labov's categories. It will be recognized, however, that many narratives do not simply proceed in an orderly fashion from 'abstract' to 'coda'. Particularly, in the case of the category 'orientation', there is much gradual unravelling, with orientational information embedded within other categories or within different features in the structural sequence.

Commentary: Narrative style, interpretation, and 'The Man with the Scar'

Abstract: There is no obvious 'abstract', with the possible exception of the title. We are not told what the story is to be about or why we should be reading it. The title, 'The Man with the Scar', is not in itself of any particular significance, though it is natural, in the search for plot-based information, to want to enquire who he is and how he came to get the scar. (Is it, for example, possible that 'scar' may not mean simply a physical scar, though this is what is initially focused as the 'theme' for the first paragraph?)

> *It was on account of the scar* that I first noticed him, for it ran, broad and red, in a great crescent from his temple to his chin. (*my emphasis*)

Orientation: Most of the information here centres on 'the man' and his physical features. This is puzzling, because there seems subsequently to be no point to much of this information. Very little is revealed by the narrator about *who* he is as an individual. In fact, throughout the story 'the man with the scar' remains nameless and without an identity. We might conclude that what the man represents may be more significant for the reader than the man himself. Very little is revealed by the first narrator (the 'I' figure in the story) about the man's character, except perhaps that he is sometimes 'the worse for liquor'. The second narrator—an acquaintance of the first narrator—subsequently reveals that he is 'an exile from Nicaragua'. The setting for the telling of the narrative is noticeably featureless and bare. Information of an orientational kind—i.e. concerning *who, what, where*—is not marked. It is notably absent from the story's opening paragraph where such information is conventionally supplied.

Complicating action: This is particularly dense in the *second* narrator's narrative. Lines 41 to 135 reveal a sequence of almost uninterrupted narrative clauses with few intervening structural features. This constitutes a significant proportion of the action of the story.

Evaluation: The action appears not to be evaluated by either narrator, though it could be said that the general's comments on bravery are evaluative of the action. Though we are, of course, dealing with a translation, the first narrator ('I') comments that the 'high-flown language' of the story told to him 'suits the story', though it is not clear whether we should regard this as a positive or negative evaluation.

Resolution: The action is in one sense 'resolved' by the second narrator when reporting the action of the general in pardoning the life of 'the man with the scar'. There is, however, no resolution of why we have been told the story of the conversation between the narrator and his acquaintance.

Coda: There is no overtly signalled coda. In fact, the way in which both narrators converge to return the reader to the point at which the narrative was entered with a re-focus on 'the scar' is perplexing in its circularity. Rather than any distinctly extractable 'message' about the man, the final 'sequence' (even 'resolution') of the action serves almost to trivialize the story, most particularly in the way it is conveyed by the first or 'I' narrator who is presented as an 'outsider' to the action in more senses than one.

We might note here briefly that appreciation of such structural effects of narrative shaping can be fostered, in a manner which involves extending activities described above, by asking for students to write their own 'endings' to the story. By 'doing it themselves' students can begin to appreciate from the inside, as it were, the relationship between narrative structure and how different readers might come to understand and interpret the story in different ways. See Appendix I for examples.

Literariness and language use: questions and topics

The question of what is specifically literary about certain texts is a complex and problematic one. The answer may be a primarily sociological one and lie with the disposition adopted by the reader towards the text. In terms of actual words employed, there can certainly be no quantitative distinction between literary and non-literary texts. However, differences in the way language is used are discernible, though it has been argued that such distinctions may be less a case of yes/no decisions than one of a gradient or cline of literariness (for fuller discussion, see Carter and Nash 1983). In the language and literature classroom it is necessary to approach such issues with an open mind and to work in the first instance from the benefits which, it was argued above, accrue from the language study of literary and non-literary texts in juxtaposition.

What follows here is a list of suggestions for discussion, topics for investigation, and issues to be raised. Such exploration is particularly suited to group or pair-based work/projects, but the question of how explicitly or abstractly such points are discussed in the classroom or remain within the conceptual underpinning of teachers' overall strategies is best left to the discretion of the individual teacher. Collectively, however, it is claimed here that engagement with these questions and the related activities can enhance the quality and depth of students' response to language, to the varied communicative values of texts, and to the different functions of linguistic items, patterns, and structures.

Although aims and objectives are harder to specify, the more advanced the language learner becomes, the more such competence becomes that more usually associated with the native-speaker. It is clear, therefore, that the questions and topics will need to be handled selectively:

1 Groups can be invited to apply Labov's model to a range of different narrative types such as jokes, anecdotes, children's stories, travelogues, reports of incidents in newspapers, journals, etc. Among the questions to be answered might be:

—What do narratives have in common? (Remember Labov's model is based on *spoken* discourse.)

—What are the stylistic differences between different narrative discourses?

—What is the effect of narratives such as 'The Man with the Scar' which are in part patterned on the expected frame and in part a deliberate break with expectations?

—Is it a signal of literariness in the narrative for the reader to be confronted with a break in frames?

—Why do some narratives play with order or 'chronology' of events?

—Is Labov right about the sequence—Abstract: Orientation: Complicating Action: Evaluation: Result or Resolution: Coda?

2 Within a narrower focus, orientation can be studied along the lines described in the previous section. An additional purpose with this context of 'literariness' is to explore the extent to which readers respond (or are invited by the author/narrator to respond) to the absence of 'expected' features of orientation. In a non-literary or 'informational' text (see Littlewood 1976) information omitted is either assumed to be known or is deemed irrelevant but, as has been suggested above, the reader of a literary text plays a generally more productive role by assigning some kind of semantic significance to 'gaps' and indeterminacies in the expected frame. This leads to greater involvement with the language of the text (where, unlike informational text, every word may be playing a significant part); it can mean that attention to the textuality of the text is much more self-conscious. Exercises such as these are designed to try to raise and extend such self-consciousness. They can also teach directly or teach awareness of the kind of *interpretative procedures* required in reading different types of discourse (see also Widdowson 1979, and the chapter in this volume by Short and Candlin).

3 In an ostensibly non-literary text like a newspaper report, the representational or referential functions of language are preponderant. In a text like 'The Man with the Scar', repetition, pattern, and relations between words are important. We become more involved with *how* the

story is told and with the *attitude* of the narrator towards what is said. Students can thus be asked to find instances of such 'pattern' in 'The Man with the Scar'; for example, what appears to be the attitude of the two narrators towards the narrative of the man with the scar? Close reference to the text in support of answers should be demanded.

4 Finally, the use of a narrative model such as that developed by Labov, together with pre-literary language activities such as, in particular, summary and prediction, can focus attention on the *form* and *shape* of the text. It can provide a basis for an analysis of how far the form of the text reflects, embodies, or otherwise enacts the meanings contained in it. The lack of explicit 'evaluation' and 'coda' in the narrative of the first narrator, for example, may be mimetic of a lack of moral interest or perception which reflects aspects of the character of the narrator himself. Or the model can be used to compare stories from different periods, and students can be invited to question why certain texts (nineteenth-century texts, for example), do have rather more explicit moral directions or codas to the reader. Note, for example, the codas in the final chapters to Jane Austen's *Mansfield Park* and George Eliot's *Middlemarch*. Or students might examine why a narrative such as Fielding's *Joseph Andrews* (1759) contains abstracts for almost every chapter.

Summary

It has been a main point of argument in this chapter that, where feasible, opportunities should be sought to integrate language and literature teaching activities. It is recognized at the same time, however, that to examine the language of the text is to examine only one feature of literary organization and of what makes up a work of literature.

From a pedagogic viewpoint a number of issues have been debated—some more explicitly than others. (Numerous further examples can be found in Carter and Long (forthcoming).) It has been argued that basic language teaching strategies can provide a 'way in' to a text, can help raise questions about its meanings, and can begin to sensitize students to its linguistic–structural organization. This is especially so if the language teaching strategies are student-centred and activity-based and can involve students in the production and generation of problems, questions, bases for interpretation, and so on. It is hoped that the suggested procedures outlined in the second section are of this order. Some teachers may wish to concentrate on this kind of integration only.

A linguistic model is introduced so that frameworks can be set up within which some questions are solved and some more precisely formulated. They exist as hypotheses to be applied to the text and then reviewed, refined, revised in the light of experience of their use. In this sense, they should not be seen as fixed and immutable. It is the responsibility of the teacher to decide how explicitly to introduce the model in the classroom, whether to introduce models *in toto* or in part, or whether to use them for their own guidance only. Much depends here on the experience of the students, their acquaintance with formal linguistics, the aims of the particular lesson, the nature of the design of the literature syllabus, etc. What is argued is that models should inform the literature class to some degree and that, since literary texts are made from language, the more linguistically principled they are, the more systematic the approach to literary text study.

Throughout this chapter, it has been argued that students need to be made aware of and given practice in the relevant procedures for making sense of the kind of reading *processes* required by different texts. This can very often involve inferential procedures of a complex kind and can vary according to the kind of control exercised by the author, the kind of assumptions made by the author, and the purposes the author has in conveying the information. It is, therefore, suggested that students be given practice at reading closely a range of texts in which they will face such styles of presentation. It is often in textual openings that such issues can be most effectively and practically focused.

Models are useful, finally, in so far as they enable students to generalize across a range of texts and to move beyond an interpretation of a single text (though such activity is in itself an interesting and motivating one) and appreciate and use the language associated with different discourse types. It is argued again that linguistic models provide the best means of sensitization to and acquisition of the relevant procedures.

Finally, I may have given the impression that no work on literary texts can begin until these skills and competences have been developed. That is clearly not true. We must also beware that such activities do not inhibit responses to the text or prevent students bringing their own experiences to bear on the formulation of that response. And foreign students are capable of fuller responses to the text than is often realized. But they are *not* native-speaker responses, and all responses need to be developed into fuller articulacy. It is my contention that some of the language activities and work with models on the literariness of texts can aid such development, and that responses can best develop with increased response to and confidence in working with the language in a variety of integrated activities, with language-based hypotheses and in classes where investigative, student-centred learning is the norm. From this pre-literary linguistic basis and integrated with the development of the kind of reading competence and appreciation outlined, students can explore the wider questions of background, author study, influence, literary tradition; they can raise evaluative questions, compare and contrast works with each other, supply information to supplement the hypotheses and investigations, and so on. It can be the case that such contextual and literary issues precede linguistic study. The view adopted in this paper is that language study should be the *first* step in an integrated programme. I hope this paper will contribute something to fuller understanding of this context of integrated language and literary work.

Notes

1 A recent paper which extends Labov's model by analysis of narrative structure is Hasan (1984). The proposed model is for 'nursery tales', but her model, which is more precise linguistically than that of Labov, can be applied to short narratives generally. Such work is appropriate for advanced students of English or linguistics. Readers may like to compare the two models with other models for narrative analysis and select that which best fits their teaching context. This in itself becomes an interesting exercise in applied linguistics, but my own preference for the Labov model is based on its usefulness for introducing a clear, simple, broad outline of narrative organization.

The Man with the Scar

IT was on account of the scar that I first noticed him, for it ran, broad and red, in a great crescent from his temple to his chin. It must have been due to a formidable wound and I wondered whether this had been caused by a sabre or by a
5 fragment of shell. It was unexpected on that round, fat and good-humoured face. He had small and undistinguished features and his expression was artless. His face went oddly with his corpulent body. He was a powerful man of more than common height. I never saw him in anything but a very
10 shabby grey suit, a khaki shirt and a battered sombrero. He was far from clean. He used to come into the Palace Hotel at Guatemala City every day at cocktail time and strolling leisurely round the bar offer lottery tickets for sale. If this was the way he made his living it must have been a poor one for I
15 never saw anyone buy, but now and then I saw him offered a drink. He never refused it. He threaded his way among the tables with a sort of rolling walk as though he were accustomed to traverse long distances on foot, paused at each table, with a little smile mentioned the numbers he had for
20 sale and then, when no notice was taken of him, with the same

smile passed on. I think he was for the most part a trifle the
worse for liquor.

I was standing at the bar one evening, my foot on the rail,
with an acquaintance—they make a very good dry Martini at
the Palace Hotel in Guatemala City—when the man with the
scar came up. I shook my head as for the twentieth time since
my arrival he held out for my inspection his lottery tickets. But
my companion nodded affably.

'*Qué tal, general?* How is life?'

'Not so bad. Business is none too good, but it might be
worse.'

'What will have have, general?'

'A brandy.'

He tossed it down and put the glass back on the bar. He
nodded to my acquaintance.

'*Gracias. Hasta luego.*'

Then he turned away and offered his tickets to the men who
were standing next to us.

'Who is your friend?' I asked. 'That's a terrific scar on his
face.'

'It doesn't add to his beauty, does it? He's an exile from
Nicaragua. He's a ruffian of course and a bandit, but not a
bad fellow. I give him a few *pesos* now and then. He was a
revolutionary general, and if his ammunition hadn't given out
he'd have upset the government and be Minister of War now
instead of selling lottery tickets in Guatemala. They captured
him, along with his staff, such as it was, and tried him by
court-martial. Such things are rather summary in these
countries you know, and he was sentenced to be shot at dawn.
I guess he knew what was coming to him when he was caught.
He spent the night in gaol and he and the others, there were
five of them altogether, passed the time playing poker. They
used matches for chips. He told me he'd never had such a run
of bad luck in his life; they were playing with a short pack,
Jacks to open, but he never held a card; he never improved
more than half a dozen times in the whole sitting and no
sooner did he buy a new stack than he lost it. When day broke
and the soldiers came into the cell to fetch them for execution
he had lost more matches than a reasonable man could use in
a lifetime.

'They were led into the patio of the gaol and placed against
a wall, the five of them side by side, with the firing party facing
them. There was a pause and our friend asked the officer in
charge of them what the devil they were keeping him waiting
for. The officer said that the general commanding the

25

30

35

40

45

50

55

60

65

government troops wished to attend the execution and they awaited his arrival.

'"Then I have time to smoke another cigarette," said our friend. "He was always unpunctual."

'But he had barely lit it when the general—it was San Ignacio, by the way: I don't know whether you ever met him—followed by his A.D.C. came into the patio. The usual formalities were performed and San Ignacio asked the condemned men whether there was anything they wished before the execution took place. Four of the five shook their heads, but our friend spoke.

'"Yes, I should like to say good-bye to my wife."

'"*Bueno*," said the general, "I have no objection to that. Where is she?"

'"She is waiting at the prison door."

'"Then it will not cause a delay of more than five minutes."

'"Hardly that, *Señor General*," said our friend.

'"Have him placed on one side."

'Two soldiers advanced and between them the condemned rebel walked to the spot indicated. The officer in command of the firing squad on a nod from the general gave an order, there was a ragged report, and the four men fell. They fell strangely, not together, but one after the other, with movements that were almost grotesque, as though they were puppets in a toy theatre. The officer went up to them and into one who was still alive emptied two barrels of his revolver. Our friend finished his cigarette and threw away the stub.

'There was a little stir at the gateway. A woman came into the patio, with quick steps. and then, her hand on her heart, stopped suddenly. She gave a cry and with outstretched arms ran forward.

'"*Caramba*," said the General.

'She was in black, with a veil over her hair, and her face was dead white. She was hardly more than a girl, a slim creature, with little regular features and enormous eyes. But they were distraught with anguish. Her loveliness was such that as she ran, her mouth slightly open and the agony of her face beautiful, a gasp of surprise was wrung from those indifferent soldiers who looked at her.

'The rebel advanced a step or two to meet her. She flung herself into his arms and with a hoarse cry of passion: *alma de mi corazón*, soul of my heart, he pressed his lips to hers. And at the same moment he drew a knife from his ragged shirt—I haven't a notion how he managed to retain possession of it—and stabbed her in the neck. The blood spurted from the cut vein and dyed his shirt. Then he flung his arms round her and once more pressed his lips to hers.

'It happened so quickly that many did not know what had occurred, but from the others burst a cry of horror; they sprang forward and seized him. They loosened his grasp and the girl would have fallen if the A.D.C. had not caught her. She was unconscious. They laid her on the ground and with dismay on their faces stood round watching her. The rebel knew where he was striking and it was impossible to staunch the blood. In a moment the A.D.C. who had been kneeling by her side rose. 115

'"She's dead," he whispered. 120

'The rebel crossed himself.

'"Why did you do it?" asked the general.

'"I loved her." 125

'A sort of sigh passed through those men crowded together and they looked with strange faces at the murderer. The general stared at him for a while in silence.

'"It was a noble gesture," he said at last. "I cannot execute this man. Take my car and have him led to the frontier. *Señor*, I offer you the homage which is due from one brave man to another." 130

'A murmur of approbation broke from those who listened. The A.D.C. tapped the rebel on the shoulder, and between the two soldiers without a word he marched to the waiting car.' 135

My friend stopped and for a little I was silent. I must explain that he was a Guatemalecan and spoke to me in Spanish. I have translated what he told me as well as I could, but I have made no attempt to tone down his rather high-flown language. To tell the truth I think it suits the story. 140

'But how then did he get the scar?' I asked at length.

'Oh, that was due to a bottle that burst when I was opening it. A bottle of ginger ale.'

'I never liked it,' said I.

Appendix I

The following 'endings' to 'The Man with the Scar' were produced by Singaporean students of English. They were written to the following instructions after the students had been introduced to the Labovian narrative model: 'In not more than fifty words write an "ending" to "The Man with the Scar" in which elements of either "evaluation" and/or "resolution" and "coda" are present.' Some examples are printed below. They were discussed with different groups. Discussion tended to focus on 'endings' in which the writer had clearly considered reference to the scar, gambling (lottery), and the man's drinking to be of significance. The degree of moral approbation/disapproval expressed in 'codas' also provided much debate.

1 'I have not liked it since,' replied my friend. 'You should have seen the accident. There was an explosion. A big glass fragment lodged itself in his face, for he was standing nearby. Perhaps this is justice. He traded his wife's life for his own. His conscience is salved now.'

2 'You mean the scar on his face? That's nothing. It's the other one—the indelible scar in his heart—that's more sinister. That biggest gamble in his life was lost dearly. You notice that he never refuses a drink? Poor fellow! No amount of brandy can drown his sorrow.'

3 I walked away and reflected on the deplorable physical and social condition of the man with the scar. Could that be the price he has to pay for double-crossing his fellow revolutionaries and for his seemingly 'brave' act of killing his wife in order to cover up for his misdeeds?

4 Since then, whenever I came to the bar, I bought some lottery tickets from the General. The scar on his face moved me to do so. Moreover, the deep gash reminded me of the fatal wound that love forced itself to inflict.

6   The Untrodden Ways

H. G. Widdowson

One of the difficulties that confront the teacher who tries to stimulate students' interest in short lyrical poems, particularly those of traditional cut, is that they are so often so slight, not to say inconsequential, in paraphrasable content. Prose fiction, drama, narrative poetry offer something substantial by way of characters and events: they tell a tale, which survives in summary and in translation. But lyrical poems do not seem to be actually *about* anything very much at all, so that when one seeks to summarize them, their content, such as it is, dissolves into banality. I sit by the sea and feel miserable. I listen to the nightingale and reflect on mortality. The swans on the water make me think of the passing of time. Typically the lyric deals with commonplace matters, trivialities and truisms which in any other mode of language use would not generally be thought worthy of comment. The poet claims a significance for personal statement which would be left unratified if the propositional content of the statement were conventionally expressed in, for example, the course of a conversation. The most likely reaction would be: 'So what?'. And this is just the kind of reaction that lyrical poems are likely to provoke in classrooms, and which the literature teacher has somehow to counter.

I want to suggest how one might oppose the 'so what?' reaction, and indeed turn it to pedagogic advantage, by considering how one might deal with a poem by Wordsworth which is particularly vulnerable to the charge of inconsequence.[1] This is one of the so-called 'Lucy' poems: 'She dwelt among th'untrodden ways'. Before doing this, however, let me illustrate the kind of difficulty, endemic in lyrical poetry, that I have been discussing by first making reference to another poem by Wordsworth entitled 'Simon Lee'.

The first fifty lines or so of this poem (arranged in eight-line verses) are devoted to a detailed description of this eponymous person. We are told about his appearance, his exuberant activities as a hunter in youth, his decline into poverty and decrepitude in age. Then, following abruptly on from a description of poor old Simon Lee's swollen ankles comes a sudden realization that the reader might be expecting some indication of what the point of this detailed description might be:

> Few months of life has he in store
> As he to you will tell,
> For still, the more he works, the more
> Do his weak ankles swell.
> My gentle Reader, I perceive
> How patiently you've waited,
> And now I fear that you expect
> Some tale will be related.

Well, frankly yes. And it does not seem an unreasonable expectation that something will follow which will give some point to this rather protracted description of Simon Lee. In terms of the normal conventions which attend the conveyance of information, the topic has been well and truly established: the reader now expects a comment of some kind. But we are destined to be disappointed. The poem continues as follows:

> O Reader! had you in your mind
> Such stores as silent thought can bring,
> O gentle Reader! you would find
> A tale in everything.
> What more I have to say is short,
> And you must kindly take it:
> There is no tale; but should you think,
> Perhaps a tale you'll make it.

That's all very well, the gentle reader might reasonably object (not disarmed by these apostrophes and appeals to gentleness), but you are the poet, not me. Why should I have to adopt your role and discover significance for myself by silent thought? If I had that capability, I would not need all this stuff about Simon Lee: I could do my own poems by thinking (silently) about anything that comes to hand—train timetables, fire instructions, the back of bus tickets. But to give a description of the kind you have is to make an implicit claim for significance, and you cannot shuffle off the responsibility for substantiating it on to the reader. So here is this old huntsman, frail and sick and poor. So what?

The problem with 'Simon Lee' is that Wordsworth sets up expectations of narrative consequence which he bathetically fails to satisfy. But there are ways of avoiding the creation of such narrative expectations, and here we come to the poem I want to consider in some detail: 'She dwelt among th'untrodden ways'. This was written a year after 'Simon Lee' and we might assume that Wordsworth had by then acquired more command of his craft. The poem runs as follows:

> She dwelt among th'untrodden ways
> Beside the springs of Dove,
> A maid whom there were none to praise
> And very few to love.
>
> A violet by a mossy stone
> Half-hidden from the eye!
> —Fair as a star, when only one
> Is shining in the sky.
>
> She lived unknown, and few could know
> When Lucy ceased to be;
> But she is in her grave, and oh,
> The difference to me!

Now this poem is about Lucy just as the previous one is about Simon Lee. In both cases we are meant to see that they are significant because of what they *are*, not because of what they *do*.

But in the case of the Lucy poem, narrative expectation is avoided. The first two verses present a series of expressions which are in apposition to each other, and this establishes a kind of fixity, an arrest of forward movement: the poem stands still and focuses attention on the nature of the appositional associations. So the sorts of questions which are provoked are not 'What did the maid do?', 'What happened to her?', but rather 'Who is this maid?', 'What does she represent?', 'What is the nature of these resemblances signalled by the appositions, what is the significance of the comparisons?'. The poem calls for the kind of response which would be evoked by a portrait rather than a story. It calls for contemplative scrutiny. The difference is between static focusing, which seeks significance in the representation of a certain state of being, as distinct from narrative projection, which seeks significance in dynamic relationship between events. This difference can be demonstrated by altering the first verse of the poem to read:

> A maid whom there were none to praise
> And very few to love
> Dwelt among th'untrodden ways
> Besides the springs of Dove.

Now the reader *does* expect some tale to be related. We now suppose that the point of mentioning this person is not primarily because she herself represents anything of any special intrinsic interest, but because of some event or other in which she was involved. The interest shifts from being to action, from state to event. That there were none to praise and very few to love her is provided as given information to be taken as read without further need of explanation, the syntax reflecting its subordination to the narrative interest. Following on from this reconstituted version, the second verse now seems very odd, since it abruptly arrests the narrative movement and obliges the reader to change from a projective to a focusing mode of interpretation in order to realize the significance of the appositions. This requirement for a shift in perspective results in distortion.

The general point I wish to make, then, is that lyrical poems, of which this one by Wordsworth might be taken as a representative example, depend for their effect on the static elaboration of perceptions and thoughts which are not especially noteworthy, and are indeed not infrequently positively trite when reduced to conventional terms by paraphrase. What such poems appear to do is to explore a third dimension of depth, so to speak, from a fixed point, and in this sense they are essentially paradigmatic expressions which establish non-sequential associations which become necessarily inconsequential when recast in the form of expressions other than those of the original. They are inherently metaphorical in character. The problem for pedagogy is how to persuade students, normally accustomed to recognize significance in terms of sequence in narrative and consequence in argument, to adopt a different perspective and see significance in the third-dimension associations represented in lyrical poems. Since such metaphorical associations are of their very nature unconventional and unique to particular poetic contexts, this will perforce call for a close attention to the language through which they are represented. Every poem is, in this sense, a tracing of untrodden ways by means of language.

I want now to demonstrate in fairly informal fashion how one might guide students towards an acknowledgement of this associative significance in the case of the Lucy poem we have been considering. The first step is to concede the inconsequence of content by presenting (or inviting the students to present) a reformulation of it in conventional terms, rephrasing what appears to be inexplicit or obscure in order to capture the gist in a conversational idiom. A reformulated version of the first verse of the poem might, for example, look like this:

A girl once lived in a remote place near the source of a river called the Dove. Nobody praised her and very few people loved her.

The class can now be asked to participate in the discovery of the differences between the two versions. Guided by the customary benevolent counsel of the teacher, such discussions might be expected to yield observations of the following sort.

She is replaced by *A girl*. This seems to be more natural. Why should this be so? Why is it that it seems odd to begin with a pronoun, to open with '*She* lived in a remote place'? Here we seek to elicit the point that the use of the pronoun assumes prior knowledge—which is obviously not warranted in this case and so causes puzzlement: she? who? If we read on, we shall find the pronoun refers to *a maid* (verse 1) and more specifically *Lucy* (verse 3). The person referred to is gradually identified. But this is of course the reverse of the usual procedure, which is to identify a person who is subsequently referred to. We would normally expect *Lucy* to appear first, and *she* afterwards to carry the reference forward. The use of the pronoun for *establishing* reference sets the poem in an unconventional key from the very beginning and immediately represents the person so curiously referred to in a strange and ambivalent light. For to refer to her as *she* is to imply that she is known to the reader, but at the same time of course she cannot be; and furthermore we are told quite explicitly (in verse 3) that 'she lived *un*known'. In this first verse we are told where she lived but not who she was. She is located but not identified. She has, as it were, a local habitation but no name. There is something elusive about her right from the start.

Maid is rewritten *girl*. An unmarked modern term replaces a marked archaic one. Is anything lost by the replacement? At this point students might be shown parts of the entry for *maid* in a dictionary. This, for example appears in the *Shorter Oxford*:

Maid: (1) a girl; a young (unmarried) woman. (2) a virgin;
specifically of the Virgin Mary.

What specifically marks *maid* and makes it distinct from *girl* is then that it has religious connotations and suggests some association between this mysterious *she* and the Virgin Mary.

Dwelt becomes *lived*. Again, an archaic term is replaced by a modern one and again reference to the relevant entry in a dictionary will reveal that something is lost in the process. The following distinct definitions, for example, appear in the *Oxford Advanced Learner's Dictionary of Current English* (henceforth *OALDCE*):

live: (1) have existence as a plant or animal (2) make one's home;
reside

This distinction between an existential and a residential meaning of *live* which is lexically marked in several languages (cf. French *vivre/habiter*, German *leben/wohnen*) is effaced by the replacement of *dwelt*, which carries only the residential meaning.[2] Does this matter? It might. Where else does the word *live* occur? At the beginning of the third verse. What meaning does it have? Apparently the existential meaning. The attention of the students might then be drawn to the fact that *dwelt* and *lived* appear in structurally parallel expressions at the beginning of the first and third verses respectively:

She dwelt among th'untrodden ways . . .
She lived unknown . . .

One might surmise, therefore, that some equivalence or contrast is implied here through the similarity of structure and that there is indeed some significance for the poem's meaning in the distinction between *dwelt* and *lived*.

Among th'untrodden ways becomes *in a remote place*. Does the paraphrase capture the meaning of the original? What anyway does *ways* mean? *Path*ways, perhaps, that is to say (according to the *OALDCE*):

ways made (across fields, through woods, etc.) by people walking

But these are *untrodden* ways. Does this mean then that they have *not* been made by people walking? If so, then they cannot, by definition, be ways in this sense at all. Alternatively, *untrodden* might mean 'not trodden any more, unfrequented', rather than 'not made by being trodden'. But then this makes another mystery. Why are they unfrequented now? Is this maid the last survivor of a previously populous place and if so, what happened to all the others? Or has she been deliberately deserted and are the ways unfrequented *because* she is there? Why then is she shunned? And why, in any case, should she be deserving of *praise*? Who is she and what has she done that should cause both solitude and praise? And why is it that even the very few that love her do not praise her as well?

Here we do not just have what the paraphrase gives us, a girl living alone by a river, but a creature of mystery and ambivalence discernible only through the particular expressions of the original poem. She is known and yet unknown. She inhabits a world which is either impossible or unexplained. She is associated with solitude and praise, but without evident reason: they seem to be intrinsic to her as natural attributes, part of her being. On the evidence of the second verse, she is both half-hidden as a violet and yet in contrast clearly visible as a star; she naturally inhabits the earth, but the heavens at the same time: she both exists and resides in a duality. What kind of image is called up, bearing in mind the connotations of the word *maid*? And notice too the expression *the springs of Dove*. What does the dove conventionally symbolize? Consider yet another entry from *OALDCE*:

dove: kind of pigeon; symbol of peace

Change *the springs of Dove* to *the springs of Peace* and what does that suggest? And notice too that in sound and spelling *Dove* differs from *Love* only in the first consonant: *the springs of Dove—the springs of Love*. There are associations here which fuse the two senses of *springs* (water coming from the ground/causes of origin), and fuse *Dove* and *Peace* symbolically and *Dove* and *Love* by resemblance of sound and graphic shape.

And so the paraphrase version is used to draw attention to the particular linguistic features of the original and their possible implications. As a result, the apparently simple content becomes complex. Conflicts and contradictions emerge in the third dimension of association, and these can be seen as analogous, on a different plane of significance, to the relations which are realized through events and characters in sequential narrative.

It might be objected that some of the observations I have induced by supposed student participation are over-elaborate and fanciful. But that does not matter. My purpose in this paper is not to present a comprehensive interpretation (even if such a thing were possible) but to set up conditions whereby students can infer their own, to indicate the *kind* of enquiry into meaning that is needed to counter the 'so what?' reaction, and to trace the poem's untrodden ways by the realization of associative significance beyond paraphrasable content.

Notes

1 Cox and Dyson in their textbook of practical criticism report their experience of teaching this poem through seminar discussion. The 'so what?' reaction was, it would seem, very much in evidence: 'A vociferous group insisted that the poem was trite, conventional, banal, not much different from "Twinkle, twinkle, little star".' (Cox and Dyson, 1965: 31)

2 The pedagogic use of paraphrases and dictionary entries, as proposed here, naturally draws attention to the properties of the language as such and to their conventional uses. It not only therefore (if successful) provides access to poetic meaning but also, reciprocally, promotes the learning of language.

7 Non-native Literatures in English as a Resource for Language Teaching

Braj B. Kachru

In recent years language teachers have shown increasing awareness about teaching language as a 'meaning system' related to various societal functions. The dichotomy between *form* and *function* is less emphasized in the curriculum and classroom teaching. A welcome outcome of this awareness has been the growing body of theoretical and methodological research relevant to the classroom in the areas of, for example, ethnography of communication, language pragmatics, and the sociology of language. It seems to me that a natural consequence of such a changed attitude is to reconsider the role of literature in the language classroom. A discussion of this topic, therefore, is both timely and of significance to language teachers.

I will not deal with the earlier controversy which resulted in what is known as the language/literature dichotomy, or its implications for language teaching. There is a large body of literature on this topic written by linguists, literary scholars, and those who stayed on the fence. Since I do not believe in this dichotomy, I will presuppose that contextually appropriate and linguistically graded literary texts have an important job to do in the classroom. Therefore, in what follows I will take the next step and discuss the appropriateness of using in the language classroom a rather specialized body of English literature which is written by *non-native* users of English. A non-native user is one who has acquired an institutionalized variety of English as a second language (L2). (For a detailed discussion, see Kachru 1985 and Smith 1981.)

Those of us who have taught English as a second language know that it is a complex undertaking. We also know that no broad generalizations which apply to all linguistically and culturally pluralistic countries are possible. Therefore, at present we have to resist the temptation of universalistic models, methods, and approaches (Kachru 1982a). A distinction has to be made between various language teaching situations in, for example, Africa, South Asia, South East Asia, and the Philippines.

However, I shall focus on the non-native English literature of South Asia. A number of South Asian English writers use English as the only language of creativity, though there are some who are creative both in their mother tongue and in English. In discussing such creative writers, the first question posed by the antagonists of English and the curious outsider is: why do such writers choose English as the language of their creativity? This question is asked both innocently, and often with suspicion about the nationalistic, linguistic, and cultural roots of such writers. There are also some who have doubted the appropriateness of a non-native language for recreating typically Indian (or Asian) social, cultural, or emotional contexts; the doubts being about the *authenticity* of a non-native medium of such creativity. The responses to such questions and criticisms are as varied as is the number of such writers. This debate was captured in an anthology by Lal (1969), for which he asked 132 'practising poets' (in English) two significant questions, among others. The answers to these questions are revealing and apply to most of the non-native English literatures, for example, those of Africa, South East Asia, and the Philippines. First, 'what are the circumstances that led to your using the English language for the purpose of writing poetry?' Second, 'do you think English is one of the Indian languages?' The responses by the poets obviously vary in their seriousness and detail. Kamala Das considers it a 'silly' question, since in her view, 'English being the most familiar, we use it. That is all.' Das makes an appropriate observation: 'The language one employs is not important. What is important is the thought contained in the words' (Lal 1969: 102–3). B. V. Desani, who is well known as the writer of *All About H. Hatterr* and *Hali*, believes that English is 'the sole language of the Indian *élite*' (126). Nissim Ezekiel attacks 'linguistic patriots in India [anti-English group] . . . [who] conduct virtually their entire social and personal lives in English, while . . . championing the mother tongue' (171). For A. K. Ramanujan, 'whether people can, will, or should write in a particular language' is not a matter of controversy. He believes that 'people who write in a particular language don't have a choice in the matter' (444–5).

Kamala Das has presented the same feelings succinctly in the following poem:

I am Indian, very brown, born in
Malabar, I speak three languages, write in
Two, dream in one. Don't write in English, they said,
English is not your mother-tongue. Why not leave
Me alone, critics, friends, visiting cousins,
Everyone of You? Why not let me speak in
Any language I like? The language I speak
Becomes mine, its distortions, its queernesses
All mine, mine alone. It is half English, half

Indian, funny perhaps, but it is honest,
It is as human as I am human, don't
You see? It voices my joys, my longings, my
Hopes, and it is as useful to me as cawing
Is to crows or roaring to the lions, it
Is human speech, the speech of the mind that is
Here and not there, a mind that sees and hears and

Is aware . . .

The body of such writing is fast increasing in various genres, styles, and registers (see Iyengar 1962 and Kachru 1983a). It is the only pan-South Asian or pan-African literature available to the world readership with what may be termed Nigerian, Indian, or Kenyan sensibility. This is, of course, *nativized* English, since the cultural context and the functional context are 'non-English'. Therefore, the proposal that the notion of English literature should be broadened and termed 'literatures in English' (as suggested by the distinguished Indian critic C. D. Narasimhaiah) is very relevant and meaningful.

The attitude towards such non-native English writers has gone through various phases, both in their own countries and in other parts of the English-speaking world. However, one must mention that in the writers' own countries they were—and to some extent continue to be—suspect; otherwise we would not be asking the above questions. And for a long time the native users of English did not consider the non-native writers of English as part of the English literary tradition. Such writers were regarded as contextually and linguistically esoteric. But the sheer persistence and the range and quality of their writing gained slow but well-deserved recognition. Even in South Asia it took at least several decades, and the constant effort of scholars and academic administrators such as V. K. Gokak, C. D. Narasimhaiah, K. R. Iyengar, and Kamesh Mohan to win a rightful place for Commonwealth literature (or South Asian English literature) in the curriculum. The resistance came mainly from the Indian professors of English whose attitude towards such writing was to some degree based on the attitude of their British teachers. In turn the British attitude was not so indifferent as that of American scholars. But then, at different periods, the attitudes are manifested in different ways. After all, till recently, the British attitude towards American English was not much different from the British attitude towards, for example, Indian English or African English. However, there is one satisfaction: that linguistic hurts tend to heal faster, and generally are not remembered for too long other than in works preserved for posterity, such as H. L. Mencken's *American Language*. In Mencken's title, note the use of 'language' instead of 'English'. This was done deliberately to demonstrate both linguistic emancipation and resentment (see Kachru 1981). The non-native varieties of English had their Menckens too, but I will not go into that here. This much about the preliminaries.

In pedagogical terms, then, what does the use of such literary texts by non-native writers entail? It is essential that some research be done to grade such texts linguistically and in terms of their content. This is necessary to determine the appropriateness of such texts for the learner, especially in terms of lexis, syntax, and cultural content. Consider, for example, Raja Rao's *The Serpent and the Rope* and R. K. Narayan's *The Bachelor of Arts*. There is no doubt that Rao's novel (if it is a novel) is more complex both in terms of the formal devices which Rao uses, and the cultural content. The style is strongly influenced by Sanskrit and Kannada. The complex theme and the underlying linguistic influences on its style give it a distinct *Indianness*. And there is no doubt that Rao makes a conscious effort to preserve such Indian identity. On the other hand, in terms of the style and the theme, Narayan's novel is less complex. Thus, there is a cline of 'Indianness' in such texts, and the teachers have to determine the suitability and proportion of doses for each class.

In the 'grading' of such texts one has to make a distinction between the *stages* and *strategies* of use. The stages of use refer to the acquisitional stages of the learner, and the strategies refer to the devices which a teacher adopts for making the literary text contextually understood. A literary text, then, may have to be explained with reference to the following specific characteristics:

1 *variety* (e.g. Indian English, Singapore English, Nigerian English)
2 *register* (e.g. the caste, or religious, journalistic, or political styles)
3 *author* (e.g. the style of Raja Rao as opposed to G. V. Desani or M. R. Anand)
4 *text* (e.g. in Raja Rao, certain formal features of *Kanthapura* can be marked separate from, for example, *The Serpent and the Rope*).

The next step is to explain how a non-native writer of English uses various linguistic devices to contextualize a non-native language in his own 'un-English' culture. I have earlier used the term 'nativization' for such processes (Kachru 1980). There is thus a relationship between the use of linguistic nativization processes and the resultant acculturation of English. The devices used for nativization are of various types. I shall merely refer to some such devices discussed in literature:

1 *Lexical innovations*: These innovations include lexicalization of various types in the text, particularly the borrowing of local words into English, and hybridization of words from two distinct lexical sources (e.g. *lathicharge*, 'to attack with a baton' (usually used by police to control a mob); *policewala*, 'a policeman'). (For a detailed discussion of this topic, see Kachru 1983b: 147–64.)

2 *Translation equivalence*: In earlier studies I have shown (e.g. Smith 1981 and Kachru 1965 and later) that the creative writers use translation from L1 into English as one of the productive devices for correlating the speech event with its appropriate formal item, for example:

a 'Cherisher of the poor, what does your honour fancy?'
b 'May thy womb be dead.'
c 'You spoiler of my salt.'

The device used in these examples is interesting and effective in many ways: (a) is used by Khushwant Singh in *Train to Pakistan*. The expression *cherisher of the poor*, translated from Urdu, functions as a mode of address. It indicates power and authority and is used for a superior. The example (b) is from Bhawani Bhattacharya's *He Who Rides a Tiger*. This expression of abuse, meaning 'may you have no progeny', is specifically used for a woman. The last example, from Mulk Raj Anand's *Untouchable*, is an approximate translation of Punjabi , Hindi, Urdu *namak haram*. This uncomplimentary expression is used for a person who has been ungrateful. I must, however, add a note of caution here. In spoken Indian English, these expressions are rarely used, if at all. On the other hand, in Indian English creative writing, translation and 'transcreation' are a very productive way of creating contextually and stylistically appropriate innovations for Indianizing the text. (See Kachru 1983b: 107–9.)

3 *Contextual redefinition* of lexical items of English in *new* contexts, especially the use of kinship terms, attitudinal terms, etc. One has to redefine the use of the terms such as *mother, sister, brother-in-law*, as used by M. R. Anand in his novels *Coolie, Untouchable*, etc.

4 *Rhetorical and functional styles*: The communicative styles are organized in such a way in English that they become functionally appropriate in terms of the situations, settings, and the participants in a speech act. The concept of what is contextually a 'proper' style is partly derived from the native literary or oral tradition, in some cases also determined by the style repertoire of literary languages such as Sanskrit, Arabic, or Persian. The native style repertoire is then 'recreated' in English. The result is that the non-native English literatures thus acquire a distinct stylistic characteristic. As I have stated elsewhere (Kachru, 1983a), the native English speakers find such functional styles 'deviant' and use attitudinally marked terms such as *latinity, phrase-mongering, polite diction, moralistic tone, bookishness* to characterize these. Such labels seem to ignore that the transfer of styles and rhetorical devices are language and culture dependent, and may be one way to manifest the user's identity through language. In other words, in the nativized discourse-types the attempt is to

contextualize the styles by various formal devices. It is, however, true that the more culture-bound the style becomes, the more *distance* is created between the native varieties of English and the non-native varieties. Such distinctness is not restricted to literary texts, but is seen in the newspaper headlines, the highly contextualized matrimonial advertisements or in the obituaries published in the newspapers. The captions such as the following are not a rarity but a regular feature of national newspapers.

d Kisan sammelan coupons missing (*The Tribune* 22.11.78)
e Krishi bank branch needed (*The Bangladesh Observer* 21.6.79)
f Shariate courts for attack (*Dawn* 12.3.79)

The matrimonial advertisements are almost unintelligible to a person who does not share the native culture and the nativized use of English. Consider the following:

g Non-Koundanya well qualified prospective bridegroom below 30 for graduate Lyengar girl, daughter of engineer. Mirugaserusham. No dosham. Average complexion. Reply with horoscope. (*The Hindu* 1.7.79).
h Wanted well-settled bridegroom for a Kerala fair, graduate Bharad-waja gotram. Astasastram girl . . . Subsect no bar. Send horoscope and details. (*The Hindu* 1.7.79).

The announcements of death in English are equally culture-specific; one has to understand the context and also how the English language is used to convey it. A person leaves 'for the heavenly abode' (*Hindustan Times* 20.5.79), due to 'the sad demise'. There will, therefore, be, for example 'kirtan and ardasa for the peace of the departed soul' (*Hindustan Times* 30.6.79). Another way to present such news is that 'the untimely tragic death . . . of . . . happened . . . on . . . uthaoni ceremony will take place on . . . ' (*Hindustan Times* 30.6.79). The cultural and religious pluralism reflects in another way too. If the dead person is a Muslim, then 'his soyem Fateha will be solemnised on . . . ' and 'all the friends and relatives are requested to attend the Fateha prayers' (*Dawn* 14.3.79).

One can multiply examples in other contexts, too, but that is not essential. What we see in these examples in a restricted sense reflects in literature (novels, short stories, etc.) in a larger way. It becomes essential for delineation of character types, plots, situations, etc. Consider, for example, the following four excerpts from four South Asian creative writers which provide illustrations of specific uses of English. The first descriptive excerpt is from Raja Rao's *Kanthapura:*

The day rose into the air and with it rose the dust of the morning, and the carts began to creak round the bulging rocks and the coppery peaks, and the sun fell into the river and pierced it to the pebbles, while the carts rolled on and on, fair carts of the Kanthapura fair ... fair carts that came from Maddur and Tippur and Santur and Kuppur ... carts rolled by the Sampur knoll and down into the valley of the Tippur stream, then rose again and groaned ... (p. 56)

The second passage is from Mulk Raj Anand's *Untouchable*, a novel which makes extensive use of caste-specific and character-specific speech functions by 'transcreating' these into English.

'Ari, ari bitch! Do you take me for a buffoon? What are you laughing at slut? Aren't you ashamed of showing your teeth to me in the presence of men, you prostitute?' shouted Gulabo, and she looked down towards the old man and the little boys who were of the company. Sohini now realized that the woman was angry. 'But I haven't done anything to annoy her,' she reflected. 'She herself began it all and is abusing me right and left. I didn't pick the quarrel. I have more cause to be angry than she has!'

'Bitch, why don't you speak! Prostitute, why don't you answer me?' Gulabo insisted.

'Please, don't abuse me,' the girl said, 'I haven't said anything to you.'

'You annoy me with your silence, you illegally begotten! You, eater of dung and drinker of urine! You, bitch of a sweeper woman! I will show you how to insult one old enough to be your mother.' And she rose with upraised arms and rushed at Sohini.

Waziro, the weaver's wife, ran after her and caught her just before she had time to hit the sweeper girl.

'Be calm, be calm, you must not do that,' she said as she dragged Gulabo back to her seat. 'No, you must not do that.' (p. 37)

The third example is from Ahmed Ali, a Muslim novelist. In his *Twilight in Delhi*, he provides an excellent example of contextualization of English in a Muslim family.

Dilchain had, in the meantime, discovered a small earthen doll buried under the oven when she was cleaning it one day. She went and showed it to Begam Habib.

'It is the effect of witchcraft,' she said, 'which is responsible for Mian's illness.'

The tender hearts of women were filled with dread. They sent Dilchain to Aakhoonji Saheb, who wrote verses from the Koran on seven snow white plates in saffron water. The plates were to be washed with a little water, and the water from one plate was to be taken for three days, a drop in the morning . . .

But a strange thing happened inside the senana. A pot full of ill-omened things came flying in the air and struck against the bare trunk of the date palm whose leaves had all fallen. Another day some cooked cereal was found lying under the henna tree . . .

Poor women from the neighbourhood came, fluttering their burqas and dragging their slippers under them, and sympathized . . .

Thus they came and sympathized and suggested cures and medicines. One said to Begam Habib:

'You must go to the tomb of Hazrat Mahboob Elahi and pray . . . '

'You must give him water from the well at Hazarat Nizamuddin's tomb,' another suggested. 'It has magical qualities and has worked miracles . . . ' (pp. 278–9)

The final excerpt is again descriptive, by a woman writer, Anita Desai. It is taken from *Games at Twilight and Other Stories*.

Morning had stirred up some breeze off the sluggish river Jumma beneath the city walls, and it was carried over the rooftops of the stifled city, pale and fresh and delicate. It brought with it the morning light, as delicate and sweet as the breeze itself, a pure pallor unlike the livid glow of artificial lights. This lifted higher and higher into the dome of the sky, diluting the darkness there till it, too, grew pale and gradually shades of blue and mauve tinted it lightly.

In a review (*The New York Times Book Review* June 22, 1980: 13) the reviewer, Alice Adams, says that '. . . any story by Anita Desai is well worth reading for the simple and amazing beauty of her prose'. We certainly see that in the above excerpt.

The use of such non-native literary texts, then, provides a challenge not only to the non-native teachers and learners, but also to teachers and learners who use English as their native language. Let me consider first a classroom in South Asia where both teachers and learners use English as an institutionalized non-native language. In such nativized texts the learners see English as part of their culture, and as a code of their day-to-day communication, 'modified' and nativized by the neighbour, the farmer, the money-lender, the coolie, and the politician (as in the novels of Anand or Narayan). One also sees a nativized style repertoire in English which *recreates* (or 'transcreates') the native patterns of speech and social interactions and attempts to transfer native humour and attitudes into English (as, for example, *brother-in-law* in Anand). Such texts also portray the subtle social stratification, and religious and ethnic pluralism. All of this is part of the learner and becomes a part of the language which he or she is learning.

Why teach such texts to those who use English as a native language? It seems to me that such literary texts are a repertoire of resources for providing linguistic and cross-cultural explanations to show (a) how English has been 'modified' in new non-Western contexts of Asia or Africa, (b) how stylistic innovations are determined by the cultural contexts and the localized style range, (c) what effect such innovations have on, for example, intelligibility, comprehensibility, and interpretability, and (d) what is meant by *acculturation* of English in 'non-English' social and cultural contexts. In other words, what it means to use English for cross-cultural communication.

One might then say that such texts, especially in the institutionalized varieties of English, produce a cultural identity, and the learners see a non-native language as part of the culture with which they identify. The English language thus acquires both formal and functional realism. This is not necessarily true when one teaches Charles Dickens or Jane Austen (even in the simplified versions) to students in, for example, Singapore, India, or Kenya. In most of these countries English is not taught for 'integrative' purposes, but for an 'instrumental' motivation (Kachru 1976). Therefore, the use of non-native English literatures may be more appropriate.

However, a word of caution is essential: my position is not one of an 'either/or' type. I don't mean that we should teach exclusively the non-native variety and not the native variety; this would be an extreme position. One has to establish a balance and introduce appropriate proportions (and varieties) of both types. What is equally important, one has to change the attitude and introduce some pragmatism in the classroom. An attitude still seems to persist that the non-native English literature is 'substandard'. I have heard teachers of English say, in their unmistakable Indian, Singapore, or Kenyan English, that if we must keep English, then we should teach *real* English literature. In their view, *real* refers only to British English literature. This attitude is based as much on emotionalism as would be if one claimed that only Anand, Achebe, and Rao should be taught in a classroom in India or Africa.

I have merely raised some questions here, and marginally discussed them. A detailed discussion is given in various studies mentioned above. I would also recommend the following studies for a more detailed treatment of some of these questions and descriptions of various non-native varieties of English: Bailey and Görlach (1982); Kachru (1982b); Smith (1981). We also now have some valuable bibliographies for some of these varieties of English, for example, Singh *et al.* (1981) and Narasimhaiah (1976).

8   Texts, Extracts, and Stylistic Texture

Guy Cook

Introduction

Extracts from works of prose literature are frequently used in the teaching of English as a Foreign Language at intermediate and advanced levels: as reading and listening comprehensions, passages for translation, and starting points for general discussion. It is the purpose of this chapter to examine the assumptions, both explicit and implicit, behind the use of such extracts, to judge their effectiveness as a means of improving the English of foreign learners, and to arrive at criteria concerning their choice and presentation.

Apart from the convenience of the enormous range of ready-made texts available in English literature, the most widely held assumption about the use of literary extracts in EFL is the rather vague one that they acquaint learners with the 'best' English and will somehow whet their appetites for more. As has often been pointed out, the study of literary English is seldom suited to the foreign learner's needs, and the mastery of literary texts has little bearing on the learner's needs to understand or produce more functional written or spoken forms of the language. It is, moreover, often in its deviation from the norms of English grammatical and lexical usage that literature achieves excellence. While such deviations may please the native speaker by the freshness they may bring to his or her linguistic world, they can do little but confuse the foreign learner. Authors addicted to such deviations—a category which includes the best English writers—are perhaps best avoided with all but the most advanced foreign learners. New shades of meaning or syntax can hardly be appreciated before their everyday usage has been fully assimilated.

There is a further and perhaps more crucial reason why the study of literary extracts may be of little use to the foreign learner. For obvious reasons of convenience, literary extracts are usually restricted to—at most—two or three pages. They are usually taken from the middle of a work. Yet the 'excellence' by which the choice of the extract is justified may not reside within the extract but in its relation to the preceding and following text from which it has been artificially isolated for pedagogic purposes. By the very act of extraction we have destroyed the superiority of style which we seek to demonstrate. It is this act of destruction through extraction with which this article is particularly concerned.

Analysis of an extract from 'The Dead' (James Joyce)

Examination of a particular extract may illustrate these two points more fully. The extract chosen for analysis is the last six paragraphs of 'The Dead', the final short story of James Joyce's *Dubliners*. This passage appears as a passage for comprehension in an anthology which is fairly widely used in the teaching of English as a Foreign Language in Italy, and is in many ways typical of the kind of extract used in many similar anthologies throughout Europe. (The entire extract is presented in the Appendix below.) This passage has been deliberately chosen for the purposes of this paper to illustrate how literary discourse may both lose meaning and acquire false meaning when extracted from the full text to which it belongs. It is intended to demonstrate one of the worst choices that can be made by a teacher or editor. Yet it is hoped that an analysis of the faults of this passage as an extract for use in the teaching of English as a Foreign Language may not be purely destructive, but may point to positive criteria regarding the choice and presentation of an extract. It is also hoped to show that the same stylistic features may account both for the excellence of a passage when considered as part of a text and its unsuitability for study as an extract isolated from that text.

The nature of the analysis

The analysis below will be stylistic rather than linguistic or critical. Widdowson defines stylistics as follows:

> By 'stylistics' I mean the study of literary discourse from a linguistics orientation and I shall take the view that what distinguishes stylistics from literary criticism on the one hand and linguistics on the other is that it is a means of linking the two. (Widdowson 1975: 3)

and he goes on to define the concern of the literary critic as follows:

> not principally with the way the signals of the artist are constructed but with the underlying message which an interpretation of these signals will reveal. (Widdowson 1975: 5)

The linguist on the other hand

> is primarily concerned with the codes themselves and particular messages are of interest in so far as they exemplify how the codes are constructed. (Widdowson 1975: 5)

Stylistics then is concerned both with interpretation and with the codes themselves; with both what the text means and why and how it means what it does; and this essay will attempt to be stylistic, because both the linguistic and the literary critical approaches are important in assessing the value of an extract for pedagogic purposes.

Text and extract

It is necessary to define the terms *text* and *extract*. The notion of text is semantic rather than grammatical. Though a single sentence may form a whole text this is not necessarily, and indeed rarely, so. A single sentence is always a complete grammatical unit; it is seldom semantically complete. It gains meaning either from the situation in which it is uttered or written, or from the other sentences with which it occurs. *Texture*, or the quality which binds sentences into a text, depends firstly on *register*, the necessity to combine linguistic features with situational features to create meaning, and secondly upon *cohesion*, the semantic (and in some cases lexico-grammatical) ties between one sentence and another.

> There is one specific kind of meaning relation that is critical for the creation of texture: that in which ONE ELEMENT IS INTERPRETED BY REFERENCE TO ANOTHER. (Halliday and Hasan 1976: 11)

Text then, with the exception of single-sentence texts, is a number of sentences bound together by cohesive ties, and giving meaning to each other. *Extract* may be regarded as a part of a text, artificially separated for purposes of quotation or study from the other sentences, with which, to a greater or lesser extent, it coheres.

In a literary message, texture is much more likely to be created by internal cohesion than by any reference to the situation in which the message is received. Yet the density of cohesive ties may vary greatly. The extraction and isolation of a passage from a literary text for pedagogic purposes will necessarily involve the cutting of cohesive ties and the rendering of certain semantic relations within the original text meaningless. The degree to which meaning is destroyed will depend upon the density of cohesive ties referring to parts of the text not included within the extract; the greater the density, the more meaning will be destroyed. As by far the greatest part of cohesive ties are *anaphoric* (referring to the preceding text) and not *cataphoric* (referring to the following text), the least destructive form of extraction is that which takes either the beginning of a text or at least a part of a text which represents a new introductory departure in the narrative. Extracts which conclude either a whole text or a recognizable section of text should be avoided.

False texture

Provided it does not break sentences, a literary extract is always grammatically intact, but seldom semantically intact. It may gain, in isolation, what may be termed *false texture*, as it is the natural tendency of a reader, when confronted with an extract, to treat it as a text.

> If he finds evidence in the situation, (the reader) can accept the passage in question as a complete text. If not, he has to seek textual evidence, and therefore to assume that the original passage is related to some preceding piece by cohesion—otherwise he can only regard it as incomplete. It is not suggested that he performs these operations as a systematic search in this or any other order. The important fact is that the hearer typically assumes that any passage which for external reasons OUGHT to be a text . . . is in fact a text: and he will go to enormous lengths to interpret it as complete and intelligible. This is an aspect of the very general human tendency to assume in the other person an intention to communicate, an assumption which is no doubt of very great value for survival. (Halliday and Hasan 1976: 54)

This tendency is reinforced by the common literary device of employing cataphoric cohesive ties at the opening of a narrative to stimulate interest and project the reader's attention forward. Thus 'The Sisters', the first short story of *Dubliners*, begins:

> There was no hope for him this time: it was the third stroke.

and employs three reference items: a pronominal *him*, the definite article *the* (implying a previous specification), and the quantitative ordinal *third* (implying a previous two instances). A similar system of unexplained reference might be deduced by the student (and teacher) when confronted with the opening sentence of the extract from 'The Dead':

> She was fast asleep.

and some significance derived from the fact that the exact identity of the female referred to by the pronominal *she* is not immediately specified. Yet this is not the case. The first quotation illustrates a literary device, while the second is a mere accident of where the extract was begun, the pronominal *she* having been quite clearly defined in the preceding text as Gretta, Gabriel's wife, together with a study of her character. To interpret the second quotation in terms of the first is a perversion of the original text, and an editor presenting the extract for study might be truer to the text to add a note on the name, age, and character of Gretta than to leave the original *she* unaltered.

It is hoped to establish that the extract from 'The Dead' is particularly dense in cohesive ties, and that a large part of its meaning (and merit) is destroyed by its being taken out of context, and that the absence of meaning created by decontextualization tempts the learner and the teacher to create a false text by imposing meanings on the extract which are demonstrably not present in the whole text. By examining the nature of the connections between the extract and the text from which it is taken, it is hoped to establish criteria for use in the selection of literary extracts whereby these dangers are reduced.

The conclusive nature of the extract

The extract given below is simultaneously part of two texts: the smaller text of 'The Dead' and the larger text of *Dubliners* to which 'The Dead' belongs. Any extract is one of three predominant types (though there is a considerable overlap between the three): *introductory, continuing,* or *conclusive*: and we might well take this as an order of preference when selecting extracts for teaching. The extract below is conclusive: it is at once the end of 'The Dead' and the end of *Dubliners,* and the sleepless thoughts of Gabriel which it describes bring together not only the thoughts and preoccupations of his evening, but also the main themes of the whole book.

Let us first consider the extract as conclusive to *Dubliners*. The book contains fifteen short stories concerned with various aspects of youth, maturity, and disillusion, the contrast between public and private behaviour, and varying forms of perception. Though there is no exact thematic sequence, we may say that the book moves from an investigation of immature perception to one of mature perception, that it begins and ends with a contrast of youth and death and the most intimate and private aspects of thought, while its central stories are concerned more with social interaction and the manifestations, rather than the internal workings, of personality. The events of 'The Dead', of which this extract forms a part, bring all these themes together. In the character of Gabriel all the various levels of social interaction are examined, and we see him firstly in a crowd of strangers and acquaintances, secondly with his family, thirdly alone with his wife, and fourthly completely alone; all these levels are touched upon or reinvoked in the last paragraphs of 'The Dead'. In Gretta's story of her affair with Michael Furey the contrast of youth and death reoccurs, as does the theme of the disillusion that comes with maturity. While ostensibly concerned solely with Gabriel's thoughts, the extract, taken in the context of *Dubliners*, brings together and connects the main themes of all the stories.

Let us now consider the extract as conclusive to 'The Dead'. The extract surveys the thoughts of a man who is sleepless for many reasons: the excitement of the party at his aunts' house earlier in the evening; the effects of alcohol; thwarted sexual desire; his being in a strange hotel room rather than in his own house; the disturbing effect of the revelation just concluded by his wife. These causes of his wakeful mental turmoil are not evident in the extract, though they are in the whole text of 'The Dead'. His thoughts, stimulated by the events of the evening, range backward in time to his wife's youth and the premature death of Michael Furey, and forward, to the imagined death of his Aunt Julia. Encouraged by his wife's story of her youth in another part of Ireland and a conversation held earlier in the evening about the possibility of a holiday in the West of Ireland, they range geographically too, away from Dublin, surveying the whole of Ireland—a fact which also contributes to the unity of *Dubliners*, a book which, by wide-ranging selection, creates an illusion of surveying the Irish personality *in toto*.

Given these directions in Gabriel's thoughts, it is not surprising that many phrases and sentences in the extract allude to information already given in the earlier parts of 'The Dead'. Though grammatically intact, and thus open to misinterpretation by the reader of the passage as extract, these allusions are, in fact, not open to any true interpretation without reference to the preceding text. (The word 'allusion' is used here to distinguish these more general connections from 'reference', a specifically defined form of cohesion, cf. 'Deviations' below.) We can set out these allusions, and the specific information in the preceding text with which they connect, as follows:

1 *So she had had that romance in her life: a man had died for her sake*—an allusion to Gretta's affair with Michael Furey, interpretable in isolation, but incapable of revealing the essential innocence and immaturity of that affair unless taken in context.

2 *It hardly pained him now to think how poor a part he, her husband, had played in her life*—an allusion to Gabriel's earlier thoughts, during the journey from the party to the hotel, of exactly what part he had played in her life.

3 *That time of her first girlish beauty*—a connection between Gabriel's earlier thoughts on the passing of his wife's good looks and her own story.

4 *for which Michael Furey had braved death*—a specific allusion to Michael Furey's contraction of pneumonia while standing in the cold in the hope of seeing Gretta; a pathetic and absurd manner of braving death which is not elucidated in this extract alone.

5 *He wondered at his riot of emotions of an hour before*—an allusion to Gabriel's growing sexual desire for his wife during their journey to the hotel and after their arrival. The nature of the 'emotions' has already been given.

6 *his aunts' supper*—an allusion to the party with which the first part of 'The Dead' is concerned. The warm, humorous, and crowded nature of this first part of 'The Dead' has a crucial contrastive effect when taken in conjunction with the ending: an effect which is completely lost in the isolated extract.

7 *his own foolish speech*—an allusion to the highly successful and well-received speech which Gabriel had made to his aunts' guests after supper, revealing a side of his character which is not present in the final paragraphs of the story. This phrase serves to underline the change in Gabriel's emotions which has taken place since his wife's story; the adjective 'foolish' indicates the alteration in his self-image which subsequent events have caused.

8 *the wine and dancing, the merry-making when saying good night in the hall, the pleasure of the walk along the river in the snow*—allusions to specific episodes in the preceding text, reinforcing, by contrast, the changes which have taken place in the mood of Gabriel and of the story.

9 *the shade of Patrick Morkan and his horse*—an allusion to a humorous anecdote told at the party by Gabriel about his dead grandfather, and a further indication of his change of mood. This phrase is meaningless when taken out of context, as the reader knows neither the identity of Patrick Morkan, nor the story of his horse. Readers nevertheless attempt to interpret such phrases. During the preparation of this chapter, several English Language students unfamiliar with 'The Dead' as a whole were presented with this extract and asked to interpret this phrase. Answers included: 'a reference to a poem', 'a colloquial comparison', 'a figure from Irish legend', 'an event in the day's newspaper', but never a simple 'Don't know'.

10 *when she was singing 'Arrayed for the Bridal'*—an allusion to Aunt Julia's performance at the party. The irony of her choice of song is lost in extract, for the fact that Aunt Julia is an old maid is information given in the preceding text.

11 *that same drawing room*—the 'same' as the one in which so much festivity has recently taken place: a contrast which is weakened out of context.

12 *Aunt Kate . . . crying and blowing her nose*—a re-evocation of the character of Aunt Kate, which may serve to remind the reader of Gabriel's earlier altruism and thoughtfulness towards his ageing aunts, thus making his present loneliness more poignant.

13 *the room*—a hotel room away from their home (as previously stated during conversation at the party), perhaps symbolic of the change which has come about in their marriage.

14 *He had never felt like that himself towards any woman*—considering the text as a whole, the reader might well conclude that this judgement of Gabriel's upon himself is drastically unfair.

15 *the partial darkness*—an allusion to the earlier description of the room, in which there is no light except for the glow of the streetlight outside the window, a fact which gives a visual setting for the scene of the extract, but is not present within it.

16 *he saw the form of a young man standing under a dripping tree*—an allusion to Gretta's earlier description of Michael Furey as she last saw him.

17 *A few light taps upon the window pane*—a suggestion of a phrase in Gretta's story: 'I heard gravel thrown up against the window'. The choice of the verb 'taps' personifies the snow, and suggests that the snow is like the ghost of Michael Furey throwing gravel against the window.

18 *his journey westward*—interpreted as 'death' by several readers of the extract in isolation, but in fact a specific allusion to a holiday planned earlier in the evening, though the suggestion of death is also present.

19 *Yes, the newspapers were right: snow was general all over Ireland*—an allusion to an earlier remark made by Gabriel's cousin Mary Jane: '"They say", said Mary Jane, "we haven't had snow like it for thirty years and I read this morning in the newspapers that the snow is general all over Ireland"', and an indication that his thoughts are still harking back to the party.

This list is by no means exhaustive, yet it will be seen that, even taking this list as complete, sixteen of the thirty-eight sentences in this extract contain allusions whose meaning is either created or substantially altered by a knowledge of the preceding text. An editor would be well advised to offer footnotes explaining any such allusions in an extract, and teachers to familiarize themselves, where possible, with the preceding text. The simpler solution is to select extracts which are not so packed with allusions as the one under present consideration.

Mood

Though told in the third person, the extract is concerned with the thoughts of Gabriel, the only fully conscious being present at this point in the story. His physical environment—the sleeping woman, the clothes on the floor, the snow falling outside—both reflect and cause his thoughts. His character and thoughts are so inextricably woven into the mood of the narrative that, for our purposes, it is not necessary to distinguish between them.

To a reader considering this passage as an extract, the character and mood of Gabriel (and of the extract) may appear maudlin, self-pitying, over-demanding, and fruitlessly introspective. The first sentence to describe his thoughts specifically creates exactly this impression:

> It hardly pained him now, to think how poor a part he, her husband, had played in her life.

The interjection of 'her husband' seems both demanding and bitter. Later he refers to 'his own foolish speech'. He continually dwells on the past and, when he thinks of the future, it is only to imagine the death of those he loves. Taken in the context of the extract, the description 'Generous tears filled Gabriel's eyes' seems singularly inappropriate. Generosity is not an attribute of the man portrayed by the extract, though it is of the man portrayed by the text.

Taken as a part of the text, both the character of Gabriel and the mood of these six paragraphs is radically altered. The greater part of 'The Dead' is concerned not with lonely introspection, but with a New Year's party in which Gabriel appears not only as altruistic, in his uncomplaining support of his ageing maiden aunts, but also as humorous, eloquent, considerate, self-effacing. In the part of the text immediately preceding the extract he is portrayed as loving and gentle, filled with a tender sexual desire for his wife which is cut short by her relatively inconsiderate relation of her youthful affair with Michael Furey. In this context Gabriel's sleepless introspection takes on a different meaning; his self-pity and preoccupations with the past take on added weight when the reader knows that they are not typical, and their origins are additionally explained as the aftermath of social activity, alcohol, and rejected love. The mood of the passage as an extract and as part of a text are radically different.

Passages whose mood is substantially different when they are taken from the text of which they are a part should be avoided by the teacher who wishes to present an accurate impression of the work from which they are taken. The mood of an extract may be created internally, within the extract, or externally, within the surrounding text; the former should be preferred by the teacher.

Deviations

Literature frequently contains deviations from accepted usage. These deviations may be lexical, as in the use of neologisms, archaisms, compounds, or of one part of speech as another, or they may be grammatical, involving departures from syntactical or morphological rules, or semantic, as in the use of metaphor. In the words of Widdowson:

> In literary writing one constantly comes across sentences which
> would not be generated by an English grammar but are nevertheless
> interpretable

and literature, for this reason, contains

> data which *cannot* be accounted for by 'the theories and methods developed in linguistics'. (Widdowson 1975: 14)

Many works of literature contain, in part, their own internalized grammatical, lexical, and semantic systems, comprehensible to the native speaker, but not applicable or appropriate outside themselves or suitable to non-literary discourse. The extract from 'The Dead' is no exception.

For the purposes of classifying the deviations in the extract under consideration, I have adapted the categories established by Leech (1969: Chapter 3) and allotted to each a symbol, which is given in parenthesis after each category. Two of the categories given by Leech—*phonological* and *graphological deviation*—are hardly ever applicable to prose literature and are therefore omitted. Some of the categories do not appear in the extract (e.g. *affixation*); they are nevertheless listed below as being potentially present in prose. There is not space here to give a full description of each category, though a brief example is given in the right-hand column. Deviation of *register* does not permit brief exemplification, and an example is not given. *Semantic* deviation is a much more complex phenomenon than is suggested here, but will nevertheless admit of two main divisions for our present purposes.

Categories of deviation

Category	Symbol	Example
Lexical:		
neologism	(Ln)	'brillig' (Carroll)
affixation	(La)	'foresuffer' (Eliot)
compounding	(Lc)	'widow-making' (Hopkins)
functional conversion	(Lf)	'and I shall see/ some squeaking Cleopatra *boy* my greatness' (Shakespeare)
Grammatical:		
morphological	(Gm)	'museyroom' (Joyce)
syntactical	(Gs)	'thou hast . . . fastened me flesh' (Hopkins)
Semantic:		
metaphor	(Sm)	'the mind has mountains' (Hopkins)
personification	(Sp)	'the morning rejoices' (Wordsworth)
Dialectal	(D)	'till all the seas gang dry' (Burns)
Register	(R)	
Historical period (Archaism)	(A)	'oft' (Keats)

Using the above symbols, we may now make the following analysis of the deviations within the extract from 'The Dead':

Line no.	Deviation	Type
3	'deep-drawn'	Lc
8	'he and she'	Lf
10, 28	'upon'	A
12	'girlish'	Sm
19	'dangled to'	Gs
20	'limp upper'	Ln
21	'fellow'	Sp
21	'riot of emotions'	Sm
27	'shade'	A
34	'cast about in his mind'	Sm
43	'she who lay'	Gs/A
44	'had locked in her heart for so many years that image'	Gs
53	'that region where dwell the vast hosts'	Gs
53	'vast hosts'	A/R
55	'flickering existence'	Sm
57	'the solid world itself, which these dead had one time reared and lived in'	Gs
60	'he watched sleepily the flakes'	Gs
62	'Yes, the newspapers were right'	R
65	'falling softly . . . softly falling'	Gs
69	'lay buried'	A
71	'his soul swooned'	Sm
72	'falling faintly . . . faintly falling'	Gs

(Line numbers refer to the extract, as given below in the appendix.)

Many of these deviations add to the meaning of the passage. The use of the archaisms 'upon', 'vast hosts', and 'shades' take us into the register of religious English. The personification of the boots makes them symbolic of the relations between Gretta and Gabriel. The choice of 'he and she' instead of the more usual 'they' reflects both the separation that Gabriel feels from Gretta and their conjugal relationship. The rearrangement of normal syntax creates a lyrical quality, highlights individual words, captures Irish speech patterns, and reflects the growing sleepiness of Gabriel.

Yet the semantic subtlety of these deviations is unlikely to be accessible to any but the most advanced foreign learners. They are more likely to confuse them, and to establish deviational grammar and lexis in their use of English. Yet to alter them is to deprive the extract of a large measure of its literary excellence. As Widdowson comments:

> It is not unusual to find literature teachers, both in first and second language situations, attempting to teach 'literary classics' (presumably for either moral or cultural reasons or both) to learners

whose knowledge of the system and use of English is so limited as to make the work being presented to them almost totally incomprehensible. Very often the teacher resorts to translation and paraphrase to overcome linguistic difficulties. Such a procedure not only has the effect of misrepresenting the nature of literature . . . but also of creating resistance to it in the reader's mind. (Widdowson 1975: 81)

and he concludes

it is not necessary (and indeed may be undesirable) to select works on the grounds of aesthetic excellence or because they are representative of different schools and periods: the criteria for selection are pedagogic rather than aesthetic or historical and have to do with whether the works can be used to develop sensitivity to language in the most effective way. It is possible to think of a literature course which contains none of the 'classics' at all, but which nevertheless prepares the way for a meaningful encounter with them at a later stage. (Widdowson 1975: 85)

Passages of the greatest literary merit may well be the most unsuitable for use in the teaching of English as a foreign language. In 'The Dead' the deviations add to the unity of the whole story, and further complicate the student reader's task of interpreting this brief abstract.

Cohesive ties within the extract

Let us now identify and categorize the cohesive items in the first seven sentences of the extract from 'The Dead', using the coding scheme by which cohesive ties may be tabulated, set out by Halliday and Hasan (1976). In evaluating the suitability of this extract for teaching purposes, particular attention should be paid to the column giving the distance between the cohesive item and the presupposed item. This item indicates whether the presupposed item is immediate (0) (referring to an item in the preceding sentence) or not immediate (having one or more preceding sentences not involved in the presupposition). If an item is not immediate, it may be mediated (M) ('having one or more intervening sentences that enter into a chain of presupposition') or non-mediated (N) ('having one or more intervening sentences not involved in the presupposition'); alternatively, an item may be cataphoric (K) (Halliday and Hasan 1976: 339). It will be noted that, if the number of intervening sentences between the presupposed and the cohesive items noted in this column is greater than the number of the sentence in the extract, then the reference item indicated *cannot* be immediately understood, as it presupposes an item not present in the extract at all.

Table of cohesive items in sentences 1–7 of the extract from 'The Dead'

Sentence no.	No. of ties	Cohesive item	Distance	Presupposed item
1	2	'She'	M34	'Gretta'
		'asleep'	N1	'bed'
2	4	'Gabriel'	N2	'Gabriel'
		'her'	M35	'Gretta'
		'tangled hair'	N3	'flung herself'
		'deep-drawn breath'	0	'asleep'
3	6	'So'	N5	(Gretta's story)
		'she'	M36	'Gretta'
		'that'	N5	(Gretta's story)
		'a man'	M17	'Michael Furey'
		'had died'	M5	'he died'
		'her'	M36	'Gretta'
4	7	'it'	K	'to think'
		'him'	N1	'Gabriel'
		'now'	0	S2/S3
		'he'	N1	'Gabriel'
		'her'	M37	'Gretta'
		'husband'	0	'he'
		'her life'	N6	(Gretta's story)
5	6	'He'	M2	'Gabriel'
		'her'	M38	'Gretta'
		'she'	M38	'Gretta'
		'as though'	0	'he watched her'
		'he and she'	M38/M2	'Gabriel'/'Gretta'
		'man and wife'	M38/M2	'Gabriel'/'Gretta'
6	9	'His'	M3	'Gabriel'
		'her'	M39	'Gretta'
		'face'	N3	'half-open mouth'
		'her'	M39	'Gretta'
		'hair'	N3	'hair'
		'and'	0	(first part of sentence)
		'she'	M39	'Gretta'
		'then, in that time'	M10	(Gretta's story)
		'her'	M39	'Gretta'
7	7	'He'	M4	'Gabriel'
		'himself'	M4	'Gabriel'
		'her'	M40	'Gretta'
		'face'	0	'face'
		'no longer'	0	'that time of . . . '
		'Michael Furey'	M20	'Michael Furey'
		'had braved death'	N10–18	(description of Michael Furey's actions)

(Coding scheme taken from Halliday and Hasan 1976: 339 ff.)

It will be seen from this table that, of the forty-one cohesive items in the first seven sentences of the extract, twenty-four presuppose items defined in the preceding text. Nor does the frequency of such items substantially diminish as the text progresses. As late as three sentences from the end of the extract (line 68), we find the reference item 'the', for example, in the phrase 'the lonely churchyard', which presupposes the phrase 'he was buried in Oughterard, where his people came from' in Gretta's story. In the seven sentences analysed above, the most frequent and notable examples of cohesive items which demand reference to the preceding text are the singular feminine pronominals 'she' and 'her'. Though it is possible to deduce from the whole extract that these pronominals refer to a sleeping woman who is (1) no longer young, (2) Gabriel's wife, and (3) has had a romance in her life, the character and identity of the woman and the way in which the reader arrives at a definition of that identity are radically different when derived from these sentences as (a) the beginning of an extract *or* (b) the conclusion of a text. Even such apparently non-referential items as 'Gabriel', 'asleep', 'tangled hair', 'deep-drawn breath', and 'a man' are significantly altered when taken in each of these ways. The name 'Gabriel' is apparently introduced if we read as (a), whereas if we read as (b), the name is not introductory but referential, re-invoking in the reader's mind an already defined character which now undergoes a certain degree of redefinition. The word 'asleep' is also defined by the preceding text, for we know the nature and cause of this sleep which follows the release of a long pent-up emotion, the pain of having been reminded of the past, and the excitement of the evening's party. The knowledge of this causality explains also 'tangled hair' and 'deep-drawn breath', both of which could lead to a variety of misinterpretations if read as (b). Similarly 'that romance' and 'a man', though they may lead the reader to a correct deduction that Gretta has had a lover other than Gabriel in the past, cannot, taken in extract, lead to a deduction of the essentially innocent nature of that affair which has so baffled Gabriel and adds considerable pathos to the passage. A knowledge of both Gretta's story and the manner in which it was told is essential to a correct interpretation of many of the cohesive ties in this extract. If we present this extract to foreign learners, we are asking them to participate in a process of decoding far more difficult than that undertaken by a reader who approaches this already difficult passage as a part of a whole text.

Conclusion

What then can we deduce from the foregoing analysis concerning the choice of literary extracts for use in the teaching of English as a foreign language? The extract analysed contains an unusual density of connections—in many varying ways—with the text which precedes it.

Appendix

Extract from 'The Dead' by James Joyce

1   She was fast asleep. (1)
      Gabriel, leaning on his elbow, looked for a few
moments unresentfully on her tangled hair and half-open
mouth, listening to her deep-drawn breath. (2) So she
5   had had that romance in her life: a man had died for her
sake. (3) It hardly pained him now to think how poor a
part he, her husband, had played in her life. (4) He
watched her while she slept, as though he and she had
never lived together as man and wife. (5) His curious eyes
10   rested long upon her face and on her hair: and, as he
thought of what she must have been then, in that time of
her first girlish beauty, a strange, friendly pity for her
entered his soul. (6) He did not like to say even to himself
that her face was no longer beautiful, but he knew that it
15   was no longer the face for which Michael Furey had
braved death. (7)
      Perhaps she had not told him all the story. His eyes
moved to the chair over which she had thrown some of
her clothes. A petticoat string dangled to the floor. One
20   boot stood upright, its limp upper fallen down: the
fellow of it lay on its side. He wondered at his riot of
emotions of an hour before. From what had it proceeded?
From his aunts' supper, from his own foolish speech,
from the wine and dancing, the merry-making when
25   saying good night in the hall, the pleasure of the walk
along the river in the snow. Poor Aunt Julia! She, too,
would soon be a shade with the shade of Patrick Morkan
and his horse. He had caught the haggard look upon her
face for a moment when she was singing 'Arrayed for the
30   Bridal'. Soon, perhaps, he would be sitting in that same
drawing-room, dressed in black, his silk hat on his knees.
The blinds would be drawn down and Aunt Kate would
be sitting beside him, crying and blowing her nose and
telling him how Julia had died. He would cast about in
35   his mind for some words that might console her, and
would find only lame and useless ones. Yes, yes: that
would happen very soon.
      The air of the room chilled his shoulders. He stretched
himself cautiously along under the sheets and lay down
40   beside his wife. One by one, they were all becoming

shades. Better pass boldly into that other world, in the full glory of some passion, than fade and wither dismally with age. He thought of how she who lay beside him had locked in her heart for so many years that image of her
45   lover's eyes when he had told her that he did not wish to live.

Generous tears filled Gabriel's eyes. He had never felt like that himself towards any woman, but he knew that such a feeling must be love. The tears gathered more
50   thickly in his eyes and in the partial darkness he imagined he saw the form of a young man standing under a dripping tree. Other forms were near. His soul had approached that region where dwell the vast hosts of the dead. He was conscious of, but could not apprehend,
55   their wayward and flickering existence. His own identity was fading out into a grey impalpable world: the solid world itself, which these dead had one time reared and lived in, was dissolving and dwindling.

A few light taps on the pane made him turn to the
60   window. He watched sleepily the flakes, silver and dark, falling obliquely against the lamplight. The time had come for him to set out on his journey westward. Yes, the newspapers were right: snow was general all over Ireland. It was falling on every part of the dark central
65   plain, on the treeless hills, falling softly upon the Bog of Allen and, farther westward, softly falling into the dark, mutinous Shannon waves. It was falling, too, upon every part of the lonely churchyard on the hill where Michael Furey lay buried. It lay thickly drifted on the crooked
70   crosses and headstones, on the spears of the little gate, on the barren thorns. His soul swooned slowly as he heard the snow falling faintly through the universe and faintly falling, like the descent of their last end, upon all the living and the dead.

PART TWO

Literature in Education

Introduction

In this section we examine a number of key educational issues that arise when we attempt to teach literature in schools.

The first paper, by Burke and Brumfit, outlines the main aims usually given for teaching English as a mother tongue, and relates the teaching of literature as an autonomous activity within this set of aims. The second half of the paper (not included) considers the role of independent language work. As we suggested in the introduction to this book, a defence of the teaching of literature will be the same kind of argument whether we are dealing with mother-tongue or foreign-language learners, provided we are not using literature simply as the servant of language or culture teaching.

Littlewood's paper, concerned particularly with foreign-language teaching, also accepts a distinction between literary and linguistic activity. But it is particularly concerned with relating the various demands which literary texts make on readers to the needs of foreign-language learners, and their implications for the selection of texts and—to a lesser extent—for methodology.

In the third paper, Brumfit outlines some general principles for the relationship between general reading ability in a foreign language and literary response. This leads to an attempt to outline the key methodological categories for teachers' planning of literary work. Although this discussion originated in foreign-language work, the methodological implications have been taken up in mother-tongue work as well, as we shall see in the final section of the book.

These three papers establish general principles. McKay's paper, based on American experience, gives several specific illustrations of ways in which a literary text may be used (and misused) in the classroom, as part of an argument for aesthetic response as a necessary component in normal second-language work. Although this paper reflects a different tradition of research and discussion than the three earlier ones, it is clear that similar preoccupations arose out of the use of literary texts in class.

Boyle's paper has been included in this collection because it illustrates well the range of test types that can be produced if literature is treated as a means of teaching a second or foreign language. This paper offers a particularly interesting basis for discussion, because it is well worth asking to what extent the issue of literature as *literature* is actually confronted by the types of tests illustrated. One constantly recurring problem is the recognition by teachers that the things we most strongly wish to teach in literature classes are not amenable to the kinds of testing procedures traditional in foreign-language work. Basic comprehension can be tested, as Boyle shows, and students will often be more willing to endure such tests in a foreign language than in their mother tongue. But does it make sense to test comprehension without examining the ability of students to construct and describe their own responses also?

Finally, two major problems are examined from quite different perspectives. Drawing on a wide experience of writing simple texts, often non-fiction, for second-language learners, Monica Vincent discusses the relationships between simple, simplified, and unsimplified texts. Reading, as we have seen, is a complex process, and the use of linguistically simpler texts need not make the process of reading easier. It may even add difficulties. In the section of this chapter written by Ron Carter, some problems of interpretation are outlined, and some of the major categories of difficulty proposed with reference largely to canonical English literary texts.

Ngugi, in contrast to all the previous commentators, writes as an impassioned consumer—as well, of course, as Kenya's greatest novelist. Literature cannot escape its cultural implications, and they may be perceived as limiting and dangerous. Any literature teaching is a response to a relationship between the culture of the students, whether it is ex-colonial, working class, bourgeois or whatever, and that represented by the current readers of the literature being presented. The internationally literate community of readers which has been presumed in our editorial discussion in this book is based on a set of values as much as any other construct. Ngugi confronts the implications of this head on, as does Chris Searle in *The Forsaken Lover* (Searle 1972). In the final section of this book, we shall be looking at one kind of pedagogy for literature which attempts to create an educational setting that is as open as possible. Only experience will show whether it can overcome the ideological strictures raised by Ngugi.

9 Is Literature Language? *or* Is Language Literature?

S. J. Burke and C. J. Brumfit

The English teacher's aims

Even a very superficial survey of books on the teaching of English will reveal an enormously wide range of different aims, some trivial and some vitally important. Many of the aims stated in the literature turn out to be more or less close paraphrases of each other, but we think it is possible, without making judgements about the relative importance of each of them, to fit all the stated aims into one or other of the following categories.

1 *The promotion of skills*

    a Literacy and oracy
      —aiming at accuracy
      —aiming at fluency and comfort
    b Critical and analytical ability
      —specifically in response to writing or speech
      —specifically in response to literary texts
      —specifically in discussion of the nature of language and how it works
      —by transfer, to all situations, particularly in response to aesthetic stimuli and to rational argument
    c Social skills, 'poise'
      —particularly in the context of the society of which the pupil is a member
    d Use of the imagination.

2 *Encouragement of attitudes and affective states*

    a Generally liberal, ethical, and humanitarian attitudes
      —through an active engagement with problems of writing and formulating ideas
      —through response to works of literature
    b Respect for the imagination and the intellect
    c respect for literary and cultural tradition
      —in general
      —a particular tradition.

3   *Provision of information*

   a Knowledge about literature
      —the English literary tradition
      —the western literary tradition
      —literature as a human activity
   b Knowledge about language
      —the English language
      —language as a human phenomenon.

It will be seen at once that these aims are very wide-ranging, and ambitious; some of them, indeed, seem to be more appropriate to a whole educational system than to one subject, albeit an important one. Nor, of course, can they be seen as completely independent of one another, but we would nevertheless suggest that all these aspects are, in principle, isolable, and that they can be discussed and assessed independently.

To produce a full analysis of these aims would require a chapter in itself, but it is worth pointing out that many aspects of English teaching are seen, at least in part, as means of promoting more general attitudes or skills. Let us take, for example, the critical and analytical ability of **1b**. We can represent the English teacher's part in this by the diagram in Figure 9.1 (the English teacher's interests are in italics):

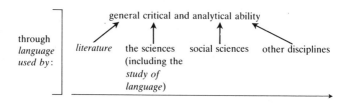

Figure 9.1

While there is, no doubt, value in the pupil's response to literature in itself, we would suggest that this is parallel with the value of the pupil's work within other subject areas, all of which require, in their different ways, extremely skilful response to—and use of—language.

Another point worth making is that a number of these aims involve concepts which are either untestable in practice (respect for tradition, etc.) or which appear to involve judgements on pupils' characters as much as on what can be taught. To what extent does a too-prescriptive definition of what is 'imaginative' or what is 'well-adjusted social behaviour' result in acceptance of cultural and artistic stereotypes? Do children learn what kind of writing is 'creative' and 'spontaneous' just as they used to imitate essays in the belles-lettres tradition? Finally, is there not a great danger in the English teacher seeing his or her (justified) concern for values, for the creation of a better society, as something which affects English teaching but somehow excludes the teaching of physics, maths or PE? Could the more messianic claims not hide a refusal to come to grips with the hard, specific problems of providing children with the linguistic tools for full self-realization, on the one hand, and with the skills for responding to literature, not in isolated sensitivity but in knowledge of the literary tradition also, on the other?

Literature as a separate subject

We assume that literature is sufficiently valuable for us to want to pass on the pleasure that reading it offers to us, but we would like to suggest that this will be done most efficiently by treating it as a completely separate subject area from English language. Let us first ask what are the difficulties lying in the way of a child who wants to become a skilled reader of literature.

For literature, as for work in any other subject, the child must be able to read accurately and easily, and in theory the first phase of schooling deals with this. The initial work on reading will be accompanied by the development of ideas which will lead into advanced and more specialized work, ideas relating to the sciences, to mathematics, to literature. By the time that literature is identifiable as an area of study in its own right, the child will have had much experience of story-telling, by adults and by children, which has been more or less consciously shaped to produce an effect on the hearer, and he or she will have experienced a wide variety of stimuli which aim to induce some sort of aesthetic response, in music and art as well as in writing. All this forms the base on which further work in literature will be built.

But literature has one major difference from other arts. Hoggart (1964: 34) describes it like this: 'Literature can never be aesthetically "pure" or abstractly contemplative. There can be no such thing as "abstract literature" as there is such as thing as abstract painting. By its nature—because its medium, language, is used by almost everybody in all sorts of everyday situations; and because it tries both to *say* and to *be*—literature is an art which invites impurities.' The result of this situation is that we can never divorce literature entirely from concepts, because we normally use language—the same language that occurs in works of literature—to express concepts; we paraphrase, we translate, we analyse. Nor can we separate literature entirely from our natural awareness of linguistic form; we are ourselves constantly engaged in a process of shaping language in order to express accurately messages which we want to convey. But in literature form acquires a special value. Most people would probably accept Northrop Frye's judgement (1957: 74) that 'in literature, questions of fact and truth are subordinated to the primary literary aim of producing a structure of words for its own sake', though it may well be argued that the structure may be as much a semantic structure as a verbal structure. From this, we would suggest that to the learner of how to read literature, difficulties may appear which result from ignorance of the language being used, of the ideas being used, or of the form being used.

We are not suggesting, of course, that these three aspects are totally independent of each other, nor that anyone reads a work of literature without being to some degree ignorant in all these three directions. But there do seem to be three elements which are to some extent separable. Consider the following examples:

a translation of *Crime and Punishment*;
Howards End;
Lord of the Flies.

Clearly the superficial nature of the language used is not fundamental to our understanding of the first (for whatever critics occasionally say, we *do* in fact read and respond to translated novels as part of our literary heritage, and relate them to our native tradition), so our response is primarily at the formal and conceptual levels. The second, while not linguistically and formally difficult, involves for the reader a subtle interaction with a conceptual framework which is far from that of the contemporary world. And with the third, while on the surface the ideas and language are not exceptionally difficult, the form poses considerable problems for those unfamiliar with the concept of allegory.

Without wishing to claim too great a separation between these three aspects, we feel that a good literature course will grade as carefully as possible the learner's progress in relation to each of them. But the use of language, concept and form in literature will be different from the use in other areas of study, and an English language course must either neglect these other areas by its concentration on literature, and at the same time over-emphasize the purely language element in literature, or include literature as no more than a small—and rather idiosyncratic— branch of language study. Neither of these situations is beneficial to the study of literature to any depth.

Let us now consider briefly what we as adults do with our literature. We talk and write about it, we adapt it and imitate it, in a wide variety of ways we relate it to our own lives and to other aspects of the world we perceive around us. Of course, in order to do these things we have to read it first, but perhaps in schools we emphasize too much the initial stage of reading to the exclusion of the more important one of using our reading.

One of the most important skills we exploit in discussing literature is that of comparison, and there is a very good reason for this. As most works of literature are conscious of form in a striking way, they are in fact exploiting tradition to achieve this effect. As we read, we are aware subconsciously of tradition, linguistic, conceptual, and formal. In other subject areas we are aware of the first two, but only in literature is the last of fundamental importance. We recognize deviance from the tradition when we become aware that our expectation has been subtly deceived, and this will be part of the pleasure of our response. To give a particular example, at the end of Keats's sonnet, 'When I have fears . . . ', we find the following:

> —then on the shore
> Of the wide world I stand alone, and think
> Till love and fame to nothingness do sink.

Surely part of the happy effect of this in context is because of our awareness of the neatness of the final couplet at the end of a Shakespearian sonnet, and a recognition that the sense unit has been unexpectedly extended to the second half of the preceding line in this poem: it is part of a tradition, yet it modifies it. Of course we bring to a reading of this poem a great many other pieces of information also, and a full and final reading of literature will never be achieved, but the more we read—and the more we experience of life outside reading, of course—the more our reading and re-reading is enriched. But it is enriched not merely at the level of language, but also at the level of form, structure of story, paragraphing, concept, and so on. This goes far beyond the boundaries of English writing; how can we understand twentieth-century English novelists without some acquaintance with Dostoyevsky, Kafka, and Proust, to give only a few obvious foreign influences?

We are asking, then, for a literature course which will lead children towards the kind of experience that the most informed and committed readers have, and we would suggest that this needs to be taught and examined quite independently of the—much more basic—language work. The kind of course we envisage would:

a treat the literary tradition that we work in as a literary and not solely a national or linguistic tradition, and also would recognize that awareness of a tradition is necessary as one part of a full understanding of literature;

b assume that the discussion of books, and the ideas in them, is valuable and necessary, and that books will be discussed collectively as much as individually, that response proceeds from an awareness of relationships between books;

c grade the skills necessary for the achievement of these objectives, so that children can respond to works of literature in an appropriate order, being given the chance to grasp significant principles of literary form without having to devote most of their energies to problems of simply translating archaic language (for example, why use *The Pilgrim's Progress* to illustrate the concept of allegory when *Lord of the Flies* could be used, or why not go straight to the nineteenth-century novel without problems of language by using modern translations of Russian or French masterpieces?);

d recognize that reading of a work of literature can be enriched by skilful use of background material, that it cannot be read in a vacuum.

Many schools do some work along these lines already. It would be good if something like this, fully developed and independent of language work, could become the norm.

10 Literature in the School Foreign-Language Course

William T. Littlewood

Introduction

There is at present a high degree of uncertainty about the role of literature in a school foreign-language course. Changes in educational and social conditions have shaken the once unquestioned status of literary study amongst our educational goals, and it also plays an ever more problematic role in a new pattern of language teaching which aims primarily to impart practical communicative skills. Recent discussions about advanced courses in schools have generally advocated less emphasis on literature in favour of language, and a revision of the principles governing the selection of texts in order to include greater consideration of pupils' actual ability, experience, and interests.[1]

Nevertheless, there is still comparatively little clarity about what role these texts should perform, and it is not uncommon to find a situation where the teacher translates passages and dictates notes, in an examination-centred approach which largely ignores the deeper insights or skills that pupils might gain from their confrontation with literature. On the other hand, it is clearly not possible to think in terms of one single role which literature should perform. A group of pupils aiming at a functional command of a language may read a modern novel because of its linguistic content, while a group of future academic specialists may discuss the basic human issues portrayed in a classical play. These are two different activities in two different situations, each equally justifiable in its own context but not to be confused: different pupils' aims require literature to serve different functions, which are best performed by different literary works.

The purpose of this chapter is to help distinguish the crucial components of these and similar situations, by relating different aspects of literature to possible aims and methods of study and to corresponding criteria for the selection of texts. It aims to provide a conceptual framework for the examination and discussion of the role of literature in different types of course. While it speaks mostly in terms of literary works used at advanced stages of learning, much of what is said can also be applied to constructed texts used at earlier levels, and indeed it is hoped that a continuity will emerge between these different types of reading material, corresponding to the continuity between stages of language learning.

Perspectives on literature

At the simplest level, literature is not qualitatively different from any other linguistic performance. It is an instance of the productive use of a limited number of linguistic structures in order to achieve communication. The main core of the linguistic system is the same, whether it is used for spoken gossip or for written literature. It is only when we consider the second level, stylistic variety, that the differences appear. Apart from 'literary styles' which differ more or less acutely (according to period, genre, and so on) from the styles of everyday usage, literature can draw on all available styles, from the most elevated to the most informal, in order to gain its effects or give its representation of life.[2]

Moving from language to content, at the third level literature is the expression of superficial subject matter, as it relates events or describes scenes: the story of a novel or the plot of a drama. When the reader begins to seek more than a cursory understanding of events and characters, the fourth level is entered, at which literature is the symbolization of the author's vision of these events and his or her world-view, and the reader is faced with the underlying theme or meaning of the work.[3]

These, then, may be considered as four levels within a literary work. It is appropriate, in the present context, to state them in linguistic terms: language as a system of structures, language in a specific stylistic variety, language as the expression of superficial subject matter, and language as the symbolization of the author's vision. According to which level is emphasized as dominant, they also constitute four ways of viewing the work: four perspectives, to which we add a fifth when we locate the work in time and place, and view it as a part of literary history or of the author's biography. The next section will look at these five perspectives in turn, and consider what their place might be in a foreign-language course.

The five perspectives and language teaching

1 The first perspective requires little discussion here. According to it, literature provides instances of language structures in use, which can form the basis for instruction and practice in the language skills, especially reading comprehension accompanied by a varying amount

of grammatical analysis and explanation. In addition, exercises and drills may be devised in order to transfer linguistic structures to the learner's active repertoire.

2 The second perspective normally becomes relevant at a later stage than the first, when students become capable of sensitivity to stylistic variation. Literature now becomes a vehicle for the learning of differences between language varieties. According to text and purpose, this may mean the introduction to the formal written register as such, or to a range of styles which the work exploits as it alternates between, say, a conversational style for dialogue, an informative style for narrative, and a poetic style for heightened effects. At a still more advanced level, the work of a regional writer may provide access to a local dialect, or classical works may be studied for the light they throw on an earlier state of linguistic development. The most delicate stage of linguistic discrimination is reached when the idiosyncratic features of the author's style are explored, which is possible only after the student has acquired knowledge of what constitutes the common core of the language and what belongs to the publicly available stylistic varieties of the language.

3 So far, the discussion in this section has centred on the linguistic content of the work: structures in language, and style in language. Most of the functions mentioned so far could be fulfilled equally well, or better, by readers or simplified texts contrived specially for language-teaching purposes. The more specific contribution of literature begins at the level of subject matter: the episodes, situations, and characters created by the literary work.

A major problem of language teaching in the classroom is the creation of an authentic situation for language. A language classroom, especially one outside the community of native speakers, is isolated from the context of events and situations which produce natural language. In the case of literature, language creates its own context. The actual situation of the reader becomes immaterial as he or she takes on what D. W. Harding calls 'the role of the onlooker', looking on at the events created by language.[4] These events create, in their turn, a context of situation for the language of the book and enable it to transcend the artificial classroom situation. Harding compares literature to make-believe and gossip, because all three are ways of representing experience to oneself and others, ways in which we 'look on at' events which are not physically present. There are three corresponding ways in which language teaching attempts to compensate for the absence of real events: by talking or 'gossiping' about them; by using role-play or 'make-believe' to simulate them; and by using reading material or 'literature' to represent them.

The world created in the work of literature is the foreign world, and literature is thus a way of assimilating (through the same experience of 'looking on') knowledge of this foreign world, and of the view of reality which its native speakers take for granted when communicating with each other.[5] In this respect, literature is one amongst several means of access to the foreign culture in the widest sense, and a continuation in intent of earlier background studies. Conversely, it is not possible to appreciate the created world of literature unless the everyday cultural background (the raw material which literature has used) has already become familiar at an earlier level of learning.

4 The fourth perspective cannot be enjoyed until after the work has been mastered at the three previous levels. Appreciation now goes beyond language or plot, in order to penetrate to the author's vision or underlying theme, which often transcends any specific place or time. At this level, it becomes unimportant whether, for example, jealousy is portrayed in a Shakespearian drama in English or a twentieth-century novel in French, though of course this becomes important again as soon as we consider the work as an integrated whole and examine how the first three levels are structured to serve the fourth.

If discussion at this level is conducted in the mother tongue, the pupils' level of ideas can be more fully stretched, but it is often argued that the native literature would provide a more suitable base for such discussion and, above all, that the valuable time would be better spent in activities of more direct benefit to the pupils' foreign linguistic competence. An alternative strategy, then, is to conduct discussion and require essays in the foreign language, accepting an inevitably lower level of ideation in the belief that the pupils' already formed ideas will stretch and expand their competence in the target language. In the transition from receptive to productive skills, the third level of literature (subject matter) might provide the basis for the pupils' use of language for 'recording' or 'reporting', while this fourth level might provide a basis for 'generalizing' or 'theorizing'.[6]

5 Finally, with the fifth perspective, we step outside the work and place it in its context as part of literary history. At its most simple, this might involve superficial chronological facts, which are often over-emphasized because of their simplicity and their reassuring 'hardness', but in themselves provide little illumination of the literary work in question. Illumination begins to emerge when we link this perspective with the preceding ones by relating features at different levels to the linguistic, social, or intellectual development of the foreign culture.

The selection of texts

The five perspectives discussed in the previous sections also provide criteria for the selection of suitable texts for specific classes and objectives.

1 Literature seen as linguistic structures provides the criterion of structural suitability. At early levels of instruction, reading material may be constructed both in order to confront pupils with texts of an appropriate level of difficulty, and to provide them with repeated instances of structures which they need to internalize. In the selection of unsimplified literary texts at a more advanced level, this second aim may still have a role to play (e.g. Camus' *L'Etranger* may be chosen because it uses the perfect tense for narrative); in particular, it may provide a reason for the avoidance of texts which use archaic structures. More frequently, however, it is a question of estimating the general difficulty of the language in relation to the pupils' linguistic competence, on the basis of intuition or past experience. A reliable method of grading texts, perhaps using cloze tests, would be welcome.

The linguistic structures are, of course, the gateway or barrier to other levels, and it is fruitless to expect pupils to appreciate literary works for which they are not linguistically ready.[7] The ideal literature syllabus might be envisaged as offering the possibility of a two-fold progression, first in terms of linguistic difficulty (and perhaps style), and second in terms of the perspective taken, so that pupils can advance from a concentration on subject matter in their early reading (with a corresponding emphasis on 'reporting' and 'recording' in their productive work), towards a gradually deepening concentration on underlying theme (with a corresponding increase in 'generalizing' and 'theorizing' in their productive work).

2 The selection of texts for their stylistic appropriateness may be conceived negatively, as the avoidance of unsuitable varieties, or positively, as the choice of suitable ones. With pupils who aim at a functional linguistic competence, we are likely to be concerned with the avoidance of archaic or highly formal varieties, and the selection of a style capable of providing a link with everyday language. Other pupils may seek a discriminating acquaintance with a wider range of styles from different levels of formality or even different historical periods.

3 The criterion provided by subject matter demands that the world created by the literary work should have interest and relevance for the pupils, and also that they should have adequate knowledge of the cultural background to appreciate it. Many features are of course common to all or most European cultures, and even to different historical periods: in the case of some works, these common features may themselves provide an adequate background to appreciation, whereas with others, cultural-specific features must be known. The crucial factor is the extent to which the reader can enter the world as an involved 'onlooker', for which there must be no cultural barriers, and the experience portrayed in the work must make contact with the pupil's experience at some point.

4 However, this contact between the domain of experience of the book, and that of the pupil, may take place not at the level of surface subject matter, but at the level of underlying theme. When asking about the relevance of a work for a group of pupils, it is important to know to what extent they will probe beyond the surface to the underlying meaning. If they will concentrate on subject matter, they need a work with which they can make contact at that level, perhaps a twentieth-century novel or a book about young people, in any case one with a clear appeal to them. If, on the other hand, they will approach the work at a deeper level and uncover the underlying theme, subject matter may become less important than the vision of life or of human nature that it embodies, and pupils may find great interest and relevance in a work whose events and characters seem at first sight remote from them, such as a classical drama written in seventeenth-century France about royal personages in Ancient Greece. However, before appealing to the universal relevance of such works and including them in a syllabus, we must ensure that the pupils are linguistically, intellectually and motivationally ready to penetrate to the underlying level at which this relevance is to be found and, having done so, to cope with the ideas that they find there.

5 The fifth perspective, though it may always be a source of interesting facts and insights, becomes a criterion for selection only at an advanced stage of study. If a work is to be meaningfully studied because of its place in literary history or within a literary or intellectual movement, pupils need a wide scope of literary experience, taking in not only the individual work but also the context in which it emerged.

Conclusion

The relative importance accorded to these different criteria can be decided only in the light of a specific situation. For pupils just emerging from the intermediate stage, language and stylistic factors may be decisive, subject matter may be a secondary but still important factor, and the fourth and fifth perspectives probably play no part at all. At a later stage, the major criterion may become subject matter, to induce pupils to read extensively; linguistic and stylistic suitability must also be examined, but the pupils' greater flexibility makes these criteria gradually less likely to provide obstacles. Many learners with functional aims may never approach texts for other than reasons of language and subject matter, and for them the fourth and fifth perspectives will not become relevant. For other learners, richness and suitability of underlying theme will later become a crucial factor; again, however, previous levels must be examined since they may be a source of undesirable frustration, as in the case of some long, difficult novels, or where the theme is of interest but the style of presentation too strange and obtrusive. The fifth perspective cannot become fully criterial until students have sufficient linguistic and intellectual experience to cope with a wide or unlimited range of works at all four levels, enabling them to select texts for reasons external to the works themselves.

To conclude, the study of literature allows a variety of emphases and perspectives. Only if we become clear about what literature has to offer, and what specific pupils require, can we begin to discuss its role and select appropriate methods and texts. Above all, any prospective text must be scrutinized according to all criteria relevant to the pupils' learning stage and requirements, and not adopted for study unless it passes through this scrutiny without hindrance.

Notes

1 See for example the Schools Council Working Paper 28 *New Patterns in Sixth Form Modern Language Studies*, Evans/Methuen Educational, 1970, also articles in *Modern Languages* by W. Grauberg, 'Set Books in the Sixth Form Course' (Vol. LI No. 2, pp. 56–9) and A. Hornsey, 'Set Books and Sixth-Form Studies' (Vol. LI No. 4, pp. 147–52).

2 For a discussion of common-core features and stylistic features, see D. Crystal and D. Davy, *Investigating English Style*, Longman, 1969, Chapter 3.

3 The use of the terms 'subject matter' and 'vision' in this context is borrowed from M. A. K. Halliday, 'Linguistic function and literary style', in his *Explorations in the Functions of Language*, Edward Arnold, 1973.

4 In 'The Role of the Onlooker', written in 1937 but reprinted in A. Cashdan and E. Grugeon (eds): *Language in Education: a Source Book*, The Open University Press/Routledge & Kegan Paul, 1972.

5 See W. M. Rivers, *Teaching Foreign-Language Skills*, University of Chicago Press, 1968, pp. 280–2.

6 These four categories of informative language use, taken from J. Moffet, are discussed in J. Britton, 'What's the Use? A Schematic Account of Language Functions' reprinted in Cashdan and Grugeon, op. cit., pp. 245–6.

7 On the importance of linguistic readiness, see for example Henry Sweet, *The Practical Study of Languages*, 1899, repr. Oxford University Press, 1964, pp. 218–19; M. A. K. Halliday, A. McIntosh and P. Strevens, *The Linguistic Sciences and Language Teaching*, Longman, 1964, pp. 183–5; D. Girard, *Linguistics and Foreign Language Teaching*, Longman, 1972, pp. 77–9.

11 Reading Skills and the Study of Literature in a Foreign Language

Christopher Brumfit

This chapter is a preliminary attempt to consider the relationship between reading in a foreign language and the teaching of literature. It is preliminary because this is an area which has been neglected in recent discussions of language teaching, while practice has continued to relate the two. Because this is a question which has been little discussed in relation to current language teaching theory, this paper will be essentially philosophical and discursive in approach. It will also attempt a consideration of approaches to literature in principle, reduced to basic categories which may be helpful to teachers, in order to set in context the difficulties of teachers of literature in foreign languages.

The problem

Recent approaches to language teaching (outlined, for example in Widdowson 1978; Brumfit and Johnson 1979) have ignored literature teaching. However, increasing recognition of the difficulties of communicative syllabuses (see contributors to Johnson and Morrow 1978; and Muller 1980) have led to a more cautious approach. It is not necessary to retreat, though, to turn again with interest to literature teaching, for literature provides us with a convenient source of content for a course in a foreign language, and a truly notional syllabus will need to be constructed round concepts and subject matter which develop in complexity (Widdowson and Brumfit 1981). Most attempts to provide motivating and communicative material for learners are strong in technique but weak in any sense of developmental structure (Moskowitz 1978; Maley and Duff 1978; Melville *et al.* 1980). Even courses intended for school use (Abbs and Sexton 1978; Jupp *et al.* 1979) suffer from fragmentation of content.

This chapter is not an attempt to argue that literature teaching ought to be used to solve these problems. It does set out to argue the role that literature teaching might have at fairly advanced levels. A clarification of this may have implications for what could happen during more elementary teaching, and is worth doing for several reasons. First, reading is the most autonomous and individualizable ability in language work, and literature is a rich and widely-appealing source of material for reading. Second, literature is one of only three areas on which a foreign language *content* syllabus could be based (the others are linguistics and civilization) which will not conflict with the claims of other subjects in the curriculum. Third, materials are readily available. But all of these reasons are subservient to the argument that there must be a content which is in itself worthwhile if advanced language teaching is to be really effective. This is not simply a matter of motivation, but of the nature of language: functional and notional development requires some basis in a developing body of information, procedures and skills to be exploited in the target language.

Literary competence

Culler writes (1975:114):

> . . . anyone wholly unacquainted with literature and unfamiliar with the conventions by which fictions are read, would . . . be quite baffled if presented with a poem. His knowledge of the language would enable him to understand phrases and sentences, but he would not know, quite literally, what to *make* of this strange concatenation of phrases. He would be unable to read it *as* literature . . . because he lacks the complex 'literary competence' which enables others to proceed. He has not internalised the 'grammar' of literature which would permit him to convert linguistic sequences into literary structures and meanings.

A true literature syllabus will not be simply the use of literary texts for advanced language purposes, but an attempt to develop or extend literary competence. But to do this involves clarifying a concept which is still contentious in terms which are simple enough to be related to classroom practice for inexperienced readers.

While it is true that there can be no final reading of a literary text—the meaning is always subject to negotiation, for it results from the relationship between reader(s) and writer—it is none the less possible to make an inappropriate response through a misunderstanding of the codes being operated. Such codes will not be solely linguistic, but will include the interplay of event with event, relationships between characters, exploitation of ideas and value systems, formal structure in terms of a genre or other literary convention, and relationships between any of these and the world outside literature itself. All of these, and other aspects too, will be subject to convention, and writers will exploit the conventions they inherit in different ways. A good reader recognizes such conventions (though not necessarily explicitly) and interprets them in relation to the world of other experience which literature must in some sense imitate or comment on.

The codes cited above—and they do not, of course, constitute a definitive list—vary in complexity and accessibility. Most works of literature are accessible in terms of plot (events) and relationships between characters, though the fact of such accessibility will lead some writers to insist on falsifying our expectations and deliberately operating with ambiguity and confusion. But certain kinds of interaction, for example with political ideas, will demand sophistication of response in terms of outside understanding of, for example, political theories. Such considerations will force us to consider literature not as an isolated activity but as one to be viewed in relation to the general cognitive development of the student. There has been some work in this direction, but there is much still to be done in clarifying the situation, even with mother-tongue readers (Whitehead *et al.* 1977; Blunt 1977; Thomson, 1979).

Relations with pedagogy

It should be clear from this discussion so far that the teaching of literature cannot simply involve an extension of ordinary reading skills. It is possible to be a competent reader and unfamiliar with literary conventions associated with a particular culture. None the less, language use requires recognition of the density of allusion that humanity is capable of and that any language exploits. All users of language share this common basis and it is from this that a specifically literary education must develop. So for a literary pedagogy to be successful, the teaching must develop the literary awareness which is implicit in learners' ability to use language at all, and sensitize learners to the conventions of the literary tradition. To attempt this in a foreign language is a demanding task, made more difficult by the confusion which reigns in the teaching of mother-tongue literature.

The teaching of literature in a foreign language must still be partially dependent on approaches taken to teaching mother-tongue literature, so some attempt to clarify this neglected area is necessary (for some indication of the range of approaches available see Brinke 1977: 175 ff; Marshall 1972: 29 ff).

Ideally, a literature syllabus in the mother tongue will not only exploit understanding of language, but will relate to other aesthetic work, art and music for example. It must, that is to say, be responsive to the total educational and cultural context, so that the form it takes will vary from situation to situation. Sometimes, indeed, for example in some Third World countries, foreign-language literatures will take upon themselves the major part of literary education, and will need to be related to traditions of oral literature, and the relation of contemporary indigenous literature with the ex-colonial cultures. Here, it will be difficult to avoid major political issues, since linguistic and cultural relations will be so bound up with issues of power and development (Brumfit 1970; Pettit 1971; Searle 1972). In the traditional foreign-language teaching contexts of European countries the differences between various local mother-tongue traditions will be crucial elements in relating to the world literary tradition. But it should be possible to specify usefully, though in general terms, the basic needs of learners of literary competence.

Relationship with advanced reading

This chapter makes no claim that the reading of literature requires different reading strategies from other kinds of reading. It does make a claim, though, that reading which exploits literary perceptions will require a different pedagogical approach. Responding to literature is not a matter of basic understanding of the language of the text. It is the significance of the text that is important to the good reader, not its ability to be translated exactly. Most native-speaking readers of (say) Shakespeare will fail to understand a proportion, even at the literal level, of what they read or hear, but this failure will not be crucial to their response unless it develops above a certain level. Accepting appropriate tolerance of uncertainty is an essential part of being a good reader. Consequently, work in literature follows naturally from integrative activities in reading, in which understanding of the text is derived from discussion by students of questions which force them to see the text as a coherent piece of discourse (see for example Munby 1968). Reading strategies which make use of explicit analytical devices will have less relevance.

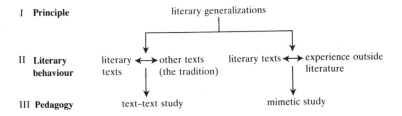

Figure 11.1

A simple pedagogical model for literature teaching

The argument to justify a simple model of the kind illustrated in Figure 11.1 is as follows:

1 The teaching of appropriate reading of literature cannot proceed primarily by linear means, for in so far as it is a mature reading process, response to the text in all its aspects must develop simultaneously.

2 The fundamental ability of a good reader of literature is the ability to generalize from the given text either to other aspects of the literary tradition or to personal or social significances outside literature.

3 These two fields of reference outside any particular text must be developed by any effective teaching theory, and techniques in literature teaching are only worthwhile in so far as they serve these two aims.

4 Students must be assisted to develop their latent abilities in both these directions, and this implies establishing criteria for grading their exposure to literature in terms of these.

5 The prime purpose of any specifically literary work in school is not to provide particular items of knowledge, but to use such knowledge as tokens in the process of generalization referred to in (2) above.

6 (a) The ability to perceive and explore relationships between literary texts and other literary texts (hence developing understanding of the notion of convention and tradition) will be developed by reading texts deliberately associated with each other for pedagogical purposes. Texts may be linked by subject matter, by formal and structural similarity, by thematic intention, or by any other appropriate device.

(b) The ability to perceive and explore relationships between literary texts and ordinary life will be developed through increasing familiarity with the various mimetic properties of literature. Pedagogically, this is best achieved by grading the complexity and subtlety of external reference in the texts used, for example by starting with relatively simple allegorical and mythical works from which generalizing to personal or external experience can be made as simple as possible.

Implications of such a model for foreign-language work

Work on foreign-language literatures must be consistent with the position outlined above, but students will be able to work at varying levels of sophistication, according to their previous experience of literature: their literary understanding will not correlate with their linguistic skills. Hence criteria for the selection of teaching materials will have to anticipate a disjuncture between linguistic and literary form. Language level alone is not an appropriate criterion. And furthermore, the work in the foreign language, if it is to be truly literary work, must be regarded as an extension of capacities already developed, at least partially, in mother-tongue literary work, but these capacities will be refined through contact with literature from a foreign culture.

Stating the arguments thus starkly runs the risk of appearing both pretentious and simplistic, but it is worth trying to be over-simple in this particular discussion, for tradition is strong and needs to be assaulted by relatively clear and unrefined arguments. It needs to be argued forcefully that literature teaching is about abilities, not knowledge, and that these abilities are totally bound up with the network of conventions which all writers choose to exploit. Foreign-language literature teaching must respond to this as much as mother-tongue literature teaching.

However, once an argument along these lines is accepted, it is possible to list the basic criteria for the selection of texts for advanced work in teaching foreign literatures. (The examples given are drawn from English literature, but the principles would apply to any.)

First, a group of criteria which relate to reading of any kind.

1 *Linguistic level.* This can of course be measured in lexical or syntactic terms. But it is essential to recognize that no descriptive linguistic model can measure significance in literary terms. Blake's poems, or Hemingway's *The Old Man and the Sea*, are examples of linguistically simple texts which pose considerable problems in literary terms.

2 *Cultural level.* Different works of literature will be close to the cultural and social expectations of different groups of learners. This may affect decisions in various ways. For example, nineteenth-century literary modes are culturally closer to the reading experience of relatively unsophisticated readers than are many contemporary works. In some Third World countries eighteenth-century writers such as Fielding or Crabbe may strike immediate chords because local society is still (just) pre-industrial.

3 *Length.* Still a crucial pedagogical factor.

Such criteria may be applied, with appropriate modification, to any reading materials, but there are three others which are significant in purely literary terms.

4 *Pedagogical role* (in relation to the literature–literature or literature–life connections). At appropriate levels works which are satisfactory on other grounds may be linked to others (Golding's *Lord of the Flies* linked to Ballantyne's *The Coral Island* on which it is a deliberate comment, for example, or linked to other books on a similar theme, such as Susan Hill's *I'm the King of the Castle*). Or books may be

deliberately read in connection with contemporary events (novels of Graham Greene, perhaps).

5   *Genre representation*. If the course is truly concerned with developing reading capacities, it cannot be restricted to short stories and poems which can be studied in class. All normal types of literature need to be available.

6   *Classic status* (or 'face validity'). Some texts may be demanded and therefore motivating for students, even though they are not essential on other grounds. The desire to read Dickens or Shakespeare may enable students to overcome difficulties which would be significant in terms of the other criteria.

Conclusion

The development of literary abilities in the way outlined here presupposes a fairly fluent capacity to read English. But the grading of literature teaching texts and strategies will have to take into account a great deal more than simple knowledge of the language. What literature teaching can offer, though, is a basis for a truly notional development of a language syllabus. The criteria for selection and use of literary texts, played off against each other, must lead to a recognition of the needs of particular groups of students. Students' authentic responses to the literary tradition will both assist the development of appropriate syllabuses, through trial and error, and will be developed through a carefully graded sequence of texts. If reading is to be viewed as an integrated process, the teaching of reading must do more than simply exercise reading in the target language. Literary texts, if used in relation to a serious view of extending literary competence, will provide a particularly suitable base from which motivated language activity can develop. In this chapter, necessarily somewhat condensed, it has been possible to give only the barest outline of a new approach. But this seems to be a direction worth exploring in further work.

12   Literature in the ESL Classroom

Sandra McKay

Should literature be part of a curriculum for English as a Second Language (ESL)? Today with the current focus in ESL on meeting the particular academic and occupational needs of the students, it is easy to view any attention to literature as unnecessary. Is there a rationale for including literature in the curriculum?

Let us first examine the common arguments *against* using literature. The most common ones are the following. First, since one of our main goals as ESL teachers is to teach the grammar of the language, literature, due to its structural complexity and its unique use of language, does little to contribute to this goal. Second, the study of literature will contribute nothing to helping our students meet their academic and/or occupational goals. Finally, literature often reflects a particular cultural perspective; thus, on a conceptual level, it may be quite difficult for students. These arguments certainly need to be addressed if we are to reach a decision as to whether or not to use literature.

Clearly, we all share the objective of promoting our students' awareness of the structure of the language. However, there are, as Widdowson (1978: 3) points out, two levels of linguistic knowledge: the level of *usage* and the level of *use*. According to his definition, *usage* involves a knowledge of linguistic rules, whereas *use* entails knowing how to use these rules for effective communication. Can a literary text contribute to a knowledge of either one?

Most present-day literary texts assume that literature can provide a basis for extending language usage. Many of these texts focus on the particular grammatical points that are salient in the text (see, for example, Fassler and Lay 1979). Furthermore, vocabulary expansion is dealt with by attention to word forms and common expressions. Povey (1972: 187), in summarizing the aims of using literature in ESL classes, argues that 'literature will increase all language skills because literature will extend linguistic knowledge by giving evidence of extensive and subtle vocabulary usage, and complex and exact syntax'. Later I will examine the wisdom of using literature as a basis for teaching usage.

Whereas literature has traditionally been used to teach language usage, rarely has it been used to develop language use. Yet the advantage of using literature for this purpose is that literature presents language in discourse in which the parameters of the setting and role relationship are defined. Language that illustrates a particular register or dialect is embedded within a social context, and thus there is a basis for determining why a particular form is used. As such, literature is ideal for developing an awareness of language use.

A second common argument against using literature is that it will do nothing toward promoting the students' academic and/or occupational goals. First of all, it is important to remember that one need not assume that literature be studied to the exclusion of other types of texts. Hence, it need not be a question of *either* literature *or* factual texts. Rather, the question is one of whether or not the study of literature can in any way contribute to academic and/or occupational goals. Certainly in so far as literature can foster an overall increase in reading proficiency, it will contribute to these goals. An evaluation of reading proficiency rests on an understanding of what is involved in the reading process. Widdowson (1979: 74) and others regard reading 'not as a reaction to a text but as *interaction* between writer and reader mediated through the text'. This interaction, it seems to me, occurs on two levels: linguistic and conceptual. In other words, reading necessitates the ability to interact with a text by decoding the language and comprehending the concepts presented. Furthermore, these two levels often interact. Johnson (1981), in examining the effects of the linguistic complexity and the cultural background of a text on the reading comprehension of Iranian ESL students, found that the relationship between these variables is complex; in some instances familiarity with the text made it easier for students to deal with complex syntactic structures, but this familiarity also resulted in students' going beyond the text in interpreting it. What is critical in selecting a text is to examine it for both its linguistic and its conceptual difficulties. Whereas readability formulas provide some index of the former, unfortunately we have little to aid us in dealing with the latter.

The perspective of reading as *interaction* presupposes, of course, that a reader is willing to interact with a particular text. It is here that the motivational factors involved in reading become critical. As Gaies (1979: 48) points out, 'since the reading process . . . is the interaction of a reader and a text, we stand in equal need of more research on the affective, attitudinal and experiential variables which would differentiate individual or groups of learners in terms of their willingness and ability to decode written input in a second language'. For some students, literature may provide the affective, attitudinal, and experiential factors which will motivate them to read. As such, literary texts can aid in the development of reading proficiency and in this way contribute to a student's academic and occupational objectives.

Finally, critics of the use of literature maintain that to the extent that literary texts reflect a particular cultural perspective, they may be difficult for ESL students to read. Clearly, this can be a problem. The question is whether or not any benefits can arise from examining the cultural assumptions of a piece of literature. Marshall (1979: 333), in using English literature with Puerto Rican students, found that as she worked to help students overcome the difficulties of the text, her own appreciation of the text was clarified and her respect for the students' own cultural framework enhanced. Thus, literature may work to promote a greater tolerance for cultural differences for both the teacher and the student. Northrop Frye (1964: 77) summarizes this benefit of literature in the following manner: 'So you may ask what is the use of studying the world of imagination where anything is possible and anything can be assumed, where there are no rights or wrongs and all arguments are equally good. One of the most obvious uses, I think, is its encouragement of tolerance.'

A second benefit of struggling with the potential cultural problem of literature is that it may promote our students' own creativity. Again as Frye puts it (1964: 129), 'It is clear that the end of literary teaching is not simply the admiration of literature; it's something more like the transfer of imaginative energy from literature to the students.' Thus, whereas students may indeed be unfamiliar with some of the cultural assumptions in literature, the advantages of confronting these assumptions may be well worth the struggle.

In summary, literature offers several benefits to ESL classes. It can be useful in developing linguistic knowledge, both on a usage level and a use level. Secondly, to the extent that students enjoy reading literature, it may increase their motivation to interact with a text, and thus ultimately increase their reading proficiency. Finally, an examination of a foreign culture through literature may increase their understanding of that culture and perhaps spur their own imaginative writing.

Selecting literature

The key to success in using literature in the ESL class seems to me to rest in the literary works that are selected. A text which is extremely difficult on either a linguistic or a cultural level will have few benefits. One common method of solving the potential problem of linguistic difficulty is the simplification of the text. There are, however, serious disadvantages to using this approach. As Honeyfield (1977: 434–5) points out, simplification tends to produce a homogenized product in which the information becomes diluted. The additional words in the text tend to spread the information out, rather than to localize the information. Furthermore, the simplification of syntax may reduce cohesion and readability. Since proficient readers rely heavily on localized information and cohesive devices, deleting these elements will contribute little to the development of reading skills.

Are there any alternatives to using simplified versions? One obvious solution is to select texts which are relatively easy according to readability counts. However, such counts typically are based on some measure of vocabulary difficulty and some index of syntactic complexity, such as sentence length. In dealing with literature, these counts, of course, give no indication of the complexity of the text in terms of plot, character, or cultural difficulty.

A second solution is to select texts from literature written for young adults. Such literature, according to Donelson and Nilsen (1980: 14–15), tends to have the following characteristics. Frequently, the theme of such literature deals with the problem of personal growth and development. Furthermore, most writing for young adults tends to be relatively short, and the characters usually limited to a small cast of characters with a young adult as the central figure. Most importantly, from an ESL perspective, many of the books tend to be stylistically less complex.

In addition to selecting literary texts that are stylistically uncomplicated, it is important to select themes with which the students can identify. Certainly, one common experience of most ESL students is their struggle with a language and culture with which they are unfamiliar. Thus, literature which deals with either of these themes should be highly relevant to them.

Using literature in the classroom

Selecting the text is only the first step. An equally important issue is how to deal with such texts in the classroom. Here, I think Rosenblatt's (1978: 24) distinction between efferent and aesthetic reading is critical. She defines efferent reading (from the Latin 'to carry away') as reading in which the reader is concerned with what she will carry away. In aesthetic reading, on the other hand, 'the reader's primary concern is with what happens during the actual reading'. In both cases the text is merely the stimulus; the reader creates her own poem as she interacts with the text, bringing her own experience to bear. For Rosenblatt, this interaction is an event in time involving a specific reader, and a specific text at a specific time and place; if any of these are changed, there is a different event. Hence, while a text may not be involving for an individual at a certain time, later the same person, by bringing additional experience to the text, may find it involving. Because of this, Rosenblatt suggests that a student be allowed to put aside a particular piece of literature, an option which we rarely allow our students. Widdowson makes a similar point when he states (1978: 80), 'to present someone with a set of extracts and to require him to read them not in order to learn something interesting and relevant about the world but in order to learn something about the language being used is to misrepresent language use to some degree'.

In short, the classroom approaches to efferent and aesthetic reading must of necessity be very different. Exploring the usage of a text which is being approached efferently is in keeping with the aim of using a text to gain information. On the other hand, since in aesthetic reading the experience is primary, this is where a classroom approach should begin and language usage should be explored only to the extent that it is relevant to that experience. The fact is that literary experiences outside of a classroom proceed in this manner. What is most important to a reader in aesthetic reading is the enjoyment attained by interacting with the text. Usage comes into play only when it impedes or highlights that experience. To do other than this in the classroom results in what Widdowson (1979: 80) terms a lack of authenticity i.e. an inappropriate relationship between the text and the reader.

Application

Let us examine how a particular literary passage might be approached aesthetically rather than efferently. The following selection is taken from *Sweet Promised Land* by Robert Laxalt (1957: 62–3). The book is a biography of Laxalt's father, a Basque shepherd who went to America when he was sixteen. As Laxalt puts it, 'My father was a sheepherder, and his home was the hills. So it began when he was a boy in the misted Pyrenees of France, and so it was to be for most of his life in the lonely Sierra of Nevada.' The following passage describes his father at the age of 63 in an exclusive New York restaurant, on the way back to his homeland for the first time since he came to America.

We made it through the soup and the salad without incident. It began when the waiter came to take away our salad plates and put on others for the main course. He collected John's and mine, and then reached for my father's. But he could not lift it, because my father was holding it to the table with both hands.

'I'm sorry,' said the waiter. 'I thought you were finished.'

'I am finished,' said my father.

'Oh,' said the waiter, and again reached for the salad plate. My father held on.

'May I take your plate, sir?' said the waiter.

'No,' said my father mildly.

The waiter stood in confused silence for a moment. 'But I have to put another plate there, sir.'

My father shook his head. 'It's all right,' he said. 'Don't go to any bother.'

The waiter blinked and then smiled weakly. 'Oh, it's no bother at all,' he said, and again reached for the plate.

This time, my father put his hands over the plate to protect it. The waiter stopped short and straightened up. He looked at us in something akin to frenzy, and John gestured with his head. The waiter retreated to the back of the room and stood there watching us from long distance. He was pale and he still had a plate in his hands.

'Pop,' said John, 'Why don't you give him your plate?'

My father shrugged. 'It's clean enough,' he said.

This time John blinked. 'I don't understand what you mean.'

'They shouldn't waste a plate,' said my father. 'This one's fine.'

John regarded my father for a long moment. 'It's really no bother,' he said. 'They've got a washer back there that does all the work.'

'Well, they might run short,' my father said.

'I'm telling you, Pop,' said John. 'There's no danger.' He took a deep drag of his cigarette and leaned forward again. 'Pop,' he said, 'You're going to get that waiter in trouble.'

'What?' said my father concernedly.

'It's this way,' said John. 'They're supposed to put a new plate on for each course. That's the way the management wants it. If the waiter doesn't do it and one of the managers sees him, he gets fired on the spot.'

'I never heard of such a thing,' my father said.

'It's true,' said John. 'That waiter's probably worried plenty by now.'

'Well hell,' said my father. 'Tell him to take it then.'

One follow-up activity that is often used in ESL texts is to begin with comprehension questions like the following.

Was this the first incident the father had with the waiter?
What did the waiter say when the father refused to give him his plate?
How many times did the waiter attempt to take the plate?

The problem with such questions is that they seek to determine, in an efferent mode, the information that the student is carrying away from the text. Whereas this knowledge may be very important in reading scientific or business texts, this passage was obviously not written to relay the information that is required above.

A second common activity is to use the text to promote language skills on the level of usage. Thus, the use of the present and past tenses might be explored. Students could be asked to circle all the verbs in the past tense, to list the irregular past tense verbs, and to explain why the present tense is used in sentences such as the following: 'They're supposed to put a new plate on for each course. That's the way the management wants it.' However, since the text was not written to exemplify a contrast between the use of the present and past tenses in English, such activities create what Widdowson terms 'an inappropriate relationship' between the reader and the text.

Another alternative, which unfortunately is less frequently used, would be to explore the language of the text in terms of language use. In this case, students could list all of the waiter's comments:

'I'm sorry. I thought you were finished.'
'May I take your plate, sir?'
'But I have to put another plate there, sir.'
'Oh, it's no bother at all.'

Then the class could discuss why the waiter used 'sir' and 'may I'. They might also be asked to suggest the tone of voice used by the waiter in making these comments. Such activities would naturally result in an exploration of the role relationship of the father and the waiter, and could ultimately lead to an examination of the central concern of the passage; namely, the father's refusal to let the waiter take his plate and even more importantly the question of *why* he refuses to do so. Since any reader interacting with the text aesthetically cannot overlook this question, this is where an examination of the passage should begin. This discussion may lead back to a closer reading of the text, as readers point to what the father says about his refusal.

In aesthetic reading, a reader often relates his or her world of experience to the text. After reading the passage, students might be asked if anything similar has ever happened to them. The following response by one student to *Sweet Promised Land* was based on such a shared experience.

> The essay which I enjoyed reading the most is *Sweet Promised Land* because it is closely related to my family. The story of *Sweet Promised Land* talks about a father who came to the United States, but he is not fully adjusted in this new culture. He doesn't let the waiter take his plate, and he also wound his wallet with a black inner-tube band. As I remember, my mother needed to do that too when we just came over to the United States. She still puts a big band around her wallet.

Since in aesthetic reading, readers often make judgments about the characters, another follow-up activity might involve having the students comment on their opinion of the father, the son, or the waiter. Furthermore, in aesthetic reading a reader often fantasizes as to what he or she would do in a similar situation. Hence, students could be asked what they would have done if they had been the father, the son, or the waiter. Such discussion, it seems to me, goes much further toward promoting an interaction between the reader and the text than an exploration of the usage in the passage.

An interaction with a literary text depends on a reader's familiarity with the cultural assumptions in it. The excerpt from *Sweet Promised Land* contains several specific cultural assumptions. It is important that students understand these, for as Allen (1975: 111) puts it, 'Literature is a facet of a culture. Its significance can be best understood in terms of its culture, and its purpose is meaningful only when the assumptions it is based on are understood and accepted.' In this passage it is assumed that the reader understands that in a high-class restaurant a waiter must at all costs be polite, that the number of dishes and the amount of work needed to keep these dishes clean is inconsequential, and that loud confrontations are generally avoided. The son is aware of these assumptions, whereas the father obviously is not. Furthermore, since the son is aware of the problem, he tries as unobtrusively as possible to resolve the conflict.

In order to prepare students to deal with these assumptions, they might be asked to indicate if the following items are typical (T) or unusual (U) in exclusive American restaurants.

1 The number of dishes is kept to a minimum so as to reduce costs.
2 Each course is brought on a separate plate.
3 It is appropriate for a waiter to insist that he do his job even if the customer is unhappy.
4 It is appropriate for a customer to insist that a restaurant alter its standard procedures to meet his wishes.
5 Any conflict between waiter and customer is resolved in as quiet a manner as possible.

If a student is unaware of any of these assumptions, the context of the passage will help to illustrate what is appropriate and what is not appropriate. In this way the passage can serve to clarify the cultural expectations of a particular social context.

Conclusion

Literature does indeed have a place in the ESL curriculum. For many students, literature can provide a key to motivating them to read in English. For all students, literature is an ideal vehicle for illustrating language use and for introducing cultural assumptions. Our success in using literature, of course, greatly depends upon a selection of texts which will not be too difficult on either a linguistic or a conceptual level. Ultimately, however, if we wish to promote truly aesthetic reading, it is essential that literature be approached not efferently, but in a manner which establishes a personal and aesthetic interaction between a reader and a text.

13   Testing Language with Students of Literature in ESL Situations

J. P. Boyle

Passing your driving test means being able to drive the car well, not simply knowing the Highway Code and a manual on engine maintenance. Language testing nowadays, like language teaching, also stresses the ability to do something with the language, not merely to know about its formal characteristics: the rules of use are seen to be important, as well as the rules of grammar. Alan Davies's Survey Articles in *Language Teaching and Linguistics: Abstracts* (1978) outline well the new awareness of the problem of testing communicative competence as well as formal knowledge. Interestingly, he ends his careful and wide-ranging survey with the question: 'Is communicative testing feasible?'

Whatever our feelings on this, most people with experience in language testing would agree that a good test will contain both questions of a general nature and questions on more specific details, in other words integrative as well as discrete-point questions. If we accept this general position and turn to the business of testing students of literature in ESL situations, some interesting test types, both of a general and specific nature, can be suggested.

But first, some preliminary remarks on the validity of considering students of literature as a special group. I am thinking of the type of situation which is not uncommon, especially in tertiary education in Commonwealth or former Commonwealth countries, where the students who choose to do a degree in English must study a great deal of literature. However, their language ability is often not too good, particularly in countries where English is being spoken less and less and the mother tongue is taking over. There is a tendency in such circumstances to play down the relevance of literature in language teaching. This tendency is reinforced when English for Specific Purposes (ESP) becomes fashionable and the generalities of literature are considered less relevant to the students' needs than the more purpose-specific language of other disciplines—science, medicine, engineering.

More than half a century ago Ezra Pound refuted such thinking:

> And this function (of literature in the state) has to do with the clarity and vigour of any and every thought and opinion. It has to do with maintaining the very cleanliness of the tools, the health of the very matter of thought itself . . . When their (writers') work goes rotten–by that I do not mean when they express indecorous thoughts—but when their very medium, the very essence of their work, the application of word to thing, goes rotten, i.e. becomes slushy and inexact, or excessive and bloated, the whole machinery of social and individual thought and order goes to pot. This is a lesson of history, and a lesson not half learned. (Pound 1928)

So the first justification for keeping language teaching—and therefore testing—in touch with literature is that literature, being language at its most vigorous and clearest, keeps language 'clean and healthy'.

A recent issue of *Forum* shows a renewed interest in returning to literature as a source of texts for enjoyable and stimulating language teaching. Admitting to a slight guilt-feeling about using literature, one writer says:

> Most of us teach literature in the language class for exactly the same reason we are ashamed that we teach literature: stories and poetry are interesting. We enjoy them. The students enjoy them. Our attention is engaged, as it is rarely engaged by word-lists and exercises, for literature touches our common humanity. (Power 1981)

And in the conclusion to the first article of the same issue of *Forum*, Albert H. Marckwardt, the author of *The Place of Literature in the Teaching of English as a Second or Foreign Language* (1978), says:

> In our wholly justifiable concern with the language per se and with taking every possible advantage of the systematic study of language to facilitate the learning process, there is a danger of overlooking or undervaluing some of the uses to which language may be put, among them its function as a literary medium.

Teaching language to students of literature is in a sense ESP, with the paradoxical twist that the speciality of literature is the consideration of human nature at its broadest, its most general. In the medical field the specialist—the surgeon, the psychiatrist, the paediatrician—is considered the high-flyer; the poor old General Practitioner definitely a cut below. In language teaching ESP is felt by some to be more high-powered than general English. But with language, as with medicine, the specialist must first be an expert in his or her general field. And with language that general field is human nature in action—the realm of literature.

In this context, then, let us see what kinds of test would be appropriate to students of literature. Rather than speak in general terms, I will give examples where possible.

Reading

1 A short story is read, e.g. Frank O'Connor's *My Oedipus Complex*. Specific comprehension questions can be asked.

a What particular delight did climbing into his mother's bed in the morning give the boy?
b What incident brought the boy and his father together?

Short passages can be quoted and their significance in the story as a whole questioned:

a 'You must be quiet while Daddy is reading, Larry,' Mother said impatiently. It was clear that she either genuinely liked talking to Father better than talking to me, or else that he had some terrible hold on her which made her afraid to admit the truth. 'Mummy,' I said that night when she was tucking me up, 'do you think if I prayed hard God would send Daddy back to the war?'
b I pretended to be talking to myself, and said in a loud voice: 'If another bloody baby comes into this house, I'm going out.' Father stopped dead and looked at me over his shoulder. 'What's that you said?' he asked sternly. 'I was only talking to myself,' I replied, trying to conceal my panic. 'It's private.'

2 The literature student must be able to discriminate in reading, between facts that are non-essential and others which are of central symbolic significance. In D. H. Lawrence's *The Horse Dealer's Daughter*, for example, the relevance of the pool (into which the doctor wades to rescue the attempted suicide) could be questioned. This type of question tests not simply accuracy in remembering all the facts of a story—'vacuum-cleaner reading', as it has been called—but the power to appreciate the importance of certain facts—like the painting of the fence in *Tom Sawyer*.

3 *Cloze/Modified cloze.* The cloze test, together with dictation, has risen in the popularity polls. The Hong Kong Examining Board is happy with initial results from modified cloze (where the blank has three or four answers and the correct one has to be chosen—a multiple-choice question). All types of cloze test seem to be reliable: deleting every nth word, or deleting on a more rational basis; allowing only the exact word or accepting reasonable alternatives. For literature students the cloze is probably more valid, certainly more relevant, if something like the following can be given. It is taken from the text of an interview with Joyce Cary, the novelist, contained in the Paris Review Interviews, *Writers at Work*.

INTERVIEWER: Have you read *The Bostonians*? There was the spellbinder.
CARY: No, I haven't read that.

INTERVIEWER: *The Princess Casamassima?*

CARY: I'm afraid I haven't read that either. Cecil is always telling me to read her and I must. But I read James a good deal. There are times you need James, just as there are times when you must have Proust—in his very different ———— of change. The essential thing ———— James is that he came ———— a different, a highly organized, hieratic society, and for him ———— was not only a very ———— and highly civilized society, but ———— It was the best the ———— could do. But it was ———— subject to corruption. This was ———— center of James' moral idea— ———— everything good was, for that ———— specially liable to corruption. Any ———— of goodness, integrity of character, ———— that person to ruin. And ———— whole civilization, because it was ———— real civilization, cultivated and sensitive, ———— fearfully exposed to frauds and ———— brutes and grabbers. This was ———— tragic theme. But my world ———— quite different—it is intensely ———— a world in creation. In ———— world, politics is like navigation ———— a sea without charts and ———— men live the lives of pilgrims.

In this example I have deleted mechanically every sixth word. To guess the correct word in some cases may perhaps seem extremely difficult, even for the native speaker, e.g. 'static', which fills the seventh blank, or 'exposed', which fills the fourteenth. However, two things must be remembered: first, that such a short passage is not a real example of a cloze test; secondly, that with a longer passage, the same mental mechanics go on as in solving crossword puzzles—clue 3 across seems impossibly difficult until you get helped by discovering the answer to clue 5 down. Similarly with cloze, a word guessed later on in the passage gives a clue to an earlier word, e.g. 'dynamic', which fills the fourth last blank, would not be impossible to get, particularly with the help of 'a world in creation' immediately following it. And once 'dynamic' has been guessed, in the context of the whole passage, the earlier seventh blank might well be correctly filled too, 'static'.

INTERVIEWER: Have you read *The Bostonians?*

CARY: No, I haven't read that.

INTERVIEWER: *The Princess Casamassima?*

CARY: I'm afraid I haven't read that either. Cecil is always telling me to read her and I must. But I read James a good deal. There are times you need James, just as there are times when you must have Proust—in his very different world of change. The essential thing about James is that he came into a different, a highly organized, hieratic society, and for him it was not only a very good and highly civilized society, but static. It was the best the world could do. But it was already subject to corruption. This was the center of James' moral idea—that everything good was, for that reason, specially liable to corruption. Any kind of goodness, integrity of character, exposed that person to ruin. And the whole civilization, because it was a real civilization, cultivated and sensitive, was fearfully exposed to frauds and go-getters, brutes and grabbers. This was his tragic theme. But my world is quite different—it is intensely dynamic, a world in creation. In this world, politics is like navigation in a sea without charts and wise men live the lives of pilgrims.

Writing

1 *Vocabulary.* The literature student has to be more at home in words which describe the finer shades of human emotion. Basic feelings can be taken as the starting point. Then the student must find six words within the range of that broad feeling, and use the six words in a sentence. For example, ANGRY might turn up such words as: *raging/cross/peeved/annoyed/furious/fuming.* JOY: *happy/glad/over-joyed/pleased/cheerful/delighted.* FEAR: *terrified/afraid/dreading/apprehensive/anxious/nervous.* LOVE: *adore/like/be fond of/be attached to/be devoted to/be infatuated with.*

Another way is to give a picture of a face which expresses a complex of emotions. The Mona Lisa would be a good example. The student has to describe the face. Or a pair of pictures can be used, e.g. a self-portrait of Rembrandt and a self-portrait of Van Gogh. Works of art are usually more useful for this, in that they are more enigmatic, less explicit than most photographs. But good photographs can readily be found too.

2 Students of literature are no different from other ESL students in their tendency to make grammatical errors. I am concentrating here on test-types which seem to be particularly relevant, but by no means saying these are the only ones. In one type of test the grammatical accuracy may be the testing-point. In another, the student's power of imagination may be the important thing. 'The snow felled on the ground like flying-saucers landing' or 'The tree falled over like an oil-rig in the North Sea capsizing' should not be marked down because of the slip, 'felled' or 'falled'. I am *not* saying the student should not be 'felled' for such errors in a *grammar* test. Since simile and metaphor are so important in literature, simple tests can be devised. The student has to complete the sentence imaginatively:

a 'His face was wrinkled like ... '
'Her hair was flowing like ... '
'The old lady's teeth were black like ... '

b More difficult would be examples with two blanks:
'His face was ... like ... '
'Her hair was ... like ... '
'The old lady's teeth were ... like ... '

c With less control will come more variety and scope, as well as more difficulty:
'His . . . was . . . like . . . '
'Her . . . was . . . like . . . '
'The old lady's . . . was . . . like . . . '

3 To test appreciation of register, discrete-point examples like the following are useful:

a 'This old (person/chap/individual/gentleman) comes up to me and he says . . . '

b 'The butler bowed and (heaved/shoved/passed/donated) over the letter.'

More creatively, the student can be asked to write a short passage which deliberately aims at humour by means of mixing registers. P. G. Wodehouse is the master and model for this.

4 More global tests of writing would include composition, more or less controlled, or a free response to a text, tape, or film.

Listening

1 *Drama* on tape/radio. After a play has been listened to, response of a general nature can be required. What was the play really about? Or more specific answers could be demanded: match each of the following with one of the characters in the play—*wily/forthright/exuberant/discreet/retiring*. A problem with this type of question, of course, is that words describing character tend to be subtle in their nuances. However, this brings us back to the type of exercise under *Vocabulary* (above).

2 *Story*. Again, after hearing a story, a global response can be required: briefly retell the story, making sure you include what seems to you to be the main point. A more specific question would be: which of the following titles best suits the story you have heard? This would be a multiple-choice question, in effect, with one of the answers more obviously defensible objectively.

3 *Poetry*. I have said very little on the use of poetry in testing the language ability of literature students. It is of limited value, it seems to me, to use a poem for structural questions, asking the student to put the poem into 'plain English'. This can take the heart out of poetry, though in some cases, with extremely difficult poets (e.g. Hopkins), this exercise will be almost necessary for ESL students. A more relevant type of test question will test the literature student's ability to appreciate the way poetry charges words with different levels of meaning. 'To read poetry adequately a student must not only have a

command of lexis in the sense that he knows how to use a number of words; he must also know a number of possible uses for any given word.' A good example would be W. B. Yeats's 'The Song of the Old Mother'.

> I rise in the dawn, and I kneel and blow
> Till the seeds of the fire flicker and glow:
> And then I must scrub and bake and sweep
> Till stars are beginning to blink and peep;
> And the young lie long and dream in their bed
> Of the matching of ribbons for bosom and head,
> And their day goes over in idleness,
> And they sigh if the wind but lift a tress:
> While I must work because I am old,
> And the seed of the fire gets feeble and cold.

The student can be asked what 'the seed of the fire' means in the poem. Many examples of this kind can easily be found. I have included this exercise under listening, because poetry is essentially an oral exercise, but clearly it could be a test-type for reading comprehension too.

4 Oller makes much of dictation as a reliable test-type. For straight dictation, probably such occasional essays as J. B. Priestley's *Delight*, for instance, would be the most suitable.

A more difficult test, of the Dicto-Comp type, would be to read a section from a modern play, preferably a radio-play, and then to ask the student to fill in the missing dialogue, as well as can be remembered. The following brief example may serve as an illustration. This example deletes too much in too short a space, and is therefore more difficult than a real test; it merely gives the idea of the test-type. It comes from a prize-winning radio play by Jennifer Phillips, *Daughters of Men*.

KATE: Age. Photos, of course you can have retouched.
ANNE: What?
KATE: Bahama had her photo taken every week.
ANNE: She told you?
KATE: No, Boy did. But he doesn't understand. You can't retouch the image in the mirror.
ANNE: But you have so much else to draw on, Kate . . . inner strengths.
KATE: And I shall be much freer.
ANNE: Oh, yes.
KATE: Without a child.
ANNE: But you won't be without.
KATE: Best to be prepared, isn't it? On the defensive. I always went round before exams at school saying I'd fail, didn't you? Saying I

had to fail because I hadn't worked at it.

ANNE: The thought of exams struck me dumb.

KATE: Your driving test! Oh, I'll never forget that. And the lead up to it. And then I practically carried you there.

KATE: Age. Photos, of course, you can have retouched.

ANNE: What?

KATE: Bahama had her photo taken every week.

ANNE: _____

KATE: No, Boy did. But he doesn't understand. You can't retouch the image in the mirror.

ANNE: But you have so much else to draw on, Kate . . . inner strengths.

KATE: _____

ANNE: Oh, yes.

KATE: Without a child.

ANNE: But you won't be without.

KATE: _____

On the defensive. I always went round before exams at school saying I'd fail, didn't you? Saying I had to fail because I hadn't worked at it.

ANNE: _____

KATE: Your driving test! Oh, I'll never forget that. And the lead up to it. And then I practically carried you there.

Speaking

1 *Reading aloud.* The difficulties of oral production tests are well outlined in J. B. Heaton's *Writing English Language Tests.* For testing appreciation of the meaning of a text, his recommendation of combining specific features with general fluency seems sound. For students of literature, the dimension of reproducing feeling or emotion in a text should also be tested, with some sort of dramatic reading. This kind of test will, of course, be affected by all sorts of extraneous factors, and these can hardly be overcome.

2 *Conversation/Discussion.* In ideal test conditions, with small numbers involved, the tester should be able, not so much to conduct a conversation with the student (this examiner/examinee situation can render real conversation pretty well impossible), but to observe two students conversing. With the importance which conversational dialogue has in both the novel and in drama, it is an area which should have a place in testing, but the problems of assessment are obvious. Probably as good a general test as any for literature students is to let them view a short play on video, after which the examiner asks them,

pair by pair, to discuss the play while he or she sits in on the discussion. A library of suitable video plays can easily be built up.

3 Other suggestions could be short talks on the work/life and times of major literary figures; and here pictures or slides, useful in all sorts of ways in testing spoken English, could be assembled by the student, and the project assessed as a whole.

Conclusion

David Daiches claims that in literature students can achieve 'the fullest possible awareness of human relevance' (1970). And an African writer in *ELT Journal* says: 'We have become so convinced that learning ESL means acquiring skills that the teaching of literature seems to have become of much less significance. ESL teachers do not seem to give much importance to the educational values of the literature they teach' (Adeyanju 1978). In a sense it is true of language teachers that, by their tests, you shall know them. This chapter has done no more than suggest a few test types which will show our students that we do respect the relevance of literature and that we do consider educational values in our teaching and our testing.

14 Simple Text and Reading Text
Part 1: Some General Issues

Monica Vincent

Simplicity, except of the most skilfully contrived kind, is hardly a characteristic of literary text. Works of literature are verbal works of art, distinguished by their sophistication, subtlety, and complexity. For a true appreciation of these 'verbal artefacts' the reader must bring to the text linguistic, conceptual, and cultural understanding of a high order. It is illuminating to consider the Common Core Recommendations for the examination of English Literature at Advanced Level in Britain.

Aim

To encourage an enjoyment and appreciation of English Literature based on an informed personal response and to extend this appreciation where it has already been acquired.

Skills tested

1 Knowledge—of the content of the books and where appropriate of the personal and historical circumstances in which they were written.
2 Understanding—extending from simple factual comprehension to a broader conception of the nature and significance of literary texts.
3 Analysis—the ability to recognise and describe literary effects and to comment precisely on the use of language.
4 Judgement—the capacity to make judgements of value based on close reading.
5 Sense of the Past and Tradition—the ability to see a literary work in its historical context as well as that of the present day.
6 Expression—the ability to write organised and cogent essays on literary subjects.

Content

Candidates will be required to offer for examination a minimum of six texts consisting of at least one play by Shakespeare, some poetry and at least one example of a genre other than poetry.

Implicit in these recommendations is an emphasis on the advanced reading skills essential for the successful study of literature by mother-tongue speakers at the end of a secondary-school career. Yet this list of aims and skills would not be considered out of place in many contexts where English is taught as a second or foreign language. There is a long and honourable tradition of seeing an appreciation of literature as the pinnacle of foreign-language achievement, intensified in the case of English by the fact that its literature is widely considered the greatest achievement of English-speaking peoples. The choice of authentic literary texts, and ways of approaching them, forms the substance of several papers in this volume. I wish to focus on a feature of English language teaching that is not, to my knowledge, at all prevalent in the study of other foreign languages and literature: the use of simple text, and its role in the development of the reading skills necessary for the eventual direct approach to authentic works of English literature.

It can, I think, be taken for granted that original works of English literature are not accessible to foreign learners of English at the start of their course, or indeed for some time to come. The native speaker does not encounter original works of English literature early in a school career, though familiarity with important authors and famous works is often achieved through special versions for children—for example, Lamb's *Tales from Shakespeare* in the nineteenth century, or more recently through film and television adaptations. Many British educators have queried the linguistic (and sometimes cultural) accessibility of our major writers, especially Shakespeare, for all students, and there has been a move away from the classical to more contemporary writing at secondary-school level. In short, literary text would seem to be considered too difficult for most native-speaker schoolchildren to read. They need something simpler.

For the foreign reader, literary text will usually be even more linguistically difficult, though some works may be culturally more accessible than they are to students in modern urban Britain. Motivation to tackle a famous writer's work is often considerably higher, and depending on age and educational level, maturity as a reader may be greater. These positive factors can, however, lead individual learners to a premature attempt to tackle literary text, and result in laborious word-by-word deciphering with the aid of a bilingual dictionary. This is neither an efficient approach to reading any material in a foreign language, nor an appropriate or desirable way in which to experience works of literature. It is a painstaking process far removed from genuine reading with response.

Similar problems arise in situations where English is a second language and the secondary school examination syllabus still consists of classical literary texts. Students spend two years studying their set books (and considerable sums on examination cribs) instead of developing a broader and deeper understanding of writing in English. Both at individual and institutional level, a worthy desire to read what is 'worthwhile' can result in an almost worthless reading process. Factors of tradition or prestige override both the common-sense criterion of providing comprehensible input, and the educational principle of designing the syllabuses to promote gradual and systematic development of the learners' capacities and experience. One question that has to be asked is 'Are we choosing the right books for the right learners at the right stage in their course?' Another is 'Have we found the right way to teach the right books?'

The traditional assumption in English language teaching, especially in situations where English was the medium of education, was to offer the same literary diet overseas as in Britain, and to attempt to make the route to it easier by the extensive use of graded Readers. English abounds in simplified versions of famous works of literature, from simple synopses of Shakespeare through many kinds of 'stories retold' to abridged novels similar in aim and scope to the condensed books featured in some monthly magazines. A glance at any publisher's list of graded Readers or a collated bibliography such as Brumfit (1979) reveals a preponderance of literary titles, including several rival versions, at different levels, of major classics such as *Oliver Twist* or *Pride and Prejudice*. What purpose does this predominance of simplified literature serve?

The first and possibly most important one is motivational. As Dr Michael West wrote:'Few things are more encouraging to a child who knows some (say) 1,500 words of English than to pick up a book written within that vocabulary and find that he is actually able to read it and enjoy a story which is (at least) an enthralling approximation of the original.' (West 1950)

The second is more pragmatic. Great writers provide good story lines, and long-dead writers provide free ones, for they are out of copyright. Pedestrian pedagogues find it easier to adapt the work of an original and imaginative writer than to generate good simple stories themselves. It is interesting to note in this connection that there is little parallel in literature with the tradition of the musical world, where great composers often write works specially for newcomers to their art. J. S. Bach's *Anna Magdalena Notebooks*, written for his young wife, and Bartok's *Microcosmos* for children are examples of works designed for those learning to play an instrument. There is also an attractive repertoire for the young listener, such as Prokofiev's *Peter and the Wolf*, or Britten's *Young Person's Guide to the Orchestra*. It seems that the abstract code of sound used to create musical works of art is more amenable to simplification than the human languages deployed in the creation of works of literature. Easy Bach is still good music, recognizably by Bach, but simplified literary texts cannot usually be classified as literature. They are qualitatively different.

The essential feature of simplification is reduction, and this can result in loss. The original book is shortened, the number of characters, situations, and events cut, the vocabulary restricted, and the use of structures controlled. More significantly, perhaps, any unusual use of language—colloquialisms, idiom, metaphor, allusion—tends to be ruthlessly expunged, and any ambiguity or uncertainty in the text resolved. My favourite example of inappropriate clarification occurs in the preliminary pages of the version of *Rebecca* by Daphne du Maurier published in the *Longman Simplified English Series*.

> The story is told by the second wife of Maxim de Winter. Their home is at Manderley, in the West of England. Rebecca was the name of Maxim de Winter's first wife.

Given the degree of simplification claimed by the series, it seems a pity to remove the opportunity for foreign readers to use their imagination to work out these key facts in the same way as native speakers do in reading the original text. As the notes on the series explain:

> There are very few words used which are outside the learner's vocabulary (the 2,000 root words of the General Service List of English Words of the Interim Report on Vocabulary Selection). These few extra words are needed for the story and are explained when they first appear. Long sentences and difficult sentence patterns have been simplified. The resulting language is good and useful English, and the simplified book keeps much of the charm and flavour of the original.

In the case of *Rebecca* it also loses one of its main literary features. There seems to be an intrinsic conflict here between the actuality of a simplified text and the express aim of the series:

> to enable thousands of readers to enjoy without great difficulty some of the best books written in the English language, and in doing so, to equip themselves in the pleasantest possible way, to understand and appreciate any work written in English.

To understand and appreciate 'any work written in English' demands a far greater command of vocabulary than 2,000 words, and an ability to tolerate and resolve uncertainty for oneself.

Most grading schemes establish a given list of structures and lexis, with rules for adding necessary extra vocabulary which the adaptor or simplifier has to follow. Some schemes, such as that used in the Heinemann *Guided Reader Series*, also try to specify how to control the flow of information, and reduce cultural overload. The status of these schemes is increasingly open to doubt. Lexical lists all seem to be based ultimately on 1930s word counts, and the approach to structural grading is also fairly dated, certainly in the older series where, for example, there is no use of the past tense, and thus no normal story narrative, in Level One Readers. There is no certainty that learners will in fact have met or mastered the language items freely allowed at any level, so it cannot therefore be assumed they will be able to work out new items from a background of known linguistic context. On the other hand, some learners may have a degree of prior knowledge or interest that enables them to make sense of much of the text, irrespective of their linguistic limitations. Why protect a French student from a device such as flash-back?

If the final result of the simplification process is merely a synopsis or report of the original work, is the effort worth it? One published novelist who decided to write an original story at the level of Longman Structural Readers, Stage 1, remarked, 'It's like trying to box in a telephone booth.' He also had a battle to retain his one 'literary' line at this basic level: 'The trees on the slope wear heavy hats of snow.' All the words had already occurred or been illustrated in the story, so the foreign reader should be able to employ the same process as in the mother tongue to understand the 'unusual' expression. Learners of English do not necessarily possess rigidly literal minds, but editorial insistence on using language only in its most obvious, everyday sense will prevent them from developing an awareness of the range of meanings possible in English, and hinder their preparation for real works of literature. Too many graded Readers are pale imitations of original writing, in thin, stilted language, lacking all the linguistic, emotional, and aesthetic qualities that characterize real literature. A diet of simplified versions of great books can be demotivating, as West himself admits:

> Simplification and abridgement have brought to life not a few books which, for the foreign reader and the English schoolchild, would otherwise be completely dead: they have also murdered not a few whose lives might have been saved. (West 1950)

West was a keen advocate of simple texts, and rightly insisted that simplification was an art to be tackled with sensitivity and professionalism. In recent years, however, the basic idea of simplifying literary, or any text, for the foreign reader has been under review, if not attack. West's view was that the right way to the right books was through simplified versions of authentic literature, finding the right level of Reader for each stage. But should works of art be cut and stitched in this way? Are simplified versions of an original work really the optimum route to authentic literature? Should learners be exposed to carefully constructed simple text of any kind, either in the rigid order of the levels of a graded Reader series, or more randomly?

There are some interesting trends in writing for the foreign reader. As twentieth-century books come out of copyright there are more relatively modern tales to be retold, and there has been a marked move towards more popular fiction: detective stories, romances, airport blockbusters, thrillers, etc., which may not be great literature but offer a good read within recognizable genres. The development of a flourishing group of Commonwealth writers in English has provided accessible reading material for secondary schools overseas and more vareity of examination choice. The response to Heinemann's *African Writers Series*, for example, has been excellent, not least from teachers who find they can encourage in their students 'an enjoyment and appreciation of English literature based on an informed personal response' not always possible with a syllabus dominated by British or American writers.

The widening of English literature to include literature in English has opened a new, promising route to literary understanding. It is also worth considering the use of translations into English of foreign works of literature, even perhaps from the learner's mother tongue, as familiarity with the author and the work may provide an excellent opportunity to read a whole, real book in English. Children will often spontaneously pick on a story they already know in their own language, such as 'Cinderella', when choosing an English book to read, because they know they will enjoy responding to a favourite story in a different linguistic form. They have discovered their own kind of simple text: a familiar story in a strange language.

Conversely, given the amount of English reading material that has been translated into other languages, it can be helpful to start people off on the path to full understanding and appreciation by encouraging them to read English literature in their own language. A translation provides far more than a report or synopsis of a work, and, if well done, will retain much of the flavour of the original. Wide reading of literature in translation makes the task of understanding a particular text in the foreign language much simpler, because the work is set in context. The reader has acquired through rapid reading in the mother tongue some conception of the nature and significance of English literary texts. Meanwhile the ability to read the English language with confidence and fluency can be simultaneously built up on other kinds of reading matter.

I would advocate the extensive use of simple texts in the early stages of developing reading skills, but with an emphasis on non-fiction 'simple accounts' (Widdowson 1979) rather than simplified versions of well-known literature. It is easier to produce good examples of explanation, description, and argument in simple English than either lively original stories or viable simplifications of existing text, and it is arguably a more authentic approach. Teachers of other subjects are all in the simplification business, all involved in the process of making ideas and information linguistically and conceptually accessible to the learner. Novelists, dramatists, and poets have other ends in view.

At an intermediate stage I would include lighter works of fiction from the various series of graded Readers to be read rapidly in the students' own time, and possibly a couple of abridged classics or fairly reputable works of the second rank for study in class. One advantage of the reduction in length and complexity of a simplified version of a standard text is that it provides an opportunity for literary-like behaviour. The characters, however limited their redrawing, can be discussed, the plot summarized, and the issues discussed. This analysis in miniature of a scaled-down work can be a useful training in how to approach a real book, and an introduction to making judgements of value.

So far I have made no mention of the current demand for the use of authentic or genuine texts, by which is meant reading material originally written for a native-speaker audience, at all times from the start of the course. This issue has been discussed elsewhere, but I would emphasize the importance of providing learners with easily-accessible reading material, in the early stages of the course. This may mean using specially written texts, though they need not be simplified according to existing grading schemes, which match the learners' conceptual and linguistic level sufficiently well to encourage an authentic response to the text. Selective scanning for information or decipherment with a dictionary are two common kinds of response to difficult authentic texts, but if our eventual aim is to facilitate the close reading of literary texts, learners must also be exposed to texts that can be tackled in detail, and in the same way as works in their mother tongue. In fact, relatively simple authentic texts tend to be chosen for use in lower-level reading classes, which would seem to be an implicit admission of the priority of simplicity over authenticity as a criterion for choice in the provision of reading material.

From a literary point of view there are two particularly interesting types of authentic text: children's literature and certain short works of adult literature. An interesting approach to developing reading skills taken by some adults has been to try working their way up through a foreign literature, by starting with children's picture books, progressing through folk and fairy tales, graduating to junior and teenage good fiction, and finally reaching 'real' literature for adults. Another tradition, especially in parts of Europe, has been to study short stories as examples of good literature. Stories are less daunting than novels simply by being shorter, and they are usually easier than either plays or poetry by being in prose. The success of relatively short books, such as *Animal Farm* or *The Old Man and the Sea*, may lie in their combination of brevity and straightforward language with demanding content. The comparative linguistic simplicity of these texts enables the learner to respond to them as works of literature, not as reading puzzles. So, the success of certain authentic texts in developing fluency and confidence in reading would seem to depend on a natural reduction of factors that can obscure or confuse, remarkably similar to the 'artificial' criteria for writing simplified Readers. Whether selected or constructed, simple texts may be the most appropriate means to the desired end of reading a wide range of more advanced material.

If the use of simple text is the right way to bring learners to the right books, are the right books necessarily works of literature? I would make two suggestions in conclusion. Literature should be interpreted far more widely, as it was in (ancient) classical times, to include well-written works of non-fiction: history, biography, philosophy, politics, and agricultural advice. This would mean that a course of simplified accounts could lead progressively and logically on to more difficult text incorporating the communicative features of non-fiction writing: exposition, narration, description, argument. Secondly, I would advocate a revision of schemes for grading simple text, with more emphasis put on vocabulary building and on the carefully contextualized inclusion, within the necessary reductions and restrictions, of features found in all kinds of normal writing, such as phrasal verbs, figurative language, and the use of inference.

A greater range of simple texts and a richer use of language within them would be more appropriate material for the development of reading skills in general, and a better bridge to works of literature in particular. Foreign students cannot suddenly start 'to recognise and describe literary effects and to comment precisely on the use of language' if they have been exposed only to unnaturally restricted language use. The extreme alternative to the use of simple text, an insistence on a diet of authentic material which has not been simplified, doctored, or filtered in any way, can create worse problems, such as desperate reliance on a dictionary at all times. Some kind of simple text remains the most suitable kind of reading material in the early stages of learning a foreign language, and some system of graded progression as the course proceeds is essential. But our concepts of simplification and grading need to be more subtle and sophisticated if we wish not only to build up our students' fluency and confidence in understanding written English, but also hope to lead them to an enjoyment and appreciation of English literature, widely conceived.

Simple Text and Reading Text
Part 2: Some Categories of Difficulty

Ronald Carter

Monica Vincent has reviewed some general issues germane to the relationship between simple texts and reading processes. In this section[1] the aim is to extend discussion by suggesting some *categories* of difficulty in canonical English literary texts. However, although discussion may lead to some refinement of our concepts of simplification and of grading texts for teaching purposes, at the present stage of research any list of categories will be necessarily provisional.

Linguistic structural criteria

As Monica Vincent has already pointed out, a first category should involve linguistic criteria. The different levels of language can each play a part here. Thus, a work like Dylan Thomas's *Under Milk Wood* may be complex at the level of phonology as a result of its dense phonaesthetic effects and phonetically inventive neologisms; or the lexical inventory of a text may cause difficulties as a result of philological change (e.g. words like *nice*, *own*, *wit*); as a result of Latinate origins (though this may make things easier for students from Latin countries); because of regionalisms (common, for example, in Hardy's prose and poetry); or because of 'lexical mixing' (see below); or simply as a result of general infrequency. Syntactic complexity can take many forms, but the most obvious feature would be sentence length and related dependencies, embeddings, and subordinations. Novelists within 'The Great Tradition' tend to fall within this category. The opening to Henry James's *The Ambassadors* (with its subtle and thematically-motivated double negatives, subject postponements and rankshifts especially prominent) serves as a well-tried example. Such syntactic complexity also abounds in George Eliot's *Middlemarch*:

> Certainly these men who had so few spontaneous ideas might be very useful members of society under good feminine direction, if they were fortunate in choosing their sisters-in-law! It is difficult to say whether there was or was not a little

> wilfulness in her continuing blind to the possibility that another sort of choice was in question in relation to her. But her life was just now full of hope and action: she was not only thinking of her plans, but getting down learned books from the library and reading many things hastily (that she might be a little less ignorant in talking to Mr. Casaubon), all the while being visited with conscientious questionings whether she were not exalting these poor doings above measure and contemplating them with that self-satisfaction which was the last doom of ignorance and folly.

But there are difficulties, too, at levels of linguistic organization which reside beyond the sentence. In many modernist texts this can involve a deliberate suspension or even absence of intersentential cohesion. Designed, as this often is, simultaneously to reproduce and represent a sense of disorientation, such incoherence can also produce an effect of confusion for which a student trained to make rational sense of text may be unwilling to seek aesthetic or thematic motivation. Examples of such modernist texts here would be T. S. Eliot's early poems, imagist poetry generally, novels by Joyce and Faulkner (especially in the case of the latter *The Sound and the Fury* where, admittedly, one aim is to represent the mentally-retarded consciousness of a main character). (The term 'modernist', by the way, designates a particular type of literary presentation and is not automatically equivalent to modern.) The organization of spoken discourse can also present problems of both understanding and interpretation, particularly in the case of texts which seek to exploit the creative possibilities and dramatic tensions inherent in the breaking of rules for turn-taking or in breaks in expected sequential patterns of support for the topic, in the duration of pauses, *non sequiturs*, etc. Several of Pinter's plays, while often simple in lexis, are demanding at such levels of language organization. Take, for example, the following extract from *The Dumb Waiter*:

Gus: I want to ask you something
Ben: What are you doing out there?
Gus: Well, I was just . . .
Ben: What about the tea?
Gus: I'm just going to make it
Ben: Well, go on, make it
Gus: Yes, I will
(*He sits in a chair. Ruminatively.*)
  He's laid on some very nice crockery this time. I'll say that. It's sort of striped. There's a white stripe.
(*Ben reads*)
Gus: It's very nice. I'll say that
(*Ben turns the page*)

Attempts to 'simplify' such examples as this would have to embrace a regularization of the exchange which would reduce the semantic density interpretable in the deliberate deviation from norms of expectation. (For further discussion of issues of translation of medium, see Davies and Widdowson 1974.) Students need to be assisted in making sense of such texts by seeking motivations for such uses of language; but much more research is required before a principled basis is available for progressive and graded introduction to different kinds of linguistic deviation.

Finally, it must be pointed out that linguistically simple texts are not necessarily readable in quite the way that students might suppose. For example, the repetition by a writer such as Hemingway of the kind of uncomplicated syntax and lexis found in early basal readers does not guarantee that such texts are easy to read with full literary understanding. Accounting adequately for the *effect* of such repetitions and for the kind of representation of content which results can create further orders of difficulty. (For fuller discussion of the linguistic constituents of readability in a range of text types, see Perera 1982; Cripwell and Foley 1984.) Such 'simple' texts may also be organized in unconventional ways in terms of narrative structure. Hemingway's short stories regularly lack conventional 'orientation', 'evaluation', and 'coda' (see the paper by Carter in this volume on related patterning in a short story by Maugham). Thus, while *linguistic* criteria will always form an important category, analysis of language and structure has clearly to be related to purposes and functions of language in use.

Marked language

Another relevant criterion of difficulty would be language which is marked for period, region, or social class; that is, language which has historical, geographical, or socio-cultural associations. Of these the language associated with social groups at particular times can be notably opaque. The oppositions created as a result in a play like John Osborne's *Look Back in Anger*—understanding of which is anyway in part dependent on a knowledge of the British class system—would be an example. More context-specific still in this regard, largely because of subtle time warps, are novels by Evelyn Waugh such as *Vile Bodies*, with its comic burlesque of the speech mannerisms of the 'bright young things' in the late 1920s ('It's just *too* sick-making!'), or *Decline and Fall*, the humour of which is dependent on a knowledge of the public school system and of the lexis in passages such as the following, with its overtones of social class:

Mr Sniggs, the Junior Dean, and Mr Postlethwaite, the Domestic Bursar, sat alone in Mr Sniggs' room overlooking the garden quad at Scone College. From the rooms of Sir Alastair Digby-Vane-Trumpington, two staircases away, came a confused roaring and breaking of glass. They alone of the senior members of Scone were at home that evening, for it was the night of the annual dinner of the Bollinger Club. The others were all scattered over Boar's Hill and North Oxford at gay, contentious little parties, or at other senior common-rooms, or at the meetings of learned societies, for the annual Bollinger dinner is a difficult time for those in authority.

It is not accurate to call this an annual event, because quite often the Club is suspended for some years after each meeting. There is tradition behind the Bollinger; it numbers reigning kings among its past members. At the last dinner, three years ago, a fox had been brought in in a cage and stoned to death with champagne bottles. What an evening that had been! This was the first meeting since then, and from all over Europe old members had rallied for the occasion. For two days they had been pouring into Oxford: epileptic royalty from their villas of exile; uncouth peers from crumbling country seats; smooth young men of uncertain tastes from embassies and legations; illiterate lairds from wet granite hovels in the Highlands; ambitious young barristers and Conservative candidates torn from the London season and the indelicate advances of debutantes; all that was most sonorous of name and title was there for the beano.

Here explanation of the social system and associations underlying words such as 'lairds', 'Conservative candidates', 'debutantes', 'senior common-room', 'learned societies', 'title', 'country seats', as well as names such as Postlethwaite, Digby-Vane-Trumpington, Scone, and Bollinger has to be supplied prior to discussion of the meaning and effect of words like 'indelicate', 'illiterate', 'crumbling', and 'beano'.

Verbal comic effects are in any case notoriously impervious to translation or simplification, and within this category Waugh would appear a difficult writer for non-native readers, although his novels appear regularly on literature syllabuses overseas. Within this category, too, we should note the difficulties inherent in explaining a phrase such as *It was necessarily a registry-office wedding* (see the paper by Short and Candlin in this volume), or items such as 'four aways' (from the British football pools), or references to landladies, 'digs', seaside 'saucer souvenirs' or the associations created in the British imagination by the towns of Stoke and Frinton (all featured in Philip Larkin's poem 'Mr. Bleaney').

In terms of the marking of regional Englishes, too, it is necessary to investigate more thoroughly, and in the light of questions raised by Kachru in this volume, the extent to which different degrees of resistance are encountered to texts involving British regional variations and international varieties of English. In other words, would students in, say, Singapore or Malaysia reading Philippine literature in English (e.g. a novel by Sionil Jose, N. V. M. Gonzalez, or Nick Joaquin) or vice versa (e.g. short stories and novels by Catherine Lim or Lloyd Fernando, or poetry by Edwin Thumboo, Arthur Yap, or Lee Tzu Pheng) be more motivated to overcome regional variants than they would to master the kind of regionalisms found in novels by Hardy and Arnold Bennett?

Content and response

This last question invokes the essentially non-linguistic criterion of the extent of identification made by a reader with the writer's *culture* in the broadest sense of the word, i.e. his or her presuppositions, themes, areas of concern, attitudes to ways of living, and so on. In terms of historical context, a further important question to ask is whether the notion is valid that modern literary texts are easier because they are more 'contemporary' and closer in theme and content, as well as in language. An extreme point of comparison here would be between W. H. Auden's poetry, with its thematic emphasis on alienation from an urbanized, impersonal world as well as its stylistically heterogeneous mixture of regional, social, and occupational registers (see the extract from 'Mundus et Infans' cited in the introduction to this book) and the poetry of eighteenth-century poets such as Goldsmith or Crabbe. Indeed, the archaisms of Goldsmith may be less impenetrable than Auden's 'modernist' syntactic ellipses and lexical mixing; but, more importantly for this category, for many students in many parts of the world, the concerns of Goldsmith or Crabbe with the break-up of rural communities can produce a more direct and imaginative response to what is read. Related points of comparison may be between different responses to English nature poetry (with its culture-specific 'responses' to sun, clouds, rain, mountains, daffodils) or between responses to those plays by Shakespeare which explore revenge morality in tightly-knit patriarchal communities. In such comparisons different responses to the content are likely to be geographically, socially, and culturally relative.

Authorial position

It is important to recognize a criterion such as *the position of the author*. The extent to which the author or an appointed narrator mediates between the text and the reader can be crucial to an understanding of or a response to the literary material. There are times, for example, when according to a number of the above criteria, George Eliot is a difficult writer; in some places, however, the reader is guided narratorially and a gloss is provided:

> When Mr. Stelling said, as the roast beef was being uncovered, 'Now, Tulliver, which would you rather decline, roast beef or the Latin for it?' Tom, to whom in his coolest moments a pun would have been a hard nut, was thrown into a state of embarrassed alarm . . . Of course he answered 'Roast beef'—whereupon there followed much laughter . . . from which Tom gathered that he had in some mysterious way refused roast beef, and, in fact, made himself appear 'a silly'.
>
> (George Eliot, *The Mill on the Floss*)

Of course, some readers may have resistance to such glossing, and this may create another order of difficulty. Such examples do not push readers into making their own inferences, as Monica Vincent recommends; but, in the ordering of a student's acquisition of reading competence, the position of the author in particular texts can affect the position of the reader. And, correspondingly, greater difficulty can result from texts with multiple points of view or which offer no single position of intelligibility or, as in the case of 'free indirect discourse' (see Leech and Short 1981: Ch. 10), where there are different clines of merger between character and authorial position.

There are, of course, many other candidates for inclusion in any set of categories of difficulty; and some may warrant greater primacy than the above-mentioned. We should perhaps consider the place of 'children's literature' in a reading programme. Is it 'easy' or 'difficult'? How far might the presentation of such texts be felt by students to be patronizing? To what extent is identification with content possible? What are the criteria by which children's literature can appeal to adults (see the chapter by Long in this volume)? Another question for consideration is to what extent the *intertextuality* of a work creates difficulties or provides an established context for reading. The issue here is one to do with breadth of reading and with reading for fluency (see the discussion in Parts Two and Three of this volume, especially papers by Pickett and Brumfit). It involves the difficulties and necessities (or otherwise) of readers interrelating texts, both formalistically, as part of a particular literary semiotic, and in terms of both tradition and treatment of content. It forces us to ask whether a text is difficult because it depends for its understanding on the relations it contracts with other texts, and whether texts can be graded relative to particular traditions, genres, or thematic parallelisms. It suggests, for example, that texts in a tradition of realist prose should normally be studied before non-representational varieties, though reading experiences will be severely restricted if students are confined to such texts. In a related way, literary texts which are dense in cultural, historical, or literary *allusion* will generate a further layer of difficulty.

This consideration of categories of difficulty could be extended in a number of ways, not least with further reference to distinctions between fiction and non-fiction and to 'literariness' in texts not conventionally considered literary (see the papers in this volume by Vincent, Short and Candlin, and Carter; and the first part of the Introduction). Several criteria of difficulty have been suggested here. Basically, a text which met each of the four main criteria above would probably be agreed to be a difficult one. But we do not know how many criteria to invoke, or in what kind of hierarchy to rank the different criteria. And although the medium of 'expression' remains a resolutely linguistic one, measurement of texts in terms of the imaginative responses they create or the extent to which specific themes provoke emotional and intellectual involvement will depend more on relative experiences of different individuals, and any selection or grading will demand more of the teacher's teaching experience. Analysis along a cline or clines of simplicity and difficulty requires teachers to be alert to stylistic analysis, but also to an increasing range of non-linguistic criteria. As Monica Vincent suggests, it involves recognition not only of what is *in* the lines, but of what is *between* and beyond the lines, too.

Note

1 The discussion here owes much to papers and debate on this topic at a conference on literature teaching held in Naples, Italy in December 1983 and organized by the British Council and the University of Naples. Although they may not wish to associate themselves with the points raised here, I am grateful to discussion generated by, among others, David Hart, Janet Kezich, John McRae, and Anita Weston.

15   Literature in Schools[1]

Ngugi wa Thiong'o

The current debate about literature in our schools has shown that we Kenyans are very concerned over the literary diet now being ladled out to our children. This is as it should be. For education is a mirror unto a people's social being. It has been a major ideological battlefield between the economic, political, and cultural forces of oppression and the forces for national liberation and unity. Hence, the education system of us Kenyans was one of the first national fortresses to be stormed by the colonial spiritual policemen preparing and subsequently guarding the way for the permanent siege of the oppressed by all the other occupation armies of British imperialism.

The debate has raised four main issues with questions that go well beyond the problem of literature alone. These issues are as follows: (1) *The relevance and adequacy of the present education system*: What is the philosophy behind it? What are its premises and guidelines? What and whose social vision is it setting out to serve? On the basis of our answers to the above, what area and what sort of literature should we be teaching in our schools? (2) *The decision-making personnel*: Who should take crucial decisions regarding our cultural and literary programmes—foreigners or nationals? Who should determine what, and how, we are teaching in our schools? (3) *The teaching staff*: Should we still recruit and retain imperialist foreigners to teach literature, language, history, and culture in our schools? Should we in fact continue employing imperialist foreigners to interpret our being to ourselves? (4) *Approaches to literature*: What is our guiding world outlook as teachers of literature? What is our attitude to literature as a reflection of society? On whose side are we when interpreting literature? To help which side in the social struggle?

The debate has tended to centre on the third issue, whether or not we should continue employing foreigners, and while this is an important matter, it has overshadowed the other three problems and has helped to obscure the main and real thrust of the report and recommendations of the working committee appointed in 1973 to assess the teaching of literature in Kenyan schools. The report of the committee in fact gave more space to the first two issues with comments, observations, and conclusions based on the assumption that literature is a very crucial reflection of a society.

The report completely rejected the notion that a child in Nairobi can only know itself by studying London first; by first immersing itself in a European writer's imaginative responses to his countryside and to his history; the notion, in other words, that a Kenyan child's route to self-realization must be via European heritages and cultures. The price we pay for these Eurocentric studies of ourselves is the total distortion and misplacement of values of national liberation, making us continue to be slaves to imperialism.

Literature, the report argues, reflects the life of a people. It reflects in word images a people's creative consciousness of their struggles to mould nature through co-operative labour and in the process acting on and changing themselves. It reflects in word images a people's consciousness of the tensions and conflicts arising out of their struggles to mould a meaningful social environment founded on their combined actions on nature to wrest the means of life: clothing, food and shelter. Literature thus contains people's images of themselves in history and of their place in the universe.

What images are presented to a Kenyan child through the literature he reads in Kenyan national schools? Let us be frank. Being a student of literature in today's Kenya means being an English student. Our children are taught the history of English literature and language from the unknown author of Beowulf to T. S. Eliot. They are made to recite, with ethereal faces and angelic voices, poems in praise or censure of the retiring unreachable haughtily coy mistress, a remnant of the courtly love games of the idle European feudal classes:

Go, lovely Rose!
Tell her, that wastes her time and me
That now she knows,
When I resemble her to thee,
How sweet and fair she seems to be.[2]

They recite poems which are an English writer's nostalgic response to his landscape:

I sing of brooks, of blossoms, birds and bowers:
Of April, May, of June, and July-flowers.
I sing of May-poles . . . [3]

They sing of the beauty of England and of the changing seasons:

Fair daffodils, we weep to see
You haste away so soon:
As yet the early-rising sun
Has not attain'd his noon.[4]

The children are mesmerized by winter in a polluted British industrial setting and so they faithfully chant about:

The yellow fog that rubs its back upon the window-panes,
The yellow smoke that rubs its muzzle on the window-panes;
Licked its tongue into the corners of the evening,
Lingered upon the pools that stand in drains,
Let fall upon its back the soot that falls from chimneys,
Slipped by the terrace, made a sudden leap,
And seeing that it was a soft October night,
Curled once about the house and fell asleep.[5]

Yes, so much for roses and daffodils and may-poles and yellow fogs, not to mention songs of London burning and Baa Baa Black Sheep!

Thus the teaching of only European literature, and mostly British imperialist literature, in our schools means that our students are daily being confronted with the European reflection of itself, the European image, in history. Our children are made to look, analyse, and evaluate the world as made and seen by Europeans. Worse still, these children are confronted with a distorted image of themselves and of their history as reflected and interpreted in European imperialist literature. They see how Prospero sees Caliban and not how Caliban sees Prospero; how Crusoe discovers and remakes Man Friday in Crusoe's image, but never how Friday views himself and his heroic struggles against centuries of Crusoe's exploitation and oppression.

This emerges more clearly if you compare literature with the state of the cinema in Kenya today. Every time we go to the movies we are confronted with the way the imperialist bourgeoisie sees the world; we are faced, so to speak, with the ideological justification of their ways to themselves and to us. Thus we never see ourselves reflected on the screen; we never react to or respond to ourselves and to our environment on the screen. Worse, we often applaud the superhuman feats of racist heroes of imperialism—a James Bond or an American cowboy wiping out a whole crowd of Third World people: Africans, Chinese, Mexicans, or the native Americans—the so-called Red Indians.

This is cultural imperialism, a very powerful instrument of oppression because it distorts a people's vision of history and of the reality of the world around them. These distorted literary reflections, reinforced by religious images of white gods and angels reigning and 'choiring' in heaven while black devils writhed in hell because of their black sins, were meant to lead us—and especially the 'educated' and the Christianized—to paths of self-doubt and self-hatred and to indecisive postures before our enemies. Okot p'Bitek in *Song of Ocol* has powerfully depicted this educated generation writhing in anguish amidst tortuous thoughts and questions:

Why
Why was I born black?[6]

The phenomenon is not of course peculiar to Africa. It is true of the whole black world, the colonized world, indeed true of those Aimé Césaire has described as 'Societies drained of their essence, cultures trampled underfoot, institutions undermined, lands confiscated, religions smashed, magnificent artistic creations destroyed, extraordinary possibilities wiped out.' Ocol's torments and his repudiation of the creative collective selfhood of African peoples is borne out by a real-life testimony from Malcolm X, who writes:

> How ridiculous I was to stand there simply lost in admiration of my hair now looking white in the mirror . . . This was my first really big step towards self-degradation: when I endured all that pain, literally burning my flesh in order to conk my natural hair until it was limp, to have it look like a white man's hair! I had joined that multitude of black men and women who are so brainwashed into believing that black people are inferior and white people superior that they will even violate and mutilate their God created bodies to try to look pretty by white standards.[7]

Well, we may not always mutilate our bodies, but how often have we mutilated our minds and our creative potential through total surrender to cultural imperialism!

It is time that we realized that the European imperialist bourgeois experience of history as reflected in their art and literature is NOT the universal experience of history. Moreover, their history has largely been one of exploitation, oppression, and elimination of other peoples. Why should we, whose experience of history as reflected in our songs and our literature is one of continuous heroic struggle against western European slavery and their imperialist pillage and plunder of our wealth, be expected to memorize and recite the story of our imperialist oppressors and thus identify with their literary glorification of imperialist plunder and murder?

I am convinced that the principles guiding the report were entirely sound: literature of the African peoples should come first. Literature of people who have struggled against racism, colonialism, against imperialist economic, political, and cultural domination—and this means mostly progressive Asian and Latin American literatures—should follow. Literature from the rest of the world—chosen on the basis of relevance to our struggle against inhibitive social structures—should be the third component of literature in our schools.

In this way we shall develop a critical mentality in our students: people who can critically assess and evaluate their total environment in Kenya and, using the tools gained therefrom, look at other worlds and similarly assess and evaluate. In literature there have been two opposing aesthetics: the aesthetic of oppression and exploitation and of acquiescence with imperialism; and that of human struggle for total liberation. The literature of all those who cherish and fight for freedom is our literature: the literature of all who hate, and therefore struggle against exploitation, oppression, diminution of the human creative spirit, is our literature: the aesthetic arising from that literature is in harmony with the aesthetic evolving from the Kenyan people's history which reached its previous highest epic peak in the Mau Mau armed struggle against British imperialism, an aesthetic which found literary expression in Mau Mau songs and poems. But the order and combination of study is important: Kenya, East Africa, Africa, Asia, and Latin America, and the rest, in that order.

The second issue—the decision-making personnel—is obviously related to the first and here again the report was clear and emphatic. No independent country should allow the most vital decisions about the study of their culture to be taken by foreigners. Decisions affecting the lives of fifteen million Kenyans can only be meaningfully taken by patriotic Kenyans and not by imperialist foreigners. I don't see why this should even be a matter of debate. It is the height of criminal folly and utter national irresponsibility and naked betrayal of millions to entrust policies on national culture to foreigners. That is why the report called for the immediate Kenyanization of the inspectorates of literature and languages. I repeat: only Kenyan nationals should decide on the running of their education system.

The third issue, concerning the employment of expatriates, is dependent on what is done about the above two issues. The feeling of the working committee was that most of the current staff in our schools were recruited and employed on the basis of the current policies that have resulted in only foreign literature in our schools. A few of these teachers have no training in literature and they can only talk about backgrounds to literature, but are incapable of adequately evaluating literature, any literature, even their own, and therefore they spend time in explaining references to daffodils, wintry snow, and may-poles. Thus they hide their ignorance behind a knowledge of their language and an acquaintance with the natural and social background to the literature.

But a few of the teachers are progressive and approach literature with a sensitivity and intelligence born of a sound training and dedication to the cause of human liberation. Such are not afraid of progressive literature. They don't feel threatened by a Kenyan national literature or any other socially relevant literatures. On the contrary, these enlightened few welcome a literature whose background the students can take for granted so that they can get on with the more exciting work of interpretation and debate. In the same way there are a few nationals who are authoritarian and who are obviously happier discussing and explaining a London they know nothing about, or a Europe learnt from imperialist literature. These literary Ocols hate this uncivilized thing called Kenyan literature, and they also hate a situation in which a student might be as much acquainted with the social background as the teacher. Fortunately these Kenyans who are sold to the culture of imperialism without even grasping its full import are increasingly being challenged by a new generation of Kenyan students and teachers who are committed to a national aesthetic of liberation.

But once again, the question about the employment of foreigners to teach literature in our schools cannot be decided on the basis of philosophical stance of the foreigners. I believe that only the nationals of a country have the right and the responsibility of running their education system, and this over-reliance on foreigners is dangerous for our country's future.

Finally I would say that the basic assumption underlying the committee's work and recommendations was the general realization, as it emerged from the discussions of the main conference, that literature, any literature, is useless unless it is committed to the values of a people 'sceptreless and free', developing to the highest possible level their limitless creative potential and enjoying to the full the fruits arising therefrom.

Imperialism, in its colonial and neo-colonial stages, is the enemy of those human values of liberation. The literature reflecting an aesthetic that glorifies the wicked deeds of the imperialist bourgeoisie and its local allies is enemy literature. The literature we teach in Kenya's schools should reflect the grandeur of our history: it should reflect Kenya's great past of heroic struggles to overcome nature and her even more heroic struggles aginst foreign domination: from the wars of resistance against the Portuguese and the Arab slave-raiders, to the patriotic wars against the British.

The history and the literature we teach should bring to the fore those immortal words in Aimé Césaire's poem *Return to My Native Land* when he argued that for a century the European imperialist bourgeoisie has fed the colonized and the oppressed with racist lies and defeatist propaganda.

> For it is not true that the work of man is finished
> That man has nothing more to do in the world
>   but be a parasite in the world
> That all we now need is to keep in step with the world.
>
> But the work of man is only just beginning and it remains
> to man to conquer all the violence entrenched in the
> recesses of his passion
>
> And no race possesses the monopoly of beauty,
> of intelligence, of force, and there is
> a place for all at the rendezvous
> of victory . . . [8]

The teaching of literature in Kenyan schools must help us to return to our native land among the masses of Kenyan peasants and workers, to build a self-reliant Kenya totally free from external and internal exploitation and oppression. The report of the working committee was only a tiny tiny step in that direction. But then, the journey of a thousand miles begins with one step.

Notes

1 This is a slightly revised article which appeared in *The Weekly Review*, 1976 as part of the fierce debate which erupted in Kenya's press after a working committee, appointed by the conference of teachers of literature, Nairobi School, 1973 to re-examine the literature syllabus in schools, released its findings and recommendations in a document entitled: *Teaching of Literature in Kenya's Secondary Schools.*

2 Edmund Waller, 'Go Lovely Rose!'

3 Robert Herrick, 'Argument of His Book'.

4 Robert Herrick, 'Daffodils'.

5 T. S. Eliot, 'The Love Song of J. Alfred Prufrock',*Collected Poems 1909–1962* (Faber, London, 1969), p. 13.

6 Okot p'Bitek, *Song of Ocol* (EAPH, Nairobi, 1970), p. 22.

7 The Autobiography of Malcolm X.

8 Aimé Césaire, *Return to My Native Land* (Penguin, Harmondsworth, 1969), p. 85.

PART THREE

Fluent Reading Versus Accurate Reading

Introduction

In the final section we have included a number of papers which address a major difficulty in literature teaching. Pickett's paper identifies the problem well:

> . . . anyone with a good literary background . . . must have felt the frustration of having to justify interpretations or aesthetic judgements by reference to a wider universe beyond the students' ken—to other works by the same writer, to works by his contemporaries, to antecedents at an earlier phase of the literary tradition, to foreign influences, to historical and social background, etc. In other words, the need to explain and enjoy a few works read in detail immediately shows up the limitations of such a practice and points up the need for vast amounts of reading at a more superficial level . . .

This issue is not simply one of quantity and its relation to quality; it also connects directly with our need to allow students to build up their own systems of relations between the various books, poems, and other works whose symbolism and frames of reference make them worthy of our attention. This process confronts directly the ideological and social issues raised by Ngugi, for it is by our reading that we weave ourselves into the web of cultural associations in which we find our own identity. Literature provides the most accessible and richest source of integration with the past and with our contemporaries. But such integration is created by each reader as the literary experience increases. There are of course many other types of reading which can ultimately provide such an integrative experience, and there are sources of such linking with our neighbours other than purely literary: philosophy, politics, art, religion, to name only the most obvious. But literature remains probably the easiest and most economical means of providing this experience of the possibilities of contact with other minds and cultural traditions within formal education.

Yet the experience demands that learners read enough to be able to start creating their own associative systems, and with enough enthusiasm to be willing to make the necessary commitment. Out of such experience scholarship may eventually grow; without it, scholarship may well be imposed from outside, an alien growth, apparently pointless.

These papers are all based on specific classroom experience. The argument between Brumfit and Pettit is based on an assessment of the needs of students in East Africa, from the differing points of view of expatriates working in Tanzania and Kenya respectively. The relationship between this discussion and Ngugi's polemic is worth examining.

These two papers are followed by a sample examination paper, representing an explicit attempt to create an examination which could not be crammed for. This complements the lower-level, more linguistically orientated examples of questions provided in Boyle's paper (Part Two).

A danger in exploring curriculum argument in this way is that of assuming that such discussion is exclusively relevant to circumstances where ideology is important in education, and publicly discussed. The other two papers relate the same curriculum design issue to the British context, with very different selections of material (in Brumfit's paper) and argument designed for a native-speaker audience. But no country or educational tradition can be free from a concern with the kinds of literary networks students are encouraged to build up. The East African situation encouraged explicit discussion of such issues. In Britain they are frequently objected to in principle. Yet our very unwillingness to address the questions as ideological ones may be the cause of our failure to teach literature effectively to so many people. The first task must be to get people reading books for meaning and making connections between them, and outwards to non-literary experiences, as a matter of personal need. Once this need is established, for any learners who wish to take this up, issues of the nature of the experience can follow. But we cannot analyse an experience we have never had, and the literary experience arises from thinking about books as meaningful, important patterning of experience, integrated with our own experience, both direct and vicarious. We cannot separate this question from the question, 'What sort of people do we want to be?'—and that is a question with fundamental ideological implications.

Pickett, however, raises a number of extremely important issues in addition. Particularly, he considers the implications of what we know of reading speed for the design of the literature curriculum. He too wishes to separate work aiming at creating committed readers from the more scholarly work of close textual examination.

There is a risk, though, of that separation being misunderstood, and it may be helpful to see it as two aspects of the necessary development of literary competence as a reader, one aiming at accuracy (i.e. careful reading of a text, avoiding misunderstanding), and the other at fluency (i.e. rapid and relaxed utilization of the capacities which have been developed through accuracy work). (See Brumfit 1984 for the development of these concepts in language teaching.) Any teaching will demand work on both aspects, but much 'set books' teaching allows only for accuracy.

16   Literature Teaching in Tanzania

Christopher Brumfit

Tanzania has committed herself to a socialist future in which education will play a vital part in developing concepts of equality, non-exploitation, independence from outside influences, etc. This means that if we are to justify the teaching of literature at all, let alone European literature, we have to show that it can contribute to the general betterment of society. Secondly we have to show that the syllabus we use is itself designed to make that contribution. As our main blue-print for education is the President's 'Education for Self Reliance' (Nyerere 1967), I shall start with three quotations from it which bear directly on the teaching of literature.

First, the general aims of education into which our literature teaching must fit: '... the educational system of Tanzania must emphasise co-operative endeavour, not individual advancement; it must stress concepts of equality and the responsibility to give service which goes with any special ability, whether it be in carpentry, in animal husbandry, or in academic pursuits' (p. 7).

Then again, he says that there are three things which education must encourage the development of: 'an enquiring mind; an ability to learn from what others do, and reject or adapt it to his own needs; and a basic confidence in his own position as a free and equal member of the society, who values others and is valued by them for what he does and not for what he obtains' (p. 8).

And later, finally: 'But the educational system of Tanzania would not be serving the interests of a democratic socialist society if it tried to stop people from thinking about the teachings, policies or the beliefs of leaders, either past or present. Only free people conscious of their worth and their equality can build a free society' (p. 9).

I think it is fair to abstract the following four points of great relevance to literature teaching from these questions:

1 The teaching must direct the pupils to service of the community.
2 It must develop generally the enquiring mind, ability to learn from others, and confidence, referred to in the second extract.
3 It must develop specifically the skill of criticism.
4 It must rely as far as possible on a co-operative approach.

The first of these depends on us recognizing—and here we have the big difference between literature teaching as often practised and what we really need—that literature is a *skills* subject, not a content subject. So perhaps are all subjects, but literature suffers more than most from the fact that it is possible to teach with high effect, for an examination, by ignoring skills and concentrating on content. But no content will be as valuable as a skill which can be used when the student has left school. As long as we are certain that we are concerned with skills, we can limit our self-justification in Tanzania to proving that the skills we train are relevant to the needs of the country.

1968 saw the introduction of new literature papers both for School Certificate and Higher School Certificate. They both also bear the new title of 'Literature in English'. I want to make a brief comment on the main changes which these syllabuses embody.

There are two. The more obvious one is that the set books are chosen with greater concern for their suitability in East Africa than for their status in English literary history—though whether Bridie plays and Neville Shute novels are in fact more suitable is doubtful. Also we now have major works of European literature in translation—Dostoevsky, Voltaire, and Brecht, among others, have been set. The other change is in the type of question asked. In general the aim is to get away from the old-style 'context' with close and unimaginative textual reference, and substitute evidence of thought about the relationship between the incident in the passage given and the other incidents in the plot, to relate the parts to the whole. This change in emphasis applies both to S.C. and to H.S.C. In addition, at H.S.C. a language paper has been made compulsory, in which the effect of linguistic conventions—and the rejection of conventions—can be examined closely.

There has been an unfortunate tendency in past years for the dim arts streams to have compulsory literature. This is not necessarily as bad as it sounds, as the ability to read well is not directly proportional to general intellectual competence. Anyway, the situation will probably improve. Again, few H.S.C. schools have been able to insist on minimum English standards for entrants to the literature course. In my most recent H.S.C. class, for example, there was one candidate who had never taken S.C. literature and had obtained the lowest grade (8) in S.C. language. He retook the language exam a year later and failed completely. All this, however, should be improving from next year when the government reorganization of H.S.C. schools takes place, with much more careful control of entry and staffing. We must still, however, be well aware of the special difficulties of the Tanzanian student when confronted with literature which, whether African or not, is firmly in a European-centred tradition. Typical H.S.C. literature entrants have read nothing but simplified readers until two years before they start their course, and have probably read not more than a dozen unabridged books of any type, apart from textbooks, during the next two years. Any syllabus must recognize this problem.

Any syllabus must also, of course, reckon with teachers who will represent a wide range of cultures (even after all the expatriates have gone) and whose experience in literature will vary widely. One of our biggest problems is the lack of suitable materials for teaching the new syllabus. Not all—perhaps not even most—H.S.C. teachers feel able to cope on their own with the amount of background knowledge necessary to teach this course.

Finally we must also remember that most schools in Tanzania are not within easy reach of bookshops; that the publishers' catalogues which are probably the only information about books to reach the schools are not reliable sources, and it can't be guaranteed that even *they* will arrive; that the chance of anybody in a school receiving, say, the *Times Literary Supplement* is very small; that the school library is often inadequately stocked; that—while the shortage of essential textbooks is, in my experience at least, a complete myth—the shortage of anything inessential is acute.

These are the problems. Before I discuss what we can do to make things easier, I would like to consider a statement of the aims of literature teaching in Tanzania. For this, I am going to reproduce, more or less, the material which I drafted and which was in broad outline approved by the Institute of Education Literature panel, as an introduction to a conference of H.S.C. literature teachers. (See further brief extract in the appendix to this chapter.)

We think that we can summarize the aims of literature teaching here thus, in order of importance:

a To consider language in action at its most effective (e.g. in works of literature), by
  i examining how language makes its effect, and
  ii considering works of literature as social phenomena.
b From **a** (ii) above, to consider what creative writing is, and to relate it to the other arts.
c To give some appreciation of literature as a world-wide phenomenon.

It will be noted that (a) and (b) will be best achieved by a consideration of works close to the environment of the students, both in content and language; the less background information required the better. Further, (c) does not ask for knowledge of world literature, but simply for a recognition that there *is* literature everywhere. In fact, of course, we concentrate fairly heavily on (a), which ideally should be systematically taught—but at present lack of material for this paper is preventing this. We should, however, also bear the other two aims in mind, referring to them when work on them is a natural follow-up to the work we are doing in (a). At School Certificate level, we are largely concerned with literature as an expression of human problems, and at H.S.C. also with the language means used to express the problems.

Very briefly, a (i) above, which can be regarded as continuation of much of School Certificate language work, is catered for by Paper 1 at H.S.C. Here, we are concerned with consideration of the effects of language in detail, and expect the student to be able to recognize how a writer achieves his effects and to be able to attempt himself to achieve a particular tone. All this leads onto a (ii), in which we look at specific works of literature. If we first consider them as 'language in action', we shall certainly have to pass soon to (b), and consider the special peculiarities of good writing. In all this work we shall be considering such vital problems as the relationship between language, literature, and propaganda, the social responsibility of the Tanzanian writer—and perhaps more important, the Tanzanian reader and critic.

In summary, then, we may produce the following effects from our course: first, increased competence in English, and an understanding of how language works; second, a basic critical competence; third, an understanding of the historical situation, of Swahili and African writing in relation to European and other traditions, and of the literary arts in relation to other arts and activities of man.

It will be noted that these aims are not on the whole aesthetic—they are all, broadly speaking, sociological, concerned with literature as a linguistic phenomenon in a particular setting. Let us try to link these aims to my four points from 'Education for Self Reliance' and then see how it might be possible to carry them out.

We cannot say that these aims will automatically direct literary training to service of the community, but they are trying to direct students to an awareness of community. The emphasis that teachers give to their work should lead to the notions of responsibility etc. which are discussed in the President's pamphlet. But above all, the critical approach will be training, we hope, the 'enquiring mind' and so on, that we quoted. The final point, that of the co-operative approach, is a matter of methodology, but it is worth stressing that the whole basis of a study of literature is the study of communication—in various forms, of various ideas—and that communication is the tie without which any co-operative endeavour is impossible.

It may perhaps be objected that most of the work we have outlined will best be taught not in English but in Swahili. Certainly. The advantage of using a language which may be better understood by the student is very great—but we face at the moment a problem of staffing. (The problem is not, as is commonly thought, a problem of subject-matter—see Dr Allen's article in the *Bulletin of the Language Association of Tanzania*, December 1968.) Eventually, no doubt, a similar course will be taught in Swahili—in Tanzania at least (though note here the problem of our link with Kenya and Uganda, who give Swahili a less dominant role in education). For the moment, though, we can use the immediate advantage of access in English to a wide range of world literature.

What should we do, then, to make our aims work in the classroom for the needs of the country? What services will the country claim from the journalists, teachers, writers, civil servants, and political leaders who may have been through our course? I do not think our course is possible at all if we are not certain that the country wants creative and independent thinkers. We must depend on 'Education for Self-Reliance' and hope that the ideas I have already quoted will remain central to educational thinking. If they do, people will be wanted who are not taken in by jargon, slogans, all the devices of propaganda; people who believe in criticism as a moral obligation, but criticism which is based on knowledge, sympathy, and practice in discriminating between subtleties of meaning; people who are not limited to a purely Tanzanian outlook, but see Africa, the freed world, and mankind, ultimately, as a whole; people who have knowledge and skills, but who use them for the betterment of others; people who recognize that while they possess knowledge and skills, they do not possess *all* knowledge and skills.

To provide the nation with such people, we are offering a course which involves the close study of records of man's impressions of life, of people in action in various parts of the world, at various times, with various beliefs. We ask the pupils to consider what is said, and how it is said. We spend much of the time analysing the language used in particular contexts, and not only literary ones. We ask them to distinguish between shades of meaning, to recognize the significance of different registers, and so on, and so on—to respond sensitively to language.

Secondly, in our concern with literature in society, we relate the activity of the writer as a responsible human being to his society and its demands. And we must, if we are to be as useful as we are asked to be, link our concern for literature with a strong concern for man, a moral concern. If we do, we shall be fulfilling the requirements of 'Education for Self Reliance'; if we don't, we shan't be. The present syllabus *can* be taught in this way. But does the exam help us to do this?

The short answer is no: it is still possible to cram the set texts—and it will always be possible to until we neutralize the effect of cramming by allowing students to take their texts into the exam. We are still heavily dependent on background knowledge of the books—partly because we only expect the candidates to read eight books in two years, and these are not enough to give any kind of scale for sensible comments about any book. The real answer to all this, I would suggest, is the type of response in the exam. It is certainly true at the moment that it is possible to be ready for the set book part of the exam comfortably after four terms.

In teaching the old syllabus for H.S.C. it was apparent that the two major problems were linguistic and logical. As long as the candidates could get by by learning a book and its notes, even the most unsuitable works—such. as *The Rape of the Lock* or Chaucer's Tales (both of which I had to teach)—produced satisfactory exam results. Now that we face the language problem more squarely, particularly in Paper One, we have to deal with, for example, the widespread inability to recognize sarcasm or to realize when a writer is trying to be funny. When a whole class of bright students failed to see that when a writer to *Drum* said 'My advice to all men in good jobs is this: change your name; wear a beard and dark glasses; and keep your money in a purse with a double lock' he was not meaning this as a serious piece of advice, we knew how far we had to go. But I don't know any solution to this problem except systematically to expose the students to as many varieties of prose writing and to as many registers and levels of formality as possible. Yet how can students who cannot recognize humorous exaggeration cope with a question which asks them to understand something as sophisticated as an unseen English lyrical poem—which they may get in the exam? Certainly some sort of language paper must attempt to deal with these difficulties.

The fundamental problem in designing the set books part of the exam is, I think, this: how can we concentrate on the skills aspect when most of the students are so lacking in background about any set texts that most of the teacher's time will be spent filling this in, and when the pupils cannot turn to consideration of the book itself without mastering a lot of necessary detail which has nothing whatsoever to do with the basic theme of the book? Then the basic pupil problem is that sensible discussion of books is only possible as a result of acquaintance with a fairly wide range of other books. If we want people to use books actively as instruments of thought and ideas, they must leave school with a wide enough basis, and with enough experience of discussion, to enable them to carry the skill away with them. My suggested solution is to design a syllabus which emphasizes wide reading, and which forces the teacher to promote general discussion of books and their ideas. The syllabus should take into account much more the subject matter of the books studied, should get the necessary background as far as possible into the book itself, and make the various set texts complement each other, and have some relevance to pupils' lives now, so that issues dealt with are not just academic. This would imply considerable reliance on African literature.

Let me finish, then, with a sketch of a syllabus which, I think, would force teachers to concentrate on the skills and not the content, and—because they could not possibly *teach* it—force them to get the pupils active. The present syllabus is still a gift for the dictated notes man.

1 A Language paper, similar to the present Paper One.

2   A paper requiring the student to read as many as possible of a large list of books, grouped round a twentieth-century theme which still has some bearing on the world today, or possibly on a more general theme such as the alienation of the moral person from society. Here are some suggested types of topic, and some books which could be used as a basic list:

The Communist Influence	*Responsibiltity of Modern Man*
Snow—*Red Star over China*	Hersey—*Hiroshima*
Reed—*Ten Days that Shook the World*	Musil—*Young Torless*
	Golding—*Lord of the Flies*
Orwell—*Animal Farm*	Camus—*The Plague*
Koestler—*Darkness at Noon*	Orwell—*Nineteen Eighty-four*
Pasternak—*Dr. Zhivago*	Solzhenitsyn—*One Day in the*
Blok—*The Twelve*	*Life of Ivan Denisovich*

These lists could obviously be extended considerably. Other themes:

Alienation	*Colonialism*
Sophocles—*Antigone*	Forster—*A Passage to India*
Ibsen—*Enemy of the People*	Kipling—*Kim*—*Selected Poems*
Laye—*Radiance of the King*	with anything by:
Kafka—*The Castle*	Achebe
Shakespeare—*Hamlet*	Ekwensi
Dostoevsky—*Crime and Punishment*	Mphahlele
	Soyinka
Golding—*The Spire*	Ngugi
Camus—*The Outsider*	Camara Laye
Pasternak—*Dr Zhivago*	Oyono
Malamud—*The Fixer*	

Better still, a section could perhaps be simply called: any African literature in English.

I am not too worried about the particular books, or the political themes, but the general idea should be clear. These are all either acknowledged works of literature or good journalism. The candidates would be expected to show a detailed knowledge of at least eight books in the exam, and some acquaintance with perhaps eight more. They should be allowed to take with them into the exam eight texts from the general list and use these. The questions should be general (e.g. '"The African returning from education overseas can never fully adapt to the needs of his homeland." Discuss, with detailed reference to at least two novels you have read'), but candidates should be expected to refer constantly and closely to the text while writing their answers.

3 A third paper could consist of a project based on these books, which candidates could be given a fortnight to write. This could involve research, but it would be marked for critical ability, and the ability to apply, not factual knowledge, but a clear critical attention to the problems of the books they had chosen to discuss.

I haven't worked this out fully, and no doubt many objections will be raised, but it does seem to me to force teachers to do many desirable things which the present exam structure does not force them to do (for example, all students would not be able to do the same work; they would have to work in independent groups, on their own areas of the syllabus), and also to force students to do many things thought desirable in our earlier aims. Above all, a lot of discussion of background will not be necessary—most of what is needed will be already in the books, and memory will become much less important. They will have to read books, not study set texts, and they will be studying literature in relation to society and particular problems.

Obviously I can only refer briefly in this chapter to many aspects of the role of literature teaching in Tanzania now. I hope I have been able both to defend it, and to define its possibilities.

Appendix—some polemical points

And finally, a few firm points on what we are *not* doing:

a. We are not teaching *English* literature, but literature.
b. We are not simply teaching eight books and a few language skills. We are attempting to teach much more than that.
c. We are not teaching pupils how to appreciate beauty, or any vague abstract idea of 'response', or how to increase 'sensitivity'.
d. We are not teaching a prescriptive critical method; there are no given rules about the function or the form of a work of literature.
e. We are not teaching the 'concept of the novel', or of the drama.
f. Our main function is not to produce writers, but readers.
g. We are not, except incidentally, preparing students to read Literature, or Linguistics, at university—many of them will not in fact do so.

We *are* hoping that as a result of our teaching, students will continue to read, think, and criticize for the rest of their lives.

17 Literature in East Africa: Reform of the Advanced Level Syllabus

R. D. Pettit

Christopher Brumfit's plan for literature teaching in Tanzania makes suggestions for the reform of the Advanced Level syllabus. It also presents, directly and indirectly, that view of the nature of literature and literary studies (to use his own word, a sociological one) from which these suggestions logically follow. Thirdly, this view is in accord with, if not directly inspired by, the socialist programme which Tanzania attempts to incarnate.

It may therefore seem something of a triumph for the integrity of literary studies that the reforms he suggests would, in very general terms, be supported by a majority of teachers in Uganda and Kenya. But this should be so: the forms of study of, 'say, medicine or the mastery of an art will develop according to the inner logic of the subject, whether in a rigorously socialist state or under, shall we say, the looser forms of socialism officially followed by Tanzania's East African partners. An official ideology may lead to *changes* in the forms of study, such as the wish Brumfit expresses for the development (very desirable) of forms of co-operative learning; but while the impulse for this comes from the ideology, the change will only be fruitful if it is in accord with the peculiar nature of the subject. (Of course, in our subject as in all others, the individual will continue to have his private struggle.) Nevertheless, literary studies should retain their own nature in any social situation, although a society may make its own stipulations about the use the followers of them will put their talents to; that is unless the Guardians of the State banish them from the Commonwealth. But while there remain advantages to the East African countries from following common courses and examinations, it should not be impossible for us to agree on what we want in them.

Before going on to Brumfit's detailed proposals, I want first to explain that the view of literature presented in his proposal is radically incomplete. He sees it as developing an open and enquiring mind: but the openness is restricted to concern with social and psychological problems. The novel is the literary form which is most suited to such problems, but even this, while it may bring their existence home to us, is not restricted to them. The *pièce-à-thèse*, such as *Flame in the Streets*, *Twelve Angry Men*, *The Ragged Trousered Philanthropists*, *The Pearl*, *A Man for all Seasons*, *Cry, the Beloved Country*, *Weep Not, Child*, *The Old Man and the Medal*, etc. is usually recognized as a wholesome yet inferior branch of literature. Why is this so? A novel or play is a construct of reality which makes its effect at different levels of consciousness. It presents a picture of life and asks us to concur in its truth and decide on the relative value of that truth. Occasionally we can enthuse over what seems absolutely true, and still more occasionally that conviction endures. A fine work makes an unconscious operation on the reader, even if the reader does not choose to make an articulate response. The deepest literature answers the question 'What do men live for?'—it does not at all necessarily pose that question—and the answers have, besides a social or psychological content, a metaphysical one: they reveal the integrity and ends of the soul, as well as of the mind and body, and its relation to God or any substitute for him. The difference between *Macbeth* or Mofolo's *Chaka the Zulu* and, say, *No Longer at Ease*, is that the first two are not only about the *reasons* for failure.

Besides this, literature is also a form of recreation. The reader or listener feels that he is at play among familiar objects. This is true of children's literature such as folktales or the Toytown stories, or of such things as the farcical parts (the best) of *A Man of the People*. It is also true of parts of more testing and exploratory works, for example the picture of the Oblonsky family in *Anna Karenina*: a distressing situation is not always radically disturbing and may be amusing. There is much humour even in archetypal works such as *Wuthering Heights* or *The Pilgrim's Progress*. This is not surprising: there are realities in which the naked soul stands before the throne of judgement; but there are also familiar landscapes and main highways, from which the complacent traveller may be entertained by the seriousness with which the static indigenae take themselves. In short, comedy, of trivial and untrivial kinds. Even those grisly literary Lokis from Ibsen to Brecht and Sartre to Kwey Armah who like to rub our noses in the existential void condescend to entertain at times.

A third quality of literature, including in a way both the previous two, and which attracts immediately the elementary critical sense, is the rendering of all the particularities and peculiar qualities of immediate experience. A writer who fails in this apparently superficial power is very seldom worth looking into for any deeper qualities. There are many writers, often favourite authors, who have created a few things in an authentic and inimitable way, for example Christopher Smart, Forest Reid, or Abioseh Nicol, while others with Epic intentions leave us unimpressed, perhaps because the grander construction is platitudinous, or inhibited in certain essential matters. We feel that the latter writer has made an order out of the elements of experience without having had the experiences. He has cheated. But the miniaturist who has captured certain parts of life as they really exist, without showing their relation to all other things, is an authentic artist: always overlooked by those who want literature to enable us to solve or understand problems.

In short there is no valid reason for positing a division between an 'aesthetic' and a 'sociological' approach to literature.

Brumfit may of course welcome some statement such as this, in that his concern was to lay the basis for certain viable proposals and illustrate the rationale behind certain themes around which the reading of novels and plays can be organized. He would perhaps have no objection to the addition to his list of such topics as 'Religious Faith and Search', 'Town and Country', 'The Relation between Morals and Manners', 'Private and Public Life', 'Serious Comedy and the Comedy of Seriousness', 'Reconstruction of the Past', and so on, even to those topics which are areas of subject matter rather than problems of life. However, there is still a serious difficulty in reconciling what should be the agreed nature of literary study, and the study of certain ideas or problems or areas of experience as they occur in a variety of works. For example a class studying *Hard Times* (University rather than Advanced Level perhaps) could profitably be set to read, individually or in groups, works such as the histories of the Hammonds and Ashton, the economic philosophy of Bentham and James Mill, other 'industrial' novels such as *North and South*, *Mary Barton*, *Coningsby*, *Alton Locke*, *The Ragged Trousered Philanthropists*, and *The Revolution in Tanner's Lane*, and documentary evidence such as Engels' *Condition of the Working Class* and Mayhew's *London Labour and London Poor*. However, there quickly comes a limit to the amount of help such reading gives to one's attitude towards *Hard Times*, in that the novel must be judged in terms of itself and one's general sense of the probabilities of life. If, however, students were studying 'Industrial Life in the Nineteenth Century', they would be involved in a sociological study in which they would be dealing with very different kinds of evidence. A novel or play is very much in the position of hearsay evidence in a Law Court and needs the most careful enquiry into its validity before it be admitted. Such developed scrupulousness is usually beyond a Higher School Certificate student. Even allowing for this, though, if a student were set such an essay title as 'Show by reference to three of the works you have studied how the relations between "masters" and "men" were inevitably dehumanized', the student's problem would not be so much to understand the nature of any particular work, or even to hold and present a clear understanding of the complexities of a historical period, but to assemble a collection of received ideas, facts and apparent facts, with as much knowledgeable connection as possible; and far from synthesizing several disciplines he would be producing a mode of thought acceptable in none.

. Of course, a teacher with a developed interest in sociology or psychology may present his students with the ideas and modes of thought of these disciplines, and use them as schematic terms of reference for the works they are studying. This approach is often very successful,[1] for fifth and sixth form students are at an age to respond strongly to ways of thinking which offer the possibility of a radical understanding of human nature and society, and of controlling or changing them; probably the frustration which many students experience with literary studies, at least from time to time, is with the more passive recognitions which appear as their terminus. But an interest in any major art field of intellectual enquiry can profitably be brought to our subject. My quarrel with the thematic approach, as I have seen and heard it presented, is not that it brings into confrontation two or more completely different systems for registering experience; rather it tends to confuse our ends and melt down our fine particularities.

This suspicion is borne out by the admittedly limited exemplification given in Brumfit's article. One question is given as an example of what could be set on a course of certain African writers: 'The African returning from education overseas can never fully adapt to the needs of his homeland.' This is an important consideration for those concerned with education and national planning, and has some relevance to students in schools in that all education tends to shake one loose from local attachments and lessen the possibility of resting in parochial satisfactions; it offers a good entrance to discussion of the group of autobiographical works of the *Child of Two Worlds* type. But it is surely a trivial question in relation to any novels or poems which are likely to have been studied, for example *The Second Round*. It is likely to be a donnée of the main centres of interest of such books, and can be answered without reference to their authors' outlooks or achievements. As those who have ever had to write on questions similar to this and the one suggested in relation to *Hard Times* know, the more conscientious you are about using your literary source material, the more dissatisfied you become with your answer. You will do much better to answer from your general knowledge of society with a few purely decorative illustrations.

A similar doubt about the kind of study envisaged occurs on considering the themes and titles suggested. Those under 'The Communist Influence' and 'The Responsibility of Modern Man' seem designed to lead to reductive conclusions about their themes, rather than comparisons revealing the natures of the separate works. Those under 'Alienation' seem very much more interesting, and could produce a realization of the essential differences of mode and civilization of the various authors, as well as fragmenting the concept offered as a theme. If these are the aims, then real literary study is possible, and I am prejudiced in continuing my doubts. However, many of the titles could go easily in one or more of the other lists, and one fears that the intention is to give a different kind of attention according to the grouping.

To be fair, though, the proposals are basically an attempt, which will be welcomed by many, to produce an HSC course more related to the growing concerns of East African students, and which cannot degenerate into a memorization of eight disparate set texts, plus commentaries, and a language paper. The present syllabus is difficult to mould into a scheme of connected studies, and does not in itself impress on students that their reading *must* go a long way beyond the syllabus, or directly give them credit for this reading in their examinations. A convinced teacher will provide direction and persuade students to read a great deal both related to the set texts and outside them. The problem which Brumfit has tried to solve, and which most teachers want solved, is somehow to embody this exploratory and educative ideal situation into the structure of studies and the examination itself. This is not just a matter of thinking in terms of African students and their environment, but also involves an understanding of the nature of the subject: it is not easy to organize the study of literary works, each with their own separate character, into meaningful groups; and impossible to design a unified course susceptible to any kind of linear programming—there are inevitable cul-de-sacs and ring-roads.

What I would like to put forward as a tentative alternative to Brumfit's proposals, or perhaps just a refinement of them, is based on the following considerations. Firstly there are different levels, even of serious reading, founded on the different degrees of attention which works require of us. The present syllabus asks for only the most intense kind. It would be deadly for literary studies to give up the kind of work which requires several re-readings and much thought before the whole is seen in relation to its parts, and the problems of the author's existential position—i.e., Is life as he or she describes it?—have been grappled with. However, there are various levels of lesser attention, and these should be distinguished and demanded by a satisfactory course. Secondly, the present structure of the A-Level syllabus ensures that very little African writing is included. A fair amount of poetry can be read at present, but at most three out of the eight set books; and even teachers anxious to give African writing a first place may find good reasons for preferring some other text to one or more of these. This is partly because the intense mode of study requires texts near the status of a classic of the language (there have been some unjustifiable choices, but the principle is good) and therefore a book of great talent and interest such as Kibera's *Voices in the Dark* does not make the grade. Another reason is that poetry texts cannot be set, and therefore Okello Oculi, Okot p'Bitek, Senghor, Christopher Okigbo and J. P. Clark are excluded.

If, however, we organized the study so that one book from the higher ranks of African and World Literature were studied in association, based on various principles, with a group of lesser works or two or three more equivalent ones (presumably sufficient agreement on the standing of different authors and works is possible for lists to be made), then it would be possible to give credit in the examination for the various levels of reading and include a very much greater proportion of African writing, including poetry. Literature studies at both East African Certificate of Education and University levels have managed to put African writing in the first place: it should be possible at A-Level.

The following outline of a syllabus and examination is more sketchy than Brumfit's. However, it would not be difficult to give it more detailed form.

Let Papers 2 and 3 be no longer confined to plays and novels respectively, but be opened to biography, journalism, and poetry as well. For each Paper two major works will be studied (perhaps out of three choices). Associated with each will be from two to six other books. Students in examination will answer, in each paper, three questions in three hours: one a context of the present kind, and two essays, either on the individual main works, or on questions calling for the discussion of general issues, literary or thematic, requiring reference to a number of the works in the group. Distinguishing names for Papers 2 and 3 can be cooked up, if necessary.

The principles of grouping should be as flexible as possible. For example, *A Grain of Wheat* could be the main text in either of the following groups:

Ngugi: A Grain of Wheat	**Ngugi: A Grain of Wheat**
Crime and Punishment	*Ordeal in the Forest*
Under Western Eyes	*Voices in the Dark*
	Mau Mau Detainee
	Mau Mau General
	Suffering Without Bitterness
	Freedom and After

Similarly for Kwey Armah's *The Beautyful Ones Are Not Yet Born*:

The Beautyful Ones	**The Beautyful Ones**
The Plague	*A Man of the People*
The Immoralist	*No Bride Price*
The Man Outside (Borchert:	*The Government Inspector*
Drausset over der Tür, Calder)	*Blind Cyclops* (Ikeddah; in *Ten One Act Plays*—Pieterse)
	One Man, One Matchet
	Song of Prisoner
	The Epidemic (O. Mirbeau; in *Spotlight*—Marland, Blackie)

Other possible groups might be:

Powys: Mr. Weston's Good Wine
Okara: *The Voice*—:
—*The Quest of the Holy Grail*
  (Penguin translation)
Bunyan: *The Pilgrim's Progress*
Ekensi: *Burning Grass*
Ibsen: *Peer Gynt*
Cervantes: *Life is a Dream*
G. Herbert: *Poems*

Shakespeare: Macbeth
Mofolo: *Chaka the Zulu*
Achebe: *Things Fall Apart*
Niane: *Sundiata*
Alaagoa: *Jaja of Opobo*
Verga: *Mastro—Don Gesualdo*
Sophocles: *Ajax*

Mark Twain: Puddenhead Wilson
Edwards: *Equiano's Travels*
Nkosi: *Rhythm of Violence*
Abrahams: *Tell Freedom*
Senghor: *Poems*
Seruma: *The Experience*
Clark: *America, Their America*

Capek: War with the Newts
Schwartz: *The Dragon*
Mrozek: *The Martyrdom of
  Peter Ohey* (in *Six Plays*—
  Constable)
Gogol: *Dead Souls*
Nwankwo: *Danda*
Agunwa: *More than One*
Aristophanes: *The Peace*
Fielding: *Jonathan Wild*

Behan: The Quare Fellow and
La Guma: The Stone Country
Mortimer: *The Dock Brief*
Maddy: *Yon Kon* (in *Ten One-
  Act Plays*)
Solzhenitsyn: *A Day in the Life
  of Ivan Denisovitch*
Dostoevsky: *Notes from the
  Underworld*
Kafka: *In the Penal Colony*

Sheridan: The School for Scandal
Murphy: *The Way to Keep Him*
  (in *Eighteenth Century After-
  pieces*—Bevis, O.U.P.)
Ene Henshaw: *Medicine for Love*
Molière: *Tartuffe*.
Goldoni: *The Superior Residence*
  (*La Casa Nova* in *Four
  Comedies*—Penguin)
Terence: *The Brothers*

J. P. Clark: Casualties
de Vigny: *Servitudes et Grandeurs Militaires*
W. B. Yeats: *Meditations in Times of Civil War and other related
  poems*
Barbusse: *Under Fire*
Remarque: *All Quiet on the Western Front*
Werfel: *The Forty Days of Musa Dagh*
Hemingway: *For Whom the Bell Tolls*

These lists are in many cases too long and require more re-reading and thought than they have been given. Supplementary lists of non-fictional library reference books would also be necessary. Such groupings really require a small group of very well-read collaborators to be produced satisfactorily. No group headings are given, as these inevitably imply restriction; however, I hope the principles behind each group are fairly clear. One principle should be that the main work in each group should be originally written in English, with exceptions made for novels in special cases. No structural alteration to the scheme would be necessary to increase the proportion of African writing as time goes by. It is also possible to produce a very large number of such lists.

Finally, Paper 1 should be extended to four hours, taken in two parts with an hour's break in between, with the questions basically as at present, but with the addition of a general literary essay, thus giving one hour for each question. Shortage of time can at present destroy the whole aim of this paper.

I am indeed grateful to Christopher Brumfit for provoking me to develop my own thoughts. His suggestion that one paper should be a project essay brings up the question of assessment. I think it is impossible under the present arrangements for assessment of students by external examination. However, such project work would be part of any scheme of work for the course I have outlined. His suggestion that texts should be brought into the examination room would be possible, once agreement were reached on the amount of annotation allowed. However, I do not feel it would make any radical difference to students and their attitude towards examinations: it would perhaps help to set more nervous students at their ease. The main objection to our kind of examination is its 'race against the clock' character, which I have been bearing in mind: such conditions of work may be suitable for examinations in Mathematics, but work against careful writing in our subject and many others. I do not share Brumfit's view that 'the present syllabus is a gift for the dictated notes man', as no good work can really be achieved without student involvement. (Even if so low a view of a substantial body of our Advanced Level teachers were correct, they would not be altered by changes in syllabus so much as by the opportunities given in our universities, Training Institutes, and In-Service Courses and Workshops.) Its main shortcomings, as already indicated, are that it does not *appear* to reward the active student who follows his literary and intellectual nose instead of wearing blinkers, and that it inhibits the study of the books most accessible to our students, i.e. African Literature; and that its terminal examination is too rigid and clock-controlled, and perhaps for this reason produces unreliable results among students who are round about the pass level, with consequent personal frustrations and preliminary fears which affect such a student's attitude to his studies. On the other hand, the present syllabus gives a valuable freedom and opportunity to the teacher to devise his own scheme of study. There is always a danger that if we provide a syllabus with 16 or 24 books to be read, they will be treated by students and, willy-nilly, by teachers as set texts in the present fashion. What we have now also follows, with admitted lapses both in choice of texts and the questions set on them, certain true principles of literary study, which could easily be lost if too-hastily devised alternatives, such as I believe mine and Brumfit's to be, are generally taken up as panaceas.

Note

1 An excellent sketch of such an approach appears in John Furness, '"A" Level English through Sociology' in *The Use of English* (Autumn 1970, Vol. 22, No. 1, London, Chatto and Windus). Some sobering thoughts on the limitations of all kinds of assessment are given in an article in the same issue, by David Clarke: 'Examinations and the aims of teaching English'.

18 Proposed Examination Paper

C. J. Brumfit and G. D. Killam

1 *Rationale*
The new proposal of examination by theme is designed to avoid set-book learning, to teach and cultivate reading and understanding of a wide range of books, and to encourage seeing clear links between book and book and between books and the experience of life.

2 *Proposed rubric*
The Paper (three hours) will require the student to read as many as possible of a large list of books, grouped round a central theme with relevance to the contemporary world. Two essays will be set, requiring the candidate to relate the themes and attitudes of the books read to each other and to his or her experience of life. Students will be expected to show close acquaintance with a few texts which will not be specified, and a general acquaintance with a large number of other texts from the list. They will also be expected to develop the ability to make rapid use of texts to support their arguments.

3 Three themes and suggested book lists will be specified each year and each candidate must state when entering for the examination which theme he or she is choosing. (One theme will be added and one deleted every year.)

4 Students may consult up to six set books during the examination.

5 *Marking scheme*
The paper should reveal:
a succinct, direct use of language and a command of essay form;
b an ability to relate the theme of the question to the books;
c an ability to justify conclusions by evidence from the texts;
d an ability to synthesize ideas gained from the various books and to relate these to relevant experience outside the books.

6 *General topics (for Papers Two and Three)*
a Man in conflict with himself and with society
b African Literature
c Responsibility of Modern Man
d Alienation
e Literature and Propaganda
f Colonialism/Imperialism

7 *Specimen booklists*
(Under the given headings 20–25 books might be selected from these lists.)

Alienation

Sophocles—*Antigone, Oedipus Rex*
Ibsen—*Enemy of the People*
Laye—*Radiance of the King*
Kafka—*The Castle, Metamorphosis*
Dostoevsky—*Crime and Punishment*
Golding—*The Spire, Free Fall*
Bellow—*Herzog*
Camus—*The Outsider*
Achebe—*Things Fall Apart*
Fugard—*The Blood Knot*
Malamud—*The Fixer*
Sartre—*Nausea*
Pasternak—*Dr Zhivago*
Pinter—*The Caretaker*
Brecht—*The Good Woman of Setzuan, The Caucasian Chalk Circle*
Ionesco—*Rhinoceros*
Miller—*Death of a Salesman, View from the Bridge*
Tressell—*The Ragged-Trousered Philanthropists*
Brontë—*Wuthering Heights*
Shakespeare—*Measure for Measure, Hamlet, King Lear*
Gogol—*Diary of a Madman*
O'Neill—*Emperor Jones*
Chekhov—*The Cherry Orchard*
Steinbeck—*Of Mice and Men*
Melville—*Moby Dick*
Faulkner—*The Sound and the Fury*
Molière—*The Misanthrope*
Beckett—*Waiting for Godot*
Gorky—*The Lower Depths*
Synge—*The Tinker's Wedding*
Frisch—*Andorra*
Eliot—*The Cocktail Party*, etc.

Colonialism/Imperialism

Forster—*A Passage to India*
Kipling—*Kim, Selected Poems*
Achebe—Anything
Ekwensi—Anything
Ngugi—*A Grain of Wheat*
Laye—*The African Child*
Oyono—*Houseboy, The Old Man and the Medal*
Bellow—*Henderson the Rain King*
Greene—*The Heart of the Matter, The Quiet American*
Camoens—*The Lusiads*
Gordimer—*A World of Strangers*
La Guma—Anything
Cleaver—*Soul on Ice*
Beti—*King Lazarus*
Cather—*Death comes to the Archbishop*
Conrad—*Heart of Darkness, Lord Jim*
Arden—*Serjeant Musgrave's Dance*
Steinbeck—*The Grapes of Wrath*
O'Casey—*Purple Dust*, etc.

8 *Specimen questions*

Alienation

1 'The individual is what society makes him.' To what extent has your reading borne out this statement? Refer closely to at least *four* works in writing your answer.

2 'The progress of society depends mainly on the person who is repelled by the society he finds himself in.' Which books you have read help us to assess the truth of this statement? Examine in detail *one* book which makes a strong case either for or against this argument.

Colonialism/Imperialism

1 Does your reading lead you to conclude that colonialism is a special unique historical phenomenon, or do you see it as simply another example of universal exploitation of the weak by the strong? Justify your conclusions by specific reference to at least eight books.

2 Discuss the different motives for the colonial activity of the various characters in the books you have read.

19 Wider Reading for Better Reading: An alternative approach to teaching literature

Christopher Brumfit

This chapter describes an attempt to reject the 'set books' approach to teaching literature at sixth-form level and above, and instead to develop with students an attitude to works of literature which should lead to a mature approach to their subsequent reading. Most people seem to agree that the set books at Advanced GCE level should be supported by the reading of a wide range of other works, but very few schools can honestly claim to establish the habit of wide, serious reading in their students. Perhaps one reason for our failure is that we do not actually ask students in schools and colleges to read in the same ways as we would expect to read ourselves. The course which is described below tries to help students to discuss books in relation to their experience of other books within similar traditions, as well as in relation to knowledge and experience gained outside literature altogether. Inevitably, the young reader's experience, both of literature and life, is limited; but this is no reason to claim that books can be discussed only in relative isolation. We have to acquire the ability, which all good readers use as they read, to compare constantly, and there is no reason why the shape of the course should not help students to do this. Certainly if this does not happen, there is a grave risk that connections and comparisons will always be those handed down by the teacher or at best drawn from secondary sources. Somehow we need to give students with a particular interest in literature the experience of reading and discovering not isolated texts but a whole body of literature—and of discussing this in relation to their experience both inside and outside literature. Perhaps it is hardly surprising that few adults read literature seriously after leaving school, when the model placed before them has often been exclusively one of *study* of individual texts more or less in isolation.

The reading experience

For many of us, the profound pleasure of reading comes partly from an experience which is simultaneously individual and communal. We read alone for much of the time, but we share the experience not only of the writers but also of other readers with whom we can discuss our reading. And we do not usually discuss isolated books, and rarely passages of books. We discuss authors against other authors, genres, national traditions, and whole epochs. Our response to literature is part of our response to history, to ethics, to politics, to understanding what we are and what other people are. In other words, we do not *have* knowledge of books, we *use* our knowledge: our response is both active and shared.

Four basic book lists

Students embarking on our course, then, were asked to read widely, to respond not to texts but to groups of texts, and to work together within a broad and flexible framework. We decided not to think in terms of set texts but of set fields, and produced four basic lists of books for students to opt for. (One of these lists can be found at the end of this chapter.) Four different criteria were used for the list selections: one taking a period—post-1945 English literature; one a genre—satire; one a theme—war literature; and one a national comparison (with a necessary time limitation)—twentieth-century American and Russian literature. Students chose to work successively on two of these fields, making their choice after looking at specimen lists of about twenty books within the general area specified by the title of the course. It was emphasized, however, that the fields were to be interpreted generously: students were completely at liberty to read and discuss any other appropriate books, and tutors expected to learn from what students read. It was not to be solely a one-way process.

The work programme

A student received the basic book list as long as possible before the beginning of term and read around the general area in any way that seemed appropriate. Contact hours could be used very flexibly by the tutor on each of the four courses. Usually, students themselves determined what would happen in the weeks ahead, with the main options available being:

a student-led seminars (led initially by groups of students, but later by individuals);
b tutor-led seminars (increasingly on topics requested by students);
c various forms of project, with small groups of students working with the tutor at any one time;
d one-to-one discussions with students.

Certain minimum requirements were laid down. Students were expected to read as many as possible of the books on the list, but the (very modest) official minimum was put at seven for each course. They were, however, expected to keep a reading record, in the form of notes on every book they read. Such notes could be on books of their own choosing, and plot retelling was not expected, though some students did prefer to make a fairly detailed record, for reference purposes. The record was to be more in the form of a reading diary, in which comments and opinions could be entered. However, the fact that it was to be looked at by tutors inevitably turned this into something of a chore, even though we did accept that some books would be non-starters for some students. It was quite legitimate to record that a book had been tried and given up, or had only been skimmed.

Written work

The other two pieces of written work demanded during each course were treated much more enthusiastically by students. The major piece of work was a long essay on a topic chosen by the student: and the shorter one was either a piece of practical analysis of a particular passage in the book, or a piece of original creative work associated with the field of the reading list.

A great deal of emphasis was given to the student's own choice of essay topic. The thought and discussion that gradually pinned down the topic, and the discipline that lay in the moulding of a precise wording both proved to be an excellent preparation for writing. Topics were also discussed publicly in seminars, if students wished, so that the problems of writing were integrated with the general reading discussions involving us all. Such discussions were particularly valuable when we were choosing appropriate topics for the shorter piece of work. Some fields lent themselves more obviously to creative work than others. It was difficult, for example, to write creatively within Russian and American literature, but imitation chapters of books read—serious parodies—were accepted, as were annotated anthologies of poems. In all options tape-recorded programmes, carefully scripted and with musical or other sound effects, could be submitted. Some students preferred to offer an intensive study of a short passage. This might take the form of a detailed examination of a particular short text, or alternatively it might involve selecting a particularly significant passage in a novel or other long work, and examining in detail its role in the structure of the whole work. Here, as with the essays, the process of selection was itself educational.

Although the emphasis was placed on direct work with the texts, students were not of course discouraged from gathering further relevant information. One group indeed compiled an enormous dossier of useful background information for their option, consisting of lists of relevant background books available in local libraries, lists of dates of publication of significant works of literature going well beyond the original list, brief biographical details of major authors, and a time-chart of world events which impinged on the authors of the works being read. Students made all the arrangements for the collection, writing up, and production of this material. While there is a risk of such information becoming more important than the reading itself, it is easy for a tutor to step in gently if this appears to be happening, and such background information may often be a stimulus to further reading.

Teaching procedures

Students spent their time, then, reading the texts, writing comments in their reading record files, preparing for the formal assignments, gathering background information, preparing for seminar presentations, or doing anything else appropriate. Those who were happiest working alone could do so, but those who responded to group activities were able to work co-operatively also. Formal seminars sometimes discussed single books—which everyone had agreed to read in time—in considerable detail; sometimes they looked at several books by one author; and sometimes they looked at several different treatments of similar themes. Tutors produced occasional lectures, but only when requested to do so by students. Other formal activities included prepared play-readings, discussion of recordings of drama and poetry, and occasions when students and tutor all arrived with short poems or prose pieces to read and discuss.

To a considerable extent the students determined the teaching procedures and the books chosen, both those read personally and those discussed publicly. The option choices provide a common frame of reference which makes useful co-operative activity possible within the group, but within these limits each student is able to move relatively freely. Some students tend towards a more sociological and some to a more aesthetic approach. At this stage, which direction they move in surely matters less than that they should develop confidence in the relevance of literature to their own development and their ability to respond seriously with enough literary experience to be able to make a relatively informed response. At the same time, however, the close liaison between tutor and student (coupled, it should be said, with a considerable degree of staff–student rapport which developed in all groups) makes it possible for a detailed examination of critical premises to take place over the year. Such strands can be taken up in later work on a formal basis.

Conclusions

It is not being claimed here that any one of the ideas described is particularly original. The great value of the course lay in establishing what might be called a 'reading community': a group of people with varying experience of life and literature, and with the agreed aim of sharing their reading in both formal and informal situations. The ability to sustain such a feeling of community is partly a responsibility of the tutor; but all the tutors on this course felt they gained more by this procedure than they had by more traditional approaches. Students become extremely supportive when there is a structure strong enough to appear authoritative but not strong enough to be authoritarian. In our reading communities we were all engaged on the same task: trying to increase our understanding of some aspect of literature. Tutors were not so much teaching, as setting up the conditions for learning and facilitating the process as it happened. We had not necessarily read all the books which students produced, but this did not matter, for we were concerned with a relationship to books, not with knowledge about a particular set of works. Knowledge became our servant, not our master.

We cannot say whether it worked. We knew that students enjoyed the whole experience and thought it worthwhile. On average, by the end of two terms, students had read twenty-seven books each, twenty-one of them 'properly'. Everyone had been intensively involved in some form of creative engagement with literature, often precisely directed. Might it not be possible that an approach such as this would lay a better foundation for both serious reading in life and academic literary study than any number of set books?

A specimen option list—satire

Arden, John: *Serjeant Musgrave's Dance*
Austen, Jane: *Northanger Abbey*
Butler, Samuel: *The Way of All Flesh*
Byron, Lord George: *Don Juan* and *The Vision of Judgement*
Chaucer, Geoffrey: *The Pardoner's Tale*
Dickens, Charles: *Hard Times*
Fielding, Henry: *Joseph Andrews*
Hardy, Thomas: *Satires of Circumstance*
Heller, Joseph: *Catch 22*
Huxley, Aldous: *Brave New World*
Opie, Iona and Peter: *The Lore and Language of Schoolchildren*
Orwell, George: *Animal Farm*
Peacock, Thomas Love: *Nightmare Abbey*
Pope, Alexander: *The Rape of the Lock*
Private Eye magazine
Shaw, George Bernard: *Major Barbara*
Smith, Edward Lucie (editor): *The Penguin Book of Satirical Verse*
Stoppard, Tom: *The Real Inspector Hound* and *After Magritte*
Swift, Jonathan: *Gulliver's Travels*
Thackeray, William Makepeace: *Vanity Fair*
Trollope, Anthony: *The Way We Live Now*
Voltaire: *Candide* (Penguin translation)
Waugh, Evelyn: *Decline and Fall* and *The Loved One*
plus any other appropriate material chosen by the students.

(Various forms of the course outlined here have been tried out in several different schools and colleges. The course as described here resulted from the intensive discussions of four tutors at what was then the City of Birmingham College of Education, now part of City of Birmingham Polytechnic. I am grateful to Miss V. Owen, Mrs J. Aldridge and Mr S. J. Burke (fellow tutors) and to many students for their contribution to these ideas.)

20 Reading Speed and Literature Teaching

G. D. Pickett

With some teaching experience in British schools recently behind me, I should like in this chapter to consider some facts of reading speed and their effect on teaching literature, largely in a mother-tongue context, but with implications for the foreign-language learner.

Paradoxes

Given the known range of reading speeds and abilities in the average class that is compelled to study English literature, are we justified in teaching literature as if all students read as well as the best of the specialists who teach the language? Furthermore, given that the justification for teaching literature is usually the Leavisite doctrine of English as a discipline of thought, and literature as a sort of general substrate of values underlying *all* education, are our methodological procedures totally at variance with our philosophical and educational premises? Just to complicate matters, the de Leeuws (1965) testify that it is the non-specialists who tend to read quickly, whereas the specialists, in whatever field, tend to read slowly because they do detailed and analytical work. As specialists ourselves, we have all had the galling experience of talking to casual readers who have voraciously romped through works it took us many arid hours to encompass. David Lodge's novel, *Changing Places* (1975), exposes the pretence to which specialists are driven as a result. If we choose to treat English as a specialist rather than as a universal study, however, does the very act of holding it up for consideration at a specialist level retard the reading necessary to master it?

It seems that either way we cannot win. As a 'universal good', literature has to accommodate the slow reader. As a specialism, it induces slow reading. Such a stultifying paradox cannot be ignored indefinitely. We are faced with the prospect that even specialists will know less and less proportionally of a growing corpus and will therefore be less entitled to generalize about it.

Facts of reading life

Let us look a little more closely at certain practical features of the reading situation. According to the de Leeuws (1965: 28), non-pathological reading speeds range from 200–650 words per minute, the former being exceptionally slow, the latter exceptionally fast. The ability is *not*, however, normally distributed in a Gaussian bell-curve with mean, median and mode at about the mid point, 425 w.p.m. i.e. (200 + 650) ÷ 2. On the contrary, most readers are at the slow end of the scale, the most frequent cases reading at speeds between 230 and 250 words per minute. Crowder (1982) cites evidence (p. 9) suggesting that adults read on the average at a rate of about 300 words per minute, but elsewhere in the same book (p. 22) states that: 'Advertisements for speed reading courses typically state correctly that an average adult is reading at about 250 words per minute'. It varies, of course, with the subject matter, the circumstances, the style, and the reader's interest, and with the numerous other factors identified by Holmes and Singer (1966). However, for the purposes of this article, I shall take the figure of 250 w.p.m. as the adult average, and base certain calculations on it. An experiment I did with 26 British sixth-formers aged about 17 who had chosen to study English literature for 'A' level showed their average to be about 230 words per minute (see Appendix).

The modern 'quality' novel favoured by publishers is about 75,000 words long. This would take the slow reader about 6.25 hours, the normal reader 5.5 hours, and the exceptionally fast reader about two hours. Research seems to indicate that once reading facility has been attained in a foreign language, an individual's speed assimilates to his or her mother-tongue reading speed. Hence the fast readers remain fast in a foreign language and can outstrip a slow reader using that language as his or her mother tongue. However, the fast readers at the top end of the scale become such a tiny minority that they hardly come within the purview of public educational provision, and they are not my concern in this article, except as evidence of the great variety in even normal human faculties. The de Leeuws (1965: 29) record results with a group of public administrators who had an initial average group speed of 380 w.p.m. With a group of psychiatrists who started with an initial speed of 334 w.p.m. they were able to get up to a speed of 647 w.p.m. and 85 per cent comprehension. They had one lawyer who began with a speed of 600 w.p.m. (1965: 30). We could afford to leave such exceptionally fast readers out of our calculations, were it not for the fact that abnormally high concentrations of them are to be found in the bodies that set literary standards and devise literature syllabuses. While we must envy and aspire to their vast knowledge of the field, we must also, I believe, treat with caution their rather Olympian view of what is teachable as literature, and devise courses more accommodating to the average reader. Some suggestions for this will follow in due course.

Generalizing and specializing

The range of reading ability outlined above is a fact of life. Crowder (1982: 22–3) is sceptical of the claims of most speed-reading courses and suggests that at the very outside only maximum speeds of 800–900 w.p.m. can be reached—presumably by people like the lawyer mentioned above who already start with 600 w.p.m.! We should therefore not draw up courses and systems for teaching literature on the assumption that all can read fast and acquire the same insights as the teacher or some ideal 'good student'. If we are consciously training specialists, such an assumption does no harm, since it sets an expert pace and target. However, in most British schools this is not the case, and it is even less so in the context of foreign-language teaching. Indeed, one of the alleged benefits of literature is that it is open to all and, unlike physics, pottery, or playing the violin, part of the heritage which all can and should possess. There is a case for separating the generalist and specialist teaching of literature in a mother-tongue context; but in foreign-language teaching we have to assume that the generalist considerations are paramount, and there are, of course, others exclusive to foreign-language teaching.

This would suggest, I think, that we teach literature on the basis of a few texts analysed in detail and presented as a sample of the great heritage that beckons to the student from outside the classroom window. We take the texts as models, their analysis as a technique to be copied, and we send the students forth with the injunction: 'Go ye and do likewise'.

Yet anyone with a good literary background who has taught in this way must have felt the frustration of having to justify interpretations or aesthetic judgements by reference to a wider universe beyond the students' ken—to other works by the same writer, to works by his or her contemporaries, to antecedents at an earlier phase of the literary tradition, to foreign influences, to historical and social background, etc. In other words, the need to explain and enjoy a few works read in detail immediately shows up the limitations of such a practice and points up the need for vast amounts of reading at a more superficial level, of which we know most of our students to be incapable, owing to the time constraint. We seem to be trapped by this paradox, and one way or another dissatisfaction will result. The problem is not merely a practical one, however, but a logical one too. Most teachers dealing in detail with a work of literature recognize and stress its uniqueness, while at the same time considering it a sample. Logically, however, something unique cannot be an example of anything but a superordinate category. Thus *King Lear* is not an example of *Hamlet* or *Andromaque*, but all are examples of the category 'tragedy'. Each single work studied, therefore, draws us into a wider vortex by comparison with which its own structure is trivial. Depending on what our educational aims are, the superordinate category we want to exemplify might be 'literature', 'language', 'psychology', 'history of ideas', 'royalty', or a host of others. Only those of 'literature' and 'language' need concern us here. Any work of literature exemplifies both but stands in a different relation to each, to understand which two approaches are needed.

Two approaches

Much of the dissatisfaction that may arise in literature teaching is of our own making and results from a conflict of aims. In practice, literature teaching tends to take two forms, each contradicting some of the assumptions of the other:

a. Classwork at the class pace, usually the close reading of texts.
b. More rarely, free reading in one's own time and at one's own pace—without the obligation to read closely and form arguable judgements.

These are very different tasks, the former a species of public exemplification, the latter the private application of what has been exemplified. The former is an artificial situation confined to the classroom and to the period of formal education. The latter is the natural situation for consuming literature in real life outside of formal education. We tend to assume that the former shapes the latter, though it is usually only the former that we test. Can the former be justified, however, unless it results in the latter? The only point of learning a 'grammar' of literature, surely, is to acquire a 'competence' in it, and just as in language learning many students never acquire a communicative competence because they are put off by the formal preliminaries of learning the grammar, I suggest that many students are put off literature in later life because of the 'close reading' approach required at school. Of course, there are also those who survive it and go on to become avid readers and acute critics. I would feel happier, however, if we could actually prove a beneficial connection between classwork and free reading in later life. As the latter is essentially private and untestable, proof is unlikely to emerge, and we continue with current classroom practices as an act of faith.

Separating the combatants

I should like to argue that the connection between the two is at best not proven and at worst may be inverse; and that in view of this, it is worthwhile separating them, justifying each on quite different grounds related to concepts of what literature is and what we should teach it for, and then providing for the two quite different syllabuses in educational establishments. We might call one Literature (Intensive/Analytic) and the other Literature (Extensive/Cumulative). The examinations required for each would be quite different. At the present time, it is difficult to say whether our literature teaching has been successful or not, because it is not altogether clear what our criterion of success ought to be. We seem to have two at least. For example, the situation can arise where a slow but sensitive reader gets high marks in class work and examinations because the pace is kept at his level, but fails to take-off as a widely-read student of literature because he can never read enough privately to keep up. Conversely, we can have the case of a fast reader who reads nearly everything conscientiously, but fails to make informed and sensitive judgements as he goes along and ultimately gets little insight into literature as a whole. I know such cases among students and friends and I dare say most readers do too. From my recent experience I can attest that such was the case even in a class that had chosen to specialize in literature, and that each type of student will be more or less a success or failure depending on how we define the purpose and nature of literature teaching. To do each justice, I think we need two definitions rather than one.

Criteria of success

'Defining the purpose and nature of literature teaching' is rather a pompous way of saying 'What are we looking for when we set and mark a literature exam?' In other words, what is the construct behind a literature test?' It might be:

a. knowledge of a particular selection of set books as might be demonstrated by quotations, replies to context questions, summaries of plot, etc. (internal knowledge);

b. knowledge of the relation of such texts to an external framework such as a period of literature, a strand of literature, a whole literature, a non-literary reference like 'history' or 'society' (external knowledge);

c. sensitivity to literature as such, a sort of passive permeability to the best authors;

d. creativity on the basis of literature, a sort of secondary firing imitative of the masters;

e. an ability to think and write clearly (such as might be demonstrated in a variety of non-literary subjects);

f. a linguistic facility displayed in the handling of literary texts;

g. some purely literary ability, presumably including elements of all the above but as consistent and identifiable in its own right as the constructs of, say, intelligence, aptitude, or personality testing. For the moment we might equate this with what Culler calls 'literary competence'. The individual's pattern of performance might be what I have termed elsewhere a 'literalect' (Pickett 1981); and the approximation of this to some ideal competence might provide us with a test criterion.

A comparison of GCE Ordinary Level English Literature standards and marking constructs in 1975 (Houston 1980) revealed that marks were being awarded for three things by the four examination boards studied, to wit: knowledge of set books, relevant use of that knowledge, expression of a personal response. It was found that each of these was in fact given different weight by different boards and even at different grades in examinations set by the same board. It will therefore do no harm to study my expanded list of possible constructs (a)–(g), as they bring in more than is currently tested.

It will be seen that (a) and (b) imply some form of attainment/achievement test, whereas the remainder are, broadly speaking, aptitude tests. For (a) and (b) to be justified, what was done needs to have been worth doing. For the remainder to be justified, the aptitudes developed and predicted need to be worth having. Of the aptitude tests, (d) and (e) go together as productive skills, the ability to write well; (c) and (g) also go together as receptive skills, the ability to respond well; (f) however seems to do no more than confirm the existence of a linguistic ability that can be amply demonstrated in other ways, and in this case it is like (e), which is not wholly dependent on literature for its demonstration. We can imagine circumstances where any one of these testing approaches could be amply justified; but it is hard to imagine any situations in a student's or an adult's life where all could be justified equally. Yet I suggest that literature is frequently taught and tested because of the cumulative weight of all these justifications together, while no single one by itself would seem very persuasive. Of course there is nothing wrong with having multiple reasons of unequal weight for doing something, but by regrouping the reasons, we may find we have two tasks rather than one, and that each is suited to a different segment of the student population: the normal readers and the fast readers.

Two streams

What I suggest, in effect, is that we split literature teaching into two streams:

Intensive/Analytic—for which linguistic interests and ability will be a prerequisite;
Extensive/Cumulative—for which fast reading ability will be a prerequisite.

The entry conditions do not exclude each other, and the possession of both abilities by any student would greatly facilitate his or her success and enjoyment, whichever stream was opted for. Such students would achieve a synthesis hoped for but not specifically aimed at, in the same way that we may leave school with a 'broad education' having studied Latin, Physics, Woodwork, History, etc. as quite separate subjects. The two literature streams, however, are intended to diverge unashamedly, the first descending into the unshaped linguistic raw material out of which literature is shaped, the second ascending to those higher-order abstractions at which literature points.

The idea is not wholly new. Several examining boards in Britain have two syllabuses for English literature at GCE Ordinary level. The London University board has this to say about its Syllabus A:

> The intention of the examination is to provide students with a detailed knowledge of a small part of English literature; most of them will never again study a book with the same thoroughness, but it should provide them with the knowledge that books of value are not to be completely comprehended in a single casual reading and that close and careful reading can give a pleasure of its own. For this purpose, a full and detailed knowledge of a play, poem or work of fiction in prose, and the ability to quote freely and refer closely, is essential; it is on this knowledge that understanding of character, form and structure is based.

But for Syllabus B the philosophy is different:

> Teachers and pupils alike are showing enterprise in their choice of material and seem to be participating in a lively study of literature through careful reading, sensible discussion and effective writing. Enjoyment of what is read and the development of an honest, personal response are plainly their chief aims as they are the aims of the examiners . . . the examiners value highly the personal response, at once imaginative and scholarly, that is essential to a fruitful study of literature. Like them the examiners want reading and talking about books to lay the foundation for a lifetime of pleasure.

Duty and delight

But contrast the respective overtones of duty and delight in the two syllabuses. Those taking Syllabus A will be given a brief beatific vision of a pleasure available in theory but hardly ever in practice once full-time education is ended; one which the examiners know will rarely be acute enough for pupils to perpetuate it in later life and one which, by revealing how rich and many-layered a work of literature is, puts it virtually out of the reach of the 'casual' reader at normal speed, which is what the vast majority of them become. Syllabus B, on the other hand, lays 'the foundation for a lifetime of pleasure' based on 'honest, personal response'—which must include, one imagines, honest rejections of distasteful works. As F. W. Bateson (1972: 71) puts it, while we hope for a positive response on the whole, 'a corollary is that negative emotional responses such as the conscientious reader's total lack of interest in a book, are also a fact of criticism. The right not to be unnecessarily bored is one of the most important of our literary rights as scholar–critics.' This right is not extended to the student doing Syllabus A.

Syllabus A seems to exist mainly to demonstrate to the bored majority that there is some justification for the minority pleasure enjoyed by those who do Syllabus B. Quite apart from the 'them and us' implications of such syllabuses, it appears that neither goes far enough in its own chosen direction to grasp the positive benefits that a dual approach might secure. If we compare, for example, both the Oxford Ordinary Level syllabuses for 1983, we find that in practice the syllabus that ostensibly demands wider reading—*English Literature (General)*—could be handled with little more reading than is required for the other, viz. three set books. Though the syllabus 'presupposes wider reading than is normally possible for candidates in one year of study, and opportunity is given in the paper to show evidence of wider reading . . . and each question will normally require knowledge of more than one work', in fact we have such questions as the following in the 1983 paper:

> Show how Shakespeare combines comic and serious elements within the same play.

> Write about the work of two poets who have particularly excited your imagination or emotions. (When the two poets chosen could both come from the same anthology.)

The 1982 paper was even more amenable to the parsimonious reader:

> Show how any one novel depicts the social setting in which the story takes place.

> Write an appreciation of one longer poem which has especially interested you.

Maximizing the results of difference

This timidity in moving away from a middle ground that presumably all candidates can tackle stems, I suggest, from a failure to recognize the implications of differential reading speeds. The average Ordinary Level class will have the usual distribution of fast and slow readers, and there is no reason why the fast readers should not be given their head and told to work through a given proportion of an extensive reading list with permission to drop any work which, after they have read a quarter of it, fails to engage their interest. Class discussion will reveal just how much tastes can differ across a group of normal pupils, and it is precisely this differential pattern of response that the teacher should highlight so that, from a Babel of jarring 'literalects', emerge the harmonies of a literary competence which all can recognize, even where they dissent from it.

The slower readers, meanwhile, have another task. Whereas for the fast readers the rules of literary competence are not laid down in advance but grow from individual reading experience and collective discussion, the slower readers have their competence preselected for them, and the few works on the syllabus are expected to illustrate it, however inadequately. Unfortunately for British students, that inevitably includes Shakespeare and frequently Chaucer too. Their language is sufficiently remote from modern English that a large proportion of the class time is spent in explaining vocabulary; whatever literary pleasure eventually results has been gained at high cost in linguistic carnage. The path of duty was ever hard, however, and as they are in blood stepped in so far that 'returning were as tedious as go o'er', I suggest they push on further towards the analysis of literature and abandon the pretence of real enjoyment and literary enlightenment. If they get that too, well and good, but the success or failure of the course should not be measured by whether they do or not. Rather than agonize over the choice of this or that set book, teachers might be better employed adopting a rationale that will justify the inevitably unrepresentative choice that will have to be made if three books are to exemplify the three hundred or three thousand that might equally well have been chosen. Such an inadequate sample is not a basis for generalizing about literature, but rather a basis for particularizing about language. It may enhance language competence but can hardly, I suggest, develop a literary competence.

Language and literature

That can only come to those who are so interested in the subject that they will spend most of their free time reading; or to those who read so fast and so attentively that they can devour a great deal of literature and still have time to study certain works in depth. It is a mistake to imagine there is a continuum between language competence and literary competence, the latter being a more elaborate form of the former. Still less is there a relation of dependence between the two. One can learn a language to a very high standard without reading any literature in it. Conversely, one can be an appreciative consumer of a literature without being able to speak, except haltingly, the language in which it is couched. Of course in both cases something will be lacking and it is to obviate this lack that literature and language study are kept closely together. Their bearing on one another, however, varies as between native and foreign students. For native speakers literature will enrich their language but not make a very perceptible contribution to their linguistic competence. By the time they are adults, they will have as much of it as they are going to need.

For foreign learners, however, who do not start off with the same degree of language competence in the new language, the acquisition of a literary competence, defective as it is bound to be in the early stages, is a valuable reinforcement and development of language competence—valuable but not indispensable. If they are already well read in their own literature so much the better; yet this in itself may have a dampening effect. When one is fully conscious of how much in one's own literature—apart from the referential meaning of words—is both allusive and elusive and how even a native speaker only tentatively understands many of the great works of his or her own heritage, one must hesitate to suppose that one's knowledge of a foreign literature can ever be on a par. To be 'biliteral' is much rarer than being bilingual and is only possible to those rather rare cases of bilinguals who have an equal and complete command of both languages over all domains likely to be mentioned in literature. Having myself at various times written essays or voiced opinions on works in languages other than my own, I am acutely aware, now that I know English literature better, how incomplete my understanding must have been. Even where I understood the language, I probably missed the things that turned it into literature. Looking back, I can see that all that reading did benefit my command of the language; but it was the language in those works, not their literariness, that did it.

Response to the text

This brings us finally to the question of 'ethos' in relation to reading speed. As defined by Group μ (1981), ethos is 'an affective state raised in the receiver by a particular message and whose specific quality varies as a function of a certain number of parameters. Among them, a large place is reserved for the addressee himself.' Though ethos is a subjective impression, it 'is always motivated, in the last analysis, by objective data'. The type of syllabus I have called *Intensive/Analytic* concentrates on identifying and describing these objective data and assessing the types of ethos to which they may give rise. The *Extensive/Cumulative* syllabus starts with the configuration of ethos within the class group then, by comparison and discussion, traces the ethos back to the objective data that caused it. Both processes meet in the field known as *theoretical semics* (Eaton 1972), which studies the recorded range of subjective response to literary stimuli. This has nothing to do with judgement or appreciation, a statement as to whether the response was or was not worth having. It covers the much less debateable ground of normative reactions to literature. Granted that each individual response will be different, there are limits on the differences that will be recorded. Whether or not they like *Wuthering Heights* or *Hamlet*, most readers would agree that they lead to an affective state of sadness and purgation in the reader. It is this type of broad consensus that semics covers, and a teacher can sense this in a class before the processes of analysis and judgement come in to ruin it. I vividly remember such an occasion reading George Herbert's 'Redemption' to a class of third-formers, not normally an auspicious audience for Jacobean devotional verse, especially nowadays when we cannot take for granted a background feeling for Christian symbolism. The hush that momentarily fell on the class after the last line ('Who straight, "Your suit is granted", said, and died') was broken by an almost embarrassed voice from the back row, 'It's sad', and after that anything more that was said about the poem, however ingenious or scholarly, was pure anti-climax. The need to analyse and judge turned the real literary experience sour.

Judgement

Judgement, however, looms large in literature courses, especially those of the Extensive/Cumulative type when, at the end of the day, all that may be left is an array of likes and dislikes associated with certain authors and works. Indeed, the prior judgement of a teacher or of a 'literary establishment' is usually the basis on which texts are selected in the first place. Many teachers feel they cannot teach books they do not like, and at the beginning of the school year there is a fair amount of horse-trading among the literature staff so that each feels more or less comfortable with the selection he or she has to teach. Yet judgement rather obscures the issues of literature teaching. As Group μ (1981: 162) explain, 'we have carefully distinguished ethos and value judgement. It is acknowledged, however, that every text can arouse a certain appreciation. But this effect is metastylistic; it is logically posterior to the recognition of an ethos derived from the entire text . . . The act that consists of expressing, manifestly or not, aesthetic satisfaction or discontent before a particular text indeed supposes the presence of a scale of values that until now have escaped any precise measurement.' Indeed, these are values derived from life, not literature, and it is here that the literature teacher must bow out as specialist and assume the much more challengeable role of human being. It is the nemesis of teaching literature as a source of value that one must also be exemplary as a product of that teaching in one's daily life.

Divergent paths

As the diagram below shows, the area of literary study is bounded on one side by language, the raw substance of literature, and on the other by life, the raw substance of evaluated experience. Between these two and connecting them is the literary artefact, which is a deliberately composed message from some remote writer to an unknown reader. The process of literature study has three phases which we can separate logically though not chronologically, since in real cases the phases tend to occur simultaneously or leapfrog one another. One is *analysis,* another *ethos,* and the third *judgement.* What I am suggesting is that, in view of differential reading speeds, literature teaching could usefully be split into two as shown, the *Intensive/Analytic approach* being devoted to relating language to *ethos via analysis,* while the *Extensive/ Cumulative approach* relates life to *ethos via judgement.* The complete literary devotee and fast reader can, of course, start from either end and run the whole gamut, but that will be a decision that comes late in one's full-time education. At an earlier stage different groups of

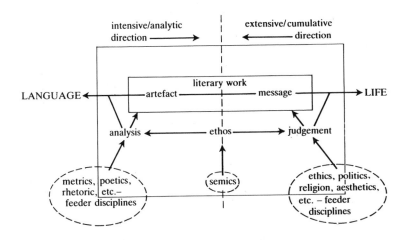

Figure 20.1: A suggested partition of literature study

students should be introduced to literature by one or the other route and the decision which to take should be made largely on the basis of reading speed and efficiency, which can easily be tested in advance.

The figures I gave above did not quite bring out the dramatic way in which a fast reader outstrips a normal reader when we consider not simply the additive processes of reading books in linear succession, but the capacity for comparisons between what has been read and the modifications to ethos-response that such comparisons entail.

Take some rough figures, for example. The average reader (250 w.p.m.) and the moderately fast reader (say 500 w.p.m.) are soon going to get further and further apart on what they have read in a ratio of at least 2:1. In forming connections and comparisons between what they have read, however, the disparity is explosive, since the differences progress geometrically, not arithmetically. For example, the reader who has four items in his or her literary experience (A, B, C and D) has 24 possibilities of ordering and comparing them in pairs (AB, BA, AD, DA, AC, CA for A alone and the same for each of B, C and D). A reader who reads twice as fast, however, will have eight comparable items to match (always assuming both have the same retention), hence 112 possibilities. If we get any more complicated than that, the disparity grows even more dramatically, e.g. combinations of all previous items with the most recently read item, as might be represented D compared with ABC; or an early work in the perspective of subsequent reading, A compared with BCD, etc.

In so far as literature is a finite corpus (and is it?) the proportion of the fast reader's acquisition to the whole will be similarly that far in advance of the slow reader's, and he or she will move into a reading situation which, again, is qualitatively different from that of the slower reader and is analogous with a walk up a mountain:

1 The fast reader reads more texts in linear progression and isolation (concentrating on each footstep up the path).

2 The later ones are read in the context of and with memory of the earlier ones, so that the fast reader's apprehension of a single text is conditioned by a richer literary experience, and his or her perspective on the earlier texts is constantly being adjusted. (Looking down the path to assess how much progress has been made.)

3 The proportion of texts read to those in the whole literature increases, so that the fast reader has an increasing consciousness of the whole corpus, not just as an aggregate of isolated texts but as an organic body embracing, defining, and articulating them. Comparisons are then not made merely from text to text (item to item), but from text/item to superordinate body. He or she is reading literature, not merely texts. (Near the summit, looking down at the whole mountain and the relations of features on it.)

Where does reading speed fit?

An interesting question arises when we try to insert reading speed somewhere into the scheme in Figure 20.1. Clearly it is not an objective quality in the text but a quality of the reader. Nevertheless, people will often say a book is 'very readable' or 'I couldn't put it down'. If the way the text is put together produces these comments, however, perhaps reading speed *is* a part of ethos. You read the book quickly because you enjoy it and it holds your attention. It does so largely because of objective qualities of the text but also, no doubt, because of some factor of peculiar sympathy between reader and writer. (These personal factors are an essential part of ethos but are virtually untraceable except where a reader chooses to mention them. Thus, for example, Edmund Gosse (1907: 122) mentions the word 'carmine' as 'my shibboleth of self indulgence; it was a symbol of all that taste and art and wealth could combine to produce.' In this case a particular word has a hold over him, but similarly subject matter, places, occupations, historical periods, and a host of other 'incidentals' may also differentially repel or attract particular readers.) Wherever we choose to put reading speed, there must be limits to its variability for individuals and I believe these will not be greater, for example, than the variations resulting from the outside circumstances of the reading act e.g. weather, temperature, time of day, humidity, background noise, etc. The test I did with my sixth-formers described above took place with two separate groups. One group did the test in the first period on a cool morning and got an average speed of 250 words per minute. The others did it in the last period on one of the hottest afternoons of the year and achieved an average speed of only 211 words per minute. Reading efficiency, expressed as the square root of the product of reading rate and percentage score on a comprehension/retention test, tended also to be higher among the morning group. Factors of the text itself that might increase reading speed noticeably will have to do with layout—paragraphing, indentation, sub-headings etc.—rather than with literary quality. Indeed these are features of writing at the opposite pole from literariness where the goal is absolute clarity, plain simple language, short sense units, and a one-to-one relationship of sign and meaning. Far from drawing attention to itself, the language tries to be the unobtrusive conveyor of a message, aspiring to Coleridge's model (1835) for good prose as opposed to poetry: 'The words in prose ought to express the intended meaning and no more; if they attract attention to themselves, it is, in general, a fault' (*Table Talk* 1,84). From this we might conclude that the more literary a text is, the slower reading will it demand. Conversely, textual qualities that conduce to fast reading may indicate defective literature.

Whatever the case may be, providing we allow a narrow band for variation, we can regard reading speeds as fairly fixed and constant. I suggest it is one of the addressee parameters of which, according to Group μ (1981: 154), ethos is a function. 'The value attached to a text is not pure entelechy [i.e. a potential realized] but a response of the reader or hearer. In other words, the latter is not content to receive an intangible aesthetic datum but reacts to certain stimuli. And this response is an appreciation.' It may be suggested, therefore, that variations within an individual's usual range of reading speeds could be an index of appreciation traceable to the objective data that contribute to ethos. However, the pleasure or displeasure at *having* read more or less quickly than usual that might then result belongs outside of ethos, just like the self-satisfaction one might feel at having read a classic. Indeed, Mark Twain defined a classic as 'a book which everyone wants to have read, but nobody wants to read', thus neatly separating the pleasures of reading and having read.

Conditions of reading

Even if we feel a book is eminently readable, we may none the less frequently 'put it down', voluntarily as well as by necessity. This is not a question of reading speed as such, but of the time one takes to finish a work and the span of pauses one permits. Ideally, one should read one book at a time so that, for a while, one is immersed in that author's world and maximally awake to references forwards and backwards in the text. To read otherwise is to risk forgetting a great deal and missing a large proportion of these cross-references in the text. The interruptions can only disturb our enjoyment of the author's imaginative world, dull the flavour of the style, dilute the concentration of his or her original vision. Yet how little of our reading is done in this way, especially in formal educational contexts where one book may be spread out thinly over several weeks of classwork! There are those who read a novel-a-night steadily for fifty years, but equally there are those who read six books intermittently but in parallel over several weeks, in bus queues, in commuter trains, at breakfast, in bed, and in a variety of other settings that must, one imagines, detract from the impact of the book. There are many other reading styles that depart from the ideal. Though I am not myself a fast reader at the best of times, I now tend to read even slower if I am enjoying a book, and put off coming to the end. I frequently leave books in the middle and come back to them years later and take up where I left off. I am not advocating this for anyone, merely illustrating the point that variations in reading style, like variations in reading speed, call in question some of our assumptions in literature teaching.

The stability of the text

Referring back to the diagram above, what remains stable in all this is the text and its analysability into the data that give rise to ethos. What must be unstable, it seems to me, is the ethos, in view of all these bad reading habits and 'addressee parameters' to which it is subject. The judgement that is based on an adulterated ethos must also be suspect. Yet despite these incidentals of the reading situation, there is remarkable consensus that the literary object is one and stable and giving rise to a constant ethos. It is as if we were playing a musical score at our own convenience, at our own pace, at our own level of skill or incompetence, and somehow the work survived. How remarkably inviolate the work of literature remains can be seen if we try to contrast it with an equivalent musical example, say, an atrocious record of Beethoven's Fifth Symphony played at the wrong speed and the rate of one movement per week. That would hardly count as a performance; yet our reading, apparently, counts as a reading.

It appears then that the literary work exists tenaciously in the inner space of our minds and becomes an object of contemplation over quite long periods quite independently of what is going on outside. This stable object of contemplation seems to require quite different treatment in our teaching from that appropriate to the ethos to which it may give rise, and the judgement that will be made upon it. The normal readers should focus on that object and study the way it comes to achieve that status; these are questions of language, psychology, and physiology. The fast readers, because they are in a position to make many more comparisons than the others and to understand how, despite differences, all that they read constitutes the social institution of literature, should concentrate on judgement and ethos, the effects of literary works on individuals and their society, and the circular relationship that binds these once again to language.

Two faces of literature

There was a time when the term 'natural philosophy' covered all of what we now call science and which is now split into the separate disciplines of physics, chemistry, biology and beyond that into biophysics, biochemistry, astrophysics, etc. There is no end to the segmentation that can be made and I am suggesting it is high time literature study underwent a similar segmentation. This is not to deny the actual unity of the whole field, merely to recognize that so much is now known about it that it might benefit from two subdisciplines that would approach the subject from opposite ends—a micro- and a macro-study, if you like. These might respectively be termed 'lingua-literature' and 'socio-literature' to clarify their terms of reference, the former analysing the artefact into its components, the latter viewing the whole artefact in its superordinate, relations.

The term 'literature' has, after all, travelled a long way during its short career in the English language. In the eighteenth century it still meant a personal intellectual quality, so that you could speak of someone as 'having a very good literature', i.e knowledge of and taste for literature. It is not until 1812 that we find it used to mean a body of books, the possession of a nation rather than of an individual, and only in the last hundred years has the term come to confer almost canonical status on the body of books referred to. This 'canonicity' is the new sociological fact that requires us to add a dimension to literary study.

We have come a long way from the time when poetry and criticism were dismissed by Pope, a professional to his fingertips, as an optional and rather trivial extra in life: 'I am afraid this extreme zeal on both sides is ill-placed; Poetry and Criticism being by no means the universal concern of the world, but only the affair of idle men who write in their closets, and idle men who read there' (Preface to *Works*, 1717 p. 1). He could hardly have imagined that it would one day be a subject widely taught and examined, engulfing millions of teenagers every year.

At the same time as literature was passing from being a personal possession to a communal one, attention was moving from the individual complete artefact to some underlying literary essence alleged to be present in all literature. We are beholden to the twentieth century and a Slavonic language for the term 'literariness', but hints of it grow right through the nineteenth century. Whereas the eighteenth century, as Sutherland points out (1948), wrote and criticized in terms of 'the poem', i.e. a completely fashioned artefact, the Romantics were more concerned with 'poetry', seen as the underlying substance in all poems and bearing the same relation to them as batter to Yorkshire puddings. The Romantics cheerfully published 'fragments', e.g. Keats's *Hyperion*, on the assumption that there was enough 'poetry' to make it worthwhile, even though it did not amount to a poem. We have extended the idea to apply to all literature and frequently speak as if literature was not only a corpus of books but also the underlying substance of those books, detectable in each of them. No doubt we need the term 'literariness' to take over this part of its meaning.

Medium and message

With the communalization and essentialization of literature has come its reification. We are taught not merely to look for the message through the artefact, but to look at the artefact as the message. As

Hawkes (1977) puts it, 'Poetic language is deliberately self-conscious, self-aware. It emphasizes itself as a "medium" over and above the "message" it contains; . . . as a result, words in poetry have the status not simply of vehicles for thoughts, but of objects in their own right, autonomous concrete entities. In Saussure's terms, then, they cease to be "signifiers" but "signifieds", and it is the poem's alienating devices of rhythms, rhyme, metre, etc. which enable this structural change to be achieved.' Lest anyone disbelieve that this structure can have an autonomous existence, let me testify to frequently forgetting the actual words of a poem but retaining its form and rhythm. Most recently, I remember reading, then forgetting, Auden's

> Lay your sleeping head, my love,
> Human on my faithless arm . . .

but carrying around the rhythm in my head like an empty bucket in search of water. Similarly another poem, Wyatt's

> There was never nothing more me pained
> Nor nothing more me moved . . .

was so strongly patterned that the sound pattern remained along with some semantic residue (the repetitious double negatives) even when the actual words were forgotten.

The reality of fiction

Now it seems to me that such mental objects, communally possessed and linked together by some common essence we call literariness, are of the same ontological status as the matter studied in the physical sciences. Indeed, Oakeshott (1959) points out that science is no less a succession of images than poetry, which he defines as 'the activity of making images of a certain kind and moving among them in a manner appropriate to their character.. . . . images of pleasure recognized as facts, and this presupposes a distinction between "fact" and "non-fact". As I understand it, the distinction between "fact" and "non-fact" is a distinction between different kinds of images and not a distinction between something that is not an image and a mere image.' In studying the act of reading, Iser (1978) suggests that the reader's self-involvement in the act of ideation before a literary text makes him value images more highly than perceptual experiences. How frequently do we hear people discussing topics of the day not with reference to some factual account in the news but to some novelist's elaboration of the topic. For instance, it would now be difficult to read the facts about espionage without giving them a colouring derived from Len Deighton or John Le Carré. Fiction is thus invading the territory traditionally reserved for fact. Increasingly we are brought to recognize that these mental literary objects now coming into focus demand the subdividing of literature study that I have been advocating. As Eaton (1980) wrote in reviewing Iser's book, 'the urgent task at the moment is to concentrate research upon how a person *does* read, rather than upon how people *ought* to read'. Obviously no dramatic changes can be expected, but a first step towards any change at all is to legitimize the separation of literature into the two aspects I have proposed. If, as Culler (1975) suggests, 'poetics is essentially a theory of reading', we need to begin with the experience of real readers; and within that experience, speed of reading is both important and observable. It is hoped that this preliminary foray into the subject will facilitate the development of such a theory.

Appendix
Reading Speed and Efficiency Experiment—June 1983

Twenty-six British lower-sixth-form boys, average age about 17, were given to read a complete story of 1,863 words by Washington Irving entitled *A Broken Heart*, which combines the factual narrative and authorial comment typical of a literary text. All started together, and finishing times for each were noted. Immediately on finishing, each did a comprehension/retention test of 24 multiple-choice items. Score was expressed as a percentage and the reading time recorded in seconds before conversion to a reading rate in words per minute. An index of reading efficiency was the score × rate, but to reduce the numbers the square root of this was taken.

Subject	Speed rank	Reading time	Rate w.p.m.	% score	Score × rate rounded	Square root of score × rate	Efficiency rank	Morning or afternoon
A	1	345 secs.	324	75.04	24313	156	3=	A
B	2	349	320	54.24	17357	131	9=	M
C	3	360	310	87.52	27131	165	1	A
D	4	383	292	41.76	12194	110	20	M
E	5	383	292	83.36	24341	156	3=	M
F	6	403	277	91.68	25395	159	2	M
G	7	407	275	62.56	17204	131	9=	M
H	8	425	263	79.20	20830	144	5	M
I	9	426	262	41.76	10941	105	22=	M
J	10	453	247	37.60	9287	96	26	M
K	11	470	238	58.40	13899	117	15=	M
L	12	480	233	79.20	18454	135	7	M
M	13	480	233	70.88	16515	128	12	A
N	14	495	226	79.20	17899	133	8	A
O	15	495	226	83.36	18839	137	5	M
P	16	508	220	70.88	15594	125	13	A
Q	17	509	219	62.56	13701	117	15=	A
R	18	535	209	62.56	13075	114	17	M
S	19	535	209	50.08	10467	102	25.	M
T	20	563	198	54.24	10739	104	24	A
U	21	564	198	62.56	12386	111	19	A
V	22	580	192	87.52	16804	129	11	A
W	23	627	178	62.56	11136	105	22=	A
X	24	682	163	87.52	14266	119	14	A
Y	25	724	154	75.04	11556	108	21	A
Z	26	805	138	91.68	12652	112	18	A

References

(Note: all scholarly references in the text are given below, together with some recent or relatively inaccessible works of literature. Well-known literary texts are not included.)

Abbs, B. and M. Sexton. 1978. *Challenges*. London: Longman.
Adeyanju, T. K. 1978. 'Teaching literature and human values in ESL: objectives and selection.' *ELT Journal* XXXII/2: 133–7.
Alatis, J., H. Altman, and P. Alatis (eds.) 1981. *The Second Language Classroom: Directions for the 1980s*. New York: Oxford University Press.
Alderson, J. C. and A. Urquhart (eds.) 1984. *Reading in a Foreign Language*. London: Longman.
Allen, H. and R. Campbell (eds.) 1972. *Teaching English as a Second Language*. New York: McGraw Hill.
Allen, P. 1975. 'The sacred hoop: a contemporary Indian perspective on American Indian literature' in Chapman 1975.

Bailey, R. W. and M. Görlach. 1982. *English as a World Language*. Ann Arbor, Michigan: Michigan University Press.
Bateson, F. W. 1972. *The Scholar Critic*. London: Routledge & Kegan Paul.
Blunt, J. 1977. 'Response to reading.' *English in Education* 11: 32–41.
Brazil, D. C. 1983. 'Kinds of English: spoken, written, literary' in Stubbs and Hillier 1983.
Breen, M. and C. N. Candlin. 1981. 'The essentials of a communicative curriculum.' *Applied Linguistics* 2/1: 89–112.
ten Brinke, S. 1977. *The Complete Mother Tongue Curriculum*. London: Longman.
Britton, J. 1971. 'What's the use?' *Educational Review* 23/3: 205–19 (reprinted in Cashdan 1972).
Brumfit, C. J. 1970. 'Literature teaching in Tanzania.' *Journal of the Language Association of Eastern Africa* 1: 38–44 (reprinted in this volume).
Brumfit, C. J. 1979. *Readers for Foreign Learners of English* (Information Guide 7). London: The British Council.
Brumfit, C. J. (ed.) 1983. *Teaching Literature Overseas: Language-Based Approaches* (*ELT Documents* 114). Oxford: Pergamon.
Brumfit, C. J. 1984. *Communicative Methodology in Language Teaching*. Cambridge: Cambridge University Press.
Brumfit, C. J. and K. Johnson (eds.) 1979. *The Communicative Approach to Language Teaching*. Oxford: Oxford University Press.

Candlin, C. N. and **C. Edelhoff.** 1982. *Challenges: Teacher's Guide.* London: Longman.

Carter, R. A. 1982a. 'Responses to language in poetry' in Carter and Burton 1982.

Carter, R. A. (ed.) 1982b. *Language and Literature: An Introductory Reader in Stylistics.* London: George Allen and Unwin.

Carter, R. A. 1985. 'Stylistics' in R. B. Kaplan (ed.): *Annual Review of Applied Linguistics V.* New York: Cambridge University Press.

Carter, R. A. and **D. Burton** (eds.) 1982. *Literary Text and Language Study.* London: Edward Arnold.

Carter, R. A. and **M. N. Long** (forthcoming). *The Web of Words: Language-Based Approaches to Literature.* Cambridge: Cambridge University Press.

Carter, R. A. and **W. Nash.** 1983. 'Language and literariness.' *Prose Studies* 6/2: 121–41.

Cashdan, A. (ed.) 1972. *Language in Education.* London: The Open University Press/Routledge & Kegan Paul.

Césaire, A. 1969. *Return to My Native Land.* London: Penguin.

Chapman, A. 1975. *Literature of the American Indians: Views and Interpretations.* New York: Meridian.

Coleridge, S. T. 1835. *Table Talk* (edited by H. N. Coleridge). Oxford: Oxford University Press.

Cox, C. B. and **A. E. Dyson.** 1963. *Modern Poetry: Studies in Practical Criticism.* London: Edward Arnold.

Cox, C. B. and **A. E. Dyson.** 1965. *The Practical Criticism of Poetry.* London: Edward Arnold.

Cripwell, K. and **J. A. Foley.** 1984. 'The grading of extensive readers.' *World Language English* 3/3: 168–78.

Crowder, R. G. 1982. *The Psychology of Reading: An Introduction.* Oxford: Oxford University Press.

Crystal, D. and **D. Davy.** 1969. *Investigating English Style.* London: Longman.

Culler, J. 1975. *Structuralist Poetics.* London: Routledge & Kegan Paul.

Culler, J. 1981. *The Pursuit of Signs.* London: Routledge & Kegan Paul.

Daiches, D. 1970. 'The place of English in the Sussex scheme' in D. Daiches (ed.): *The Idea of a New University.* Cambridge, Ma: MIT Press.

Davies, A. 1978. 'Survey articles on language testing.' *Language Teaching and Linguistics Abstracts* 11: 145–59 and 215–51.

Davies, A. and **H. G. Widdowson.** 1974. 'Reading and writing' in J. P. B. Allen and S. Pit Corder (eds.): *Techniques in Applied Linguistics.* London: Oxford University Press.

Donelson, K. and **A. Nilsen.** 1980. *Literature for Today's Young Adults.* Glenview, Ill.: Scott Foresman.

Eagleton, T. 1983. *Literary Theory.* Oxford: Basil Blackwell.

Eaton, T. 1972. *Theoretical Semics.* The Hague: Mouton.

Eaton, T. 1980. Review of Iser: *The Act of Reading. Style* XIV/2: 179–81.

Fassler, D. and **N. Lay.** 1979. *Encounters with a New World.* Englewood Cliffs, NJ: Prentice-Hall.

Fish, S. E. 1973. 'How ordinary is ordinary language?' *New Literary History* 5: 41–54.

Fowler, R. 1971. 'Introduction' in R. Fowler (ed.): *The Languages of Literature.* London: Routledge & Kegan Paul.

Freedman, A., I. Pringle, and **J. Yalden** (eds.) 1983. *Learning to Write: First Language/Second Language.* London: Longman.

Frye, N. 1957. *Anatomy of Criticism.* Princeton, NJ: Princeton University Press.

Frye, N. 1964. *The Educated Imagination.* Bloomington, Ind: Indiana University Press.

Furness, J. 1970. '"A" level English through sociology.' *The Use of English* 22/1.

Gaies, S. 1979. 'Linguistic input in formal second language learning.' *TESOL Quarterly* 13/1: 41–50.

Girard, D. 1972. *Linguistics and Foreign Language Teaching.* London: Longman.

Gläser, R. 1975. 'Emotive features in scientific and technical English' in Ringbom 1975.

Gosse, E. 1907. *Father and Son.* (Reprinted by Penguin, London, 1949.)

Grauberg, W. 1970. 'Set books in the sixth form course.' *Modern Languages* LI/2: 56–9.

Gregory, M. and **S. Carroll.** 1978. *Language and Situation.* London: Routledge & Kegan Paul.

Group μ. 1981. *A General Rhetoric* (translated by P. B. Burrell and E. M. Slotkin). Baltimore: Johns Hopkins University Press.

Halliday, M. A. K. 1973. *Explorations in the Functions of Language.* London: Edward Arnold.

Harding, D. W. 1937. 'The role of the onlooker.' *Scrutiny* 6/3: 247–58. (Reprinted in Cashdan 1972.)

Harweg, R. 1980. 'Beginning a text.' *Discourse Processes*, Vol. 3.

Hasan, R. 1984. 'The nursery tale as a genre.' *Nottingham Linguistic Circular* 13, Special Issue on Systemic Linguistics.

Hawkes, T. 1977. *Structuralism and Semiotics.* London: Methuen.

Haynes, J. 1976. 'Polysemy and association in poetry.' *ELT Journal* XXXI/1: 56–62.

Heaton, J. B. 1975. *Writing English Language Tests.* London: Longman.

Hoggart, R. 1964. 'The critical moment.' *Times Literary Supplement.*

Holmes, J. A. and **H. Singer.** 1966. *Speed and Power of Reading in High School.* Washington DC: US Department of Health, Education, and Welfare.

Honeyfield, J. 1977. 'Simplification.' *TESOL Quarterly* 11/4: 431–40.

Hornsey, A. 1970. 'Set books and sixth-form studies.' *Modern Languages* LI/4: 147–52.

Houston, J. G. 1980. *Report of the Inter-Board Cross-Moderation Study in English Literature at Ordinary Level: 1975.* Aldershot: Associated Examining Board.

Iser, W. 1978. *The Act of Reading: A Theory of Aesthetic Response.* Baltimore: John Hopkins University Press.

Iyengar, K. R. S. 1962. *Indian Writing in English.* Bombay and New York: Asia Publishing House.

Jakobson, R. 1960. 'Concluding statement: linguistics and poetics' in Sebeok 1960.

Johnson, K. 1983. 'Communicative writing practice and Aristotelian rhetoric' in Freedman, Pringle, and Yalden (eds.) 1983.

Johnson, K. and **K. Morrow** (eds.) 1978. *Functional Materials and the Classroom Teacher.* Reading: Centre for Applied Language Studies.

Johnson, K. and **K. Morrow** (eds.) 1981. *Communication in the Classroom.* London: Longman.

Johnson, P. 1981. 'Effects on reading comprehension of language complexity and cultural background of a text.' *TESOL Quarterly* 15/2: 169–81.

Jupp, T. C. *et al.* 1979. *Encounters.* London: Heinemann.

Kachru, B. 1965. 'The *Indianness* in Indian English.' *Word* 21: 391–410.

Kachru, B. 1976. 'Models of English for the third world: white man's linguistic burden or language pragmatics?' *TESOL Quarterly* 10/2: 221–39.

Kachru, B. 1980. 'The pragmatics of non-native varieties of English' in L. E. Smith (ed.) 1981.

Kachru, B. 1981. 'American English and other Englishes' in C. Ferguson and S. B. Heath (eds.) *Language in the USA.* New York: Cambridge University Press.

Kachru, B. 1982a. (ed.) *The Other Tongue: English Across Cultures.* Urbana, Ill: University of Illinois Press.

Kachru, B. 1982b. 'South Asian English' in Bailey and Görlach (eds.) 1982.

Kachru, B. 1983a. 'The bilingual's creativity: discoursal and stylistic strategies in contact literatures in English.' *Studies in the Linguistic Sciences* 13/2: 38–55.

Kachru, B. 1983b. *The Indianization of English.* New Delhi: Oxford University Press.

Labov, W., 1972. *Language in the Inner City.* Philadelphia, PA: University of Pennsylvania Press.

Lakoff, G. and **M. Johnson.** 1980. *Metaphors We Live By.* Chicago: University of Chicago Press.

Lal, P. (ed.) 1969. *Modern Indian Poetry in English.* Calcutta: Writers Workshop.

Leavis, F. R. 1969. *Lectures in America.* London: Chatto and Windus.

Leech, G. N. 1966. *English in Advertising.* London: Longman.

Leech, G. N. 1969. *A Linguistic Guide to English Poetry.* London: Longman.

Leech, G. N. 1974. *Semantics.* London: Penguin.

Leech, G. N. and **M. H. Short.** 1981. *Style in Fiction.* London: Longman.

de Leeuw, M. and **E. de Leeuw.** 1965. *Read Better, Read Faster.* London: Penguin.

Levin, S. R. 1965. 'Internal and external deviation in poetry.' *Word* 21: 225–37.

Lexalt, R. 1957. *Sweet Promised Land.* New York: Harper and Brothers.

Littlewood, W. T. 1976. 'Literary and informational texts in language teaching.' *Praxis* 1: 19–26.

Lodge, D. 1975. *Changing Places.* London: Secker and Warburg.

Maley, A. and **A. Duff.** 1978. *Drama Techniques in Language Learning.* Cambridge: Cambridge University Press.

Maney, A. S. and **R. L. Smallwood** (eds.) 1971. *MHRA Style Book.* London: MHRA.

Marckwardt, A. H. 1981. 'What literature to teach: principles of selection and class treatment.' *Forum* XIX/1.

Marshall, J. 1972. *European Curriculum Studies 5: The Mother Tongue.* Strasbourg: Council for Cultural Cooperation, Council of Europe.

Marshall, M. 1979. 'Love and death in Eden: teaching English literature to ESL students.' *TESOL Quarterly* 13/3: 331–40.

Melville, M. *et al.* 1980. *Towards the Creative Teaching of the English.* London: George Allen and Unwin.

Modern Language Association of America. 1970. *The MLA Style Book.* New York: MLA.

Moskowitz, G. 1978. *Caring and Sharing in the Foreign Language Class.* Rowley, MA: Newbury House.

Muller, K. E. 1980. 'The foreign language syllabus and communicative approaches to teaching.' *Studies in Second Language Acquisition* 3/1.

Munby, J. 1968. *Read and Think.* London: Longman.

Narasimhaiah, C. D. (ed.) 1976. *Commonwealth Literature: A Hand-Book of Select Reading Lists.* Delhi: Oxford University Press.

Nyerere, J. K. 1967. 'Education for self-reliance.' Reprinted in J. K. Nyerere: *Freedom and Socialism*. Nairobi: Oxford University Press (1968).

Oakeshott, J. 1959. *The Voice of Poetry in the Conversation of Mankind*. London: Bowes.

O'Donnell, W. R. and **L. Todd.** 1980. *Variety in Contemporary English*. London: George Allen and Unwin.

p'Bitek, Okot. 1970. *Song of Ocol*. Nairobi: East African Publishing House.

Pearce, R. 1977. *Literary Texts. Discourse Analysis Monographs No. 3*. University of Birmingham: English Language Research.

Perera, K. 1982. 'The assessment of linguistic difficulty in reading material' in R. A. Carter (ed.) *Linguistics and the Teacher*. London: Routledge & Kegan Paul.

Pettit, R. D. 1971. 'Literature in East Africa.' *Journal of the Language Association of Eastern Africa* 2: 19–26. (Reprinted in this volume.)

Phillips, J. 1979. 'Daughters of Men' in *Best Radio Plays of 1978*. London: Eyre Methuen.

Pickett, G. D. 1981. Internal discussion paper for British Council (mimeo).

Pound, E. 1928. 'How to read' in *Literary Essays, 1954*. London: Faber and Faber.

Povey, J. 1972. 'Literature in TESL programs: the language and the culture' in Allen and Campbell (eds.) 1972.

Power, H. W. 1981. 'Literature for language students: the question of value and valuable questions.' *Forum* XIX/1.

Pratt, M. L. 1977. *Towards a Speech Act Theory of Literary Discourse*. Bloomington, Ind: Indiana University Press.

Quirk, R. 1962. *The Use of English*. London: Longman.

Quirk, R., S. Greenbaum, G. Leech, and **J. Svartvik.** 1972. *A Grammar of Contemporary English*. London: Longman.

Richards, J. C. and **M. N. Long.** 1978. *Breakthrough* Book 3. Kuala Lumpur: Oxford University Press.

Rimmon-Kenan, S. 1983. *Narrative Fiction: Contemporary Poetics*. London: Routledge & Kegan Paul.

Ringbom, H. (ed.) 1975. *Style and Text: Studies Presented to Nils Erik Enkvist*. Stockholm: Abo.

Rivers, W. M. 1968. *Teaching Foreign-Language Skills*. Chicago: University of Chicago Press.

Rosenblatt, L. 1978. *The Reader, The Text, The Poem*. Carbondale, Ill: Southern Illinois University Press.

Schools Council. 1970. Working Paper 28: *New Patterns in Sixth Form Modern Language Studies*. London: Evans/Methuen Education.

Searle, C. 1972. *The Forsaken Lover*. London: Routledge & Kegan Paul.

Sebeok, T. (ed.) 1960. *Style in Language*. Cambridge, MA: MIT Press.

Short, M. H. 1981. 'Discourse analysis and the analysis of drama.' *Applied Linguistics* 2/2: 180–202.

Short, M. H. (forthcoming). 'Literature and language teaching and the nature of language' in T. D'haen (ed.) *Linguistic Contributions to Literature*. Amsterdam: Rodopi.

Singh, A., R. Verma, and I. Joshi (eds.) 1981. *Indian Literature in English, 1827–1979: A Guide to Information Sources*. Detroit, MI: Gale Research Company.

Smith, L. E. (ed.) 1981. *English For Cross-Cultural Communication*. London: Macmillan.

Soudek, M. and L. Soudek. 1983. 'Cloze after thirty years: new uses in language teaching.' *ELT Journal* 37/4: 335–40.

Stubbs, M. W. and H. Hillier (eds.) 1983. *Readings on Language, Schools and Classrooms*. London: Methuen.

Sutherland, J. R. 1948. *A Preface to Eighteenth Century Poetry*. Oxford: Oxford University Press.

Sweet, H. 1899. *The Practical Study of Language*. (Reprinted, Oxford University Press, 1964.)

Thomson, J. 1979. 'Response to reading: the process as described by one fourteen-year-old.' *English in Education* 13: 1–11.

Werth, P. 1976. 'Roman Jakobson's verbal analysis of poetry.' *Journal of Linguistics* 12: 21–73.

West, M. 'Simplified *and* abridged.' *English Language Teaching* V/2: 48–52.

Whitehead, F. *et al.* 1977. *Children and Their Books*. London: Macmillan.

Widdowson, H. G. 1975. *Stylistics and the Teaching of Literature*. London: Longman.

Widdowson, H. G. 1978. *Teaching Language as Communication*. Oxford: Oxford University Press.

Widdowson, H. G. 1979. *Explorations in Applied Linguistics*. Oxford: Oxford University Press.

Widdowson, H. G. 1983. 'Talking shop: literature and ELT.' *ELT Journal* 37/1: 30–36.

Widdowson, H. G. and C. J. Brumfit. 1981. 'Issues in second language syllabus design' in Alatis, Altman and Alatis (eds.) 1981.